BEYOND THE HIGH BLUE AIR

BEYOND THE HIGH BLUE AIR

LU SPINNEY

CATAPULT  NEW YORK

Published by Catapult
catapult.co

First published in hardcover in Great Britain in 2016 by Atlantic Books,
an imprint of Atlantic Books Ltd.

ISBN: 978-1-936787-54-8

Catapult titles are distributed to the trade by
Publishers Group West
Phone: 866-400-5351

Library of Congress Control Number: 2016952067

Printed in the United States of America

9 8 7 6 5 4 3 2 1

For everything begins with consciousness
and nothing is worth anything except through it.

—Albert Camus,
The Myth of Sisyphus

. . . But to have been
this once, completely, even if only once:
to have been at one with the earth, seems beyond undoing.

—Rainer Maria Rilke,
"The Ninth Elegy"

Miles Kemp

Contents

Author's Note

There are hundreds, if not thousands, of people like Miles who are unable to speak for themselves and give or withhold consent for inclusion in a book such as this. To protect the identity of those few I have included, their names have been changed and some details of their story altered.

Some other names have also been changed, for reasons of discretion.

Finally, there are people who were closely involved in Miles and Ron's situation but whom I have not included in detail, both to protect their privacy and because they were not, in the end, part of my story.

BEYOND

THE

HIGH

BLUE

AIR

March 19, 2006—St. Anton

Imagine a young man in his prime. He is quite tall, has clear, deep green eyes, brown hair thick and so dark it can gleam almost to black, and a longish face balanced by strongly defined cheekbones and jawline. His look is humorous, challenging, engaged; there is a vivid charge of energy to be felt in his presence. He has just turned twenty-nine and after a week's hard snowboarding he is fitter than ever; that is the reason he will be known by the doctors and nurses in the intensive care unit as the Athlete.

It is early morning on the last day of his skiing holiday and the sun is just beginning to glint and sparkle on the night-hardened snow. Inside his room it is still dark and he will have had to set an alarm to wake this early, for early rising is not his forte. There is that particular hush in the air that comes after a night of heavy snow, broken now only by the distant sound of the piste machines with their wide corrugated tires already busy preparing the empty ski slopes. Turning off the alarm, the young man lies back luxuriously in his bed to contemplate the day. Tomorrow he will be back in London and back to work, and he realizes with surprise that it's not an unpleasant thought. In fact, there is nothing right now that he doesn't feel positive about, a state of mind he used to associate only with childhood. His school years were not straightforward and in his early twenties his bent for introspection descended into a suffocating depression, during which he came to recognize the hard-eyed gremlin sitting on his shoulder overseeing his every move, judging, criticizing, never drawing breath. "The rabid prattle in my skull," he once wrote. But over these last few years the prattle has subsided and now it is gone; his mind feels as sharp as a new razor, his sight is clear. If you asked him, he would admit he feels capable of achieving great things. Indeed, he is anticipating it; in an attempt to clarify his aims he has written in his journal:

Step back. What are the principles?
Don't want to abstract. Want to create.
Want to create things of great beauty and power.
Want to change the world.

He sees his future brightly lit and gleaming ahead of him. Having reached that point where ambition and self-awareness happily coincide, he now acknowledges his weaknesses and knows his strengths. With exhilaration he feels that anything and everything is possible.

He gets up and draws back the curtains, letting sunshine cascade into the room against a backdrop of snowy mountains and blinding blue sky. With a prickle of adrenaline he remembers the day's plan—last night he and his friends had decided they couldn't leave without attempting the notoriously high jump in the snowboard park that they hadn't yet tried. For the first time in all his years of chasing the thrills of skiing and snowboarding he is going to get himself a crash helmet. That is why he has to get up early today, to give himself time to go to the ski shop where he will buy the best one available; he likes the best of things and now he can afford to be extravagant.

He packs his small bag, throwing in his clothes without a thought, no careful folding or smoothing. Then he takes a quick shower, long enough to enjoy the sting of hot water washing off the suds as he feels the tension in his muscles; keeping fit is one of his hobbies, which is why he has taken up amateur boxing back in London. This reminds him of a former girlfriend, Annabel, and he thinks now with pleasure about her body, as lean and supple as a ballerina's even though exercise was as alien to her as ballet is to him. Together with his mother and sisters, it was she who nagged him to give up boxing when he came home one evening from his weekly bout with his T-shirt covered in blood. You have such a magnificent brain, Annabel had said, it's one of the things I love about you! He considered giving in to them, for in a rueful sort of way he enjoyed the fuss they made.

Breakfast is served downstairs in the small dining room of this old Alpine hotel with its checked gingham curtains and cozy decor, everything so strangely diminutive compared to the view through the mullioned windows. When I have a chalet in the mountains, he thinks, I'll have one built to amplify the light and the vastness, to feel on the edge of such awesome beauty and to see and know it is dropping away beneath me. Soon he is joined for breakfast by his friends, Ben and Charlie, both fellow snowboarders as well as colleagues back in London, and after some laughter recalling last night's exploits they confirm the day's plans. The snowboard park, the jump and then the dash to the airport to get the flight to London. They discuss the jump, how long the descent for it should be, where to start; it is difficult to judge at what point and at what speed it should be taken to remain on balance, which is where the thrill comes in. The longer the approach down to it, the faster you go, the higher you jump. He is the only one not to own a helmet, so he leaves them finishing breakfast and makes his way to the ski shop.

This is St. Anton and the shop is appropriately stocked. The clientele of the elegant resort is a mix of ambitious snowboarders and well-heeled classical skiers and there is every fashionable accoutrement for sale. He is distracted on entering by a striking girl assessing herself in a long mirror, clearly wondering about the figure-hugging pale turquoise ski suit she is trying on. He catches her eye as he walks past and wants to say, You look beautiful in that, but he doesn't and fleetingly regrets his reserve. Soon she is forgotten and he is looking at helmets, listening carefully to the laid-back long-haired ski pro describing the merits of each. Trying them on, he is surprised by their lightness but dislikes the sensation of containment. He wonders if it might be disorienting; absolute concentration and balance are needed when making a serious jump, and the helmet could be a distraction when he is not used to it. The assistant explains the technology and shows him how the fit must be precise, the strap under the chin tightened and adjusted just so to keep it in place. And of course it needs to look cool, because undoubtedly part of the fun of snowboarding is looking cool, which he can't help thinking is compromised by a helmet. But the jump today is very high and he is going to take it as hard and as fast as he can, so this precaution is the responsible thing to do. As he pays for the sleek black choice he's made he senses the familiar excitement beginning to build. Picking up his snowboard as he leaves he feels an added surge of pleasure; he bought it while in the States a few months ago and he hasn't yet seen one like it here. There's nothing to match its curled smoothness and sleek design, not even in the racks of gleaming new boards in this shop.

Out in the sunshine he puts on his sunglasses and looks around. There is a photograph of him taken at this moment by one of the friends who has just arrived, so imagination is not necessary here: he doesn't know it but he is as handsome as he might ever wish to be, and the girl also caught on camera coming out of the shop in her new turquoise ski suit thinks so too as she gives him an inviting smile. He doesn't notice, for all he is interested in now is the perfection of the moment: even down here at resort level he can see the snow is still thick from last night's fall, so he knows the slopes higher up will be ideal for snowboarders, the thin cool air just warmed enough to be comfortable for working up a sweat. If they get cracking they might have time after the jump for a quick sandwich and a beer in the sunshine before they leave. He zips up his jacket, puts on his padded gloves, and casually tucks the snowboard under his arm as he walks with his friend across to the chair lift.

Arriving at the top he thrills to the view spread before him. Pushing himself off the chairlift, he slides across to the edge and stands quietly for a moment, taking it in. It is the thrill of being on the tip of the world, snow-covered peaks in every direction fading into the blue distance, the sense of latent power brooding within the vastness. To be made aware of his insignificance in the face of nature's grandeur but to know he is an essential part of it too; he remembers when he first thought about it in that way, a small boy talking to his mother as they sat together on the balcony of their Alpine chalet, how grown-up he felt when she took his discovery seriously.

He can hear his friends have all arrived, so he turns from the view to join them. Together they set off towards the snowboard park, moving down in unison over the freshly fallen snow.

And now he is standing at the top of a slope that leads in one steep drop to the dip and rise of the jump, a curved tusk of packed snow protruding out of the whiteness. It looks huge even from this distance and he recognizes the sudden blaze of mental clarity that accompanies adrenaline release. This is when he is at his happiest, under pressure, pushing himself to succeed. He likes the sense of breaking through ever more challenging barriers; he savors the private confirmation of his own worth. It is not conceit—depression and introspection have saved him from that; it is simply a clear conviction of his rootedness in the world, of the value of this existence, here and now, his intention to live his life to its limits.

He adjusts and fastens his new crash helmet as he was advised to by the ski pro. He checks the bindings on his snowboard; they're working fine. He is ready to go. Adrenaline and excitement mixed with a sudden sharp twist of fear; he can smell the acrid whiff of his perspiration. Then, taking a deep breath, he pushes himself off and down the slope. At first gliding and swooping from side to side as sure as a hawk descending to its prey, his path gradually straightens into an arrow of gathering speed for the final descent towards the jump. Too fast now, he fears he could lose his balance and then he has reached the dip of the jump and he knows he is not in control as he is taken by force up the ramp, skewing sideways as his board clips the edge and then he is hurtling, spinning up, up into the free blue sky ahead . . .

The thwack of board and helmet on hard ice, the cries of onlookers, the blue of sky and white of snow. Silence. Then, very slowly, the fallen figure sits up, raises himself, stands shakily. Friends gather around, supporting him, their faces grave. After such a fall how can he be all right? He speaks: Jesus, that was something. So shocking was the fall that someone feels it necessary to ask him, Do you know where you are? Do you know what day it is? St. Anton, Sunday, he says, thickly. He takes off his helmet and slowly pushes himself on his board to the edge of the slope and sits down. Motionless, head bowed, and then, suddenly, violently, he vomits onto the clean white snow. The friends' faces now in horror, watching as his eyes roll upwards and his body convulses in front of them all, back arched, limbs juddering. A doctor skiing past stops to help, the Rescue Patrol is called, paramedics are removing the young man's jacket, T-shirt, cutting through his vest in the race to keep him alive, the air reverberating with the thump, thump of a helicopter's blades.

In the helicopter the young man stops breathing. Below him the mountains glitter impassively in the slanting afternoon sun as he dies, for a moment. But the two paramedics immediately put their skills to work, passing a tube down his throat and connecting the other end to a portable ventilator. He is made to breathe again; he has been prevented from dying, but he is still critically injured. The neurosurgery team at Innsbruck University Hospital have been warned that he is coming; it is a Sunday, so the on-duty surgeons are called from their homes and when the helicopter lands on the rooftop landing pad and the young man is whisked down to the operating theater they are ready, waiting for him. Without them he would have died again, his brain bleeding and swelling, lethally compressing his brain stem, but they are excellent and dedicated neurosurgeons and for the second time in three hours his life is saved.

March 19, 2006—London

Happiness complete: a Sunday morning in early spring, pale shafts of sunshine falling through the gap where the bedroom curtains don't quite meet and I lie in bed thinking, Ron is right. He says I wake easily, like a cat, and that is how I feel right now, the languorous contentment of a cat. The sun is shining and it's a Sunday so Ron will be at home all day, Claudia and Marina are still asleep upstairs after getting back from university yesterday, Miles returns this afternoon, and Will is coming home for supper tonight. Added pleasure from the relief in remembering that Miles won't be snowboarding today, he won't have time because he'll be traveling to the airport and that means his holiday is safely over. I can feel the background fear of the past week dissolving, the fear that always lurks when Miles or Will are away snowboarding. I've seen them both doing those jumps and it doesn't bear thinking about.

Turning over lazily I find Ron is already awake, sitting up next to me reading. How gorgeous is the morning, I say, and he blows me a kiss, continuing to read. Like Miles, he's undistractable when reading, but I continue anyway. I've been lying here feeling ridiculously contented, Ronathan, I tell him. It's all your fault. It's true; how many times have the children and I talked about the happiness Ron has brought, of a kind none of us could have dreamed of during the long, painful unraveling of my marriage to their father. Meeting Ron six months afterwards was for me, still exhausted and diminished from the divorce process, like suddenly being swept up by a giant wave at the end of a tumultuous storm and then being brought in to land somewhere far away, unfamiliar but safe. The weird thing is, I continue, even if he isn't really listening, that this happiness feels fragile at times. Little slivers of dread that it's too good to be true. Anyway, guess what, it is true right now. I distract his reading further with a quick kiss on the cheek as I get out of bed. I'd like another one of those, he says, putting down his book, so I stay a little longer in the warmth beside him. But we've got all these people coming for lunch, Ronathan, I remind him, so we should really get up and get going.

Since all the children will be home for supper tonight I asked the butcher for an extra-large piece of beef to cook for lunch. That way I'll have enough for dinner too—cold peppered beef with rosemary and anchovy aioli is their favorite and it will be a celebration tonight, all four being home at once. The best of all dinner parties, I think. If Ron doesn't want a repeat of lunch I'll do a treat for him, too, maybe a creamy gratin dauphinoise, one of his favorites that now has to be rationed to keep his cholesterol down. It always seems to me a luxury rather than a burden to be the cook of the household, choosing what I want for each meal with the added pleasure of being able to gift what I cook. The rich trivia of domesticity, a sustaining thing, I think, as I crush the peppercorns in the heavy ceramic bowl, surprised afresh by the mouthwatering spicy scent from such a dull kitchen staple.

We prepare for lunch in a companionable duo. Ron has laid the table and is now sorting out the drinks. I found an interesting-looking bottle of whisky while I was down in the cellar, he says, one I haven't tried yet. The boys and I can have fun tonight seeing what we make of it. I think now about Miles's frank acknowledgment of the adjustment he had to make when Ron came into our lives. In the turmoil of my collapsing marriage with his father he had stepped right into the breach as the oldest child and provided, aged only twenty-one, a solid wall of support for me and his three younger siblings. It wasn't easy for me when you first met Ron, he told me when we talked about it some time later, I had to make an adjustment, my role in the family changed. But he's a top guy, Mum, the best thing that could have happened.

THE MAIN COURSE is coming to an end, the ice cream and caramelized oranges are ready and waiting and there is nothing left to do now except enjoy myself. When the phone rings I answer it in the kitchen and the background noise of people and laughter makes it difficult to hear the young man asking me if I am Miles's mother. Yes, I reply, why, what's happened? I know already, I know from the tone of the man's voice even before I hear that Miles is gravely injured; later he will tell me the most harrowing moment of his life so far was being with Miles on the mountain slope as his body convulsed away from him into unconsciousness. I'm Ben, a friend of Miles's, he says. He has had a serious accident on his snowboard. What injury? I ask, but again somehow I know. A head injury. He's in an air ambulance now, on his way to Innsbruck University Hospital. Another friend and I are taking the train to Innsbruck to be there with him. I'm sorry, I have to go now, but I will call you again as soon as I get there.

The line clicks dead. I remain standing, frozen, still holding the phone to my ear, not daring to sever the thread that connects me across sea and forests and mountains to Miles, to the person who was with him at that fateful moment when I was not. From one instant to another the world has changed. We are no longer safe; with frightening clarity I see each one of the people I love as though standing on the edge of a precipice, isolated, friable, their outlines sharply etched above the abyss that now threatens us all. With what complacency have I existed before this moment.

My mind seems to have cut loose in a peculiar floating calm while my body absorbs the shock in a visceral plunge of nausea. Upstairs in the bathroom I study my reflection in the mirror with detached interest, as though peering through the window of a stranger's house and seeing someone who looks faintly but inter-estingly familiar. Going back into the kitchen I'm still floating as in a dream, an out-of-body experience, watching myself as I put my hand up to stop the lunch party conversation. I'm so sorry, you'll have to leave. Miles has had an accident snowboarding. A head injury. I can hear my voice, flat, expressionless, see Ron's face as he stands up, the confusion and shock, and register the intake of breath as Jennifer, a psychiatrist, reveals something else in her expression of horror, a doctor's knowledge.

Ron sees our guests out while in a distant land Ben and Charlie are traveling over the mountains to Miles. Above them a rescue helicopter (red, I imagined, but now I've seen the photograph I know it was white) is taking Miles low over the same mountains towards the waiting surgeons. In the helicopter the sound of Miles breathing on the portable respirator as his brain is silently bleeding and swelling, the noise of the blades chopping the air outside, the Austrian paramedics talking in low tones (or shouting above the noise?) working to keep him alive while below them the snow-covered Alps gleam in the late afternoon sunshine. Too terrible to think of myself vainly crushing peppercorns at the moment that he stood, thrilling with adrenaline, on the top of that ski slope, unaware he was poised on the threshold of consciousness. He fell to earth and only his brain was hurt; from such a height and at such a speed that it shattered in the crash helmet like an egg in an empty biscuit tin, shearing the axons and damaging all those fragile, magnificent neurons. And not a bruise on the rest of his body—how can one make sense of that?

Late that Sunday night we too fly over the mountains, enduring the banter of the easyJet air hostess and the jovial passengers setting off on carefree holidays. The children's father, David, has joined us, and landing at midnight, blank with exhaustion, we hire a car and drive through the bleak streets beyond the airport to the first hotel we come across. It looks brutal, an unloved concrete façade punctuated by straight lines of barred identical windows. The foyer is too hot and the man behind the reception desk ominously relaxed, as if he has been expecting us to arrive here in this place at this time. He leads us to our rooms through stifling circular corridors, the air as stale as a tomb.

The Austrian surgeon we telephoned from London before we left had advised us to stop on our journey overnight. Get some rest before you arrive, he said, it would be better for you to come feeling fresh in the morning. We will take care of him. He sounded concerned and kindly and we had not questioned his advice, but now I wish we had. Rest is irrelevant and anyway impossible; the only imperative is to reach Miles. Lying on my back on the hotel bed in Munich, the day's events sift down slowly in my mind like the last silent ashes falling after an eruption. Everything lies color-less, shapeless, now coated in a thick layer of dread. Through the window above my bed a pale sliver of moon gleams coldly; it will be shining down on Miles, too, I think, and I sense the first tremor of a strange new anger. I've known that moon since early child-hood, growing up on a farm in Africa hundreds of miles from any city; most nights were as black as pitch, but when the moon was up it shone with a fierce beauty that dazzled the African darkness. Later, when we moved to live by the Indian Ocean, it gilded and soothed the waves with its ethereal light. I felt protected by this moon of mine, felt a private oneness with its ancient, soundless presence that continued into adulthood. It is my childish secret, so that even living in London, on the rare nights it breaks through the cloud, I get out of bed and go to a window to let it drench me in its light. But now I find I can no longer look at it, cannot stand to look at it. Fuck the moon, I think, fuck the fucking moon; and feel betrayed.

AFTER A FITFUL sleep I wake before dawn. In the gray half-light the plainly furnished room with its barred window could be a prison cell, and with sudden, cold precision I know that my life before this morning is no longer accessible. A barrier has come down in the night; I have been shut off from the world as it was and which now appears so far removed, a distant, light-filled place of ease and foolish innocence. Across the room Claudia and Marina are still asleep in the narrow double bed. I don't know what our future holds, but I can't suppress a deep sense of dread that threatens to extinguish the hope I so desperately want to maintain.

An early breakfast in the empty hotel dining room and we set off in the car, soon leaving Munich behind us. We could be aliens in a spaceship, so unrecognizable does the world look as we speed through it, so safe, tranquil, *ordinary*, as though nothing has happened. I'm surprised people are not staring and pointing at us as we go by, strange creatures from another planet gazing out on their ordered world of fields and forests and sturdy Bavarian farmhouses with smoke curling from warm kitchens into the pale morning air. When the mountains rise into view their menace seems equally unreal; they are where this thing happened to Miles and I marvel at their indifference, the carefree destruction at their heart as they tower so calmly over us. When finally Innsbruck appears spread out in the valley below us it could be a surreal postcard. Picturesque Tyrolean rooftops and glinting church domes just catching the light as the sun rises over the encircling snow-covered peaks, a macabre fairy-tale scene in the midst of which Miles lies, injured and alone. Silence in the car as we descend into the town, each one of us tense, braced for landing. We have no idea, we have absolutely no way of even beginning to know, what we are about to face; the future is a void.

1

We have arrived too late. Everything has happened; we are simply witnesses to the aftershock. Charlie and Ben are waiting in the hotel foyer and the two young men, fit and tanned after a week's snowboarding, are tense, tight-faced with the knowledge of where they are about to take us. They arrived in Innsbruck yesterday evening and were waiting at the hospital for Miles when he came out of the operating theater. Ben says the sight of him then was too difficult to be able to describe it to us; he was glad we had not yet arrived.

I hate that I don't have those memories. I wish I could see a slow-motion replay of the accident, see his face close up afterwards, know what was going through Miles's brain as it was splintering—I cannot bear that it was unshared. I cannot bear the isolation of that moment, the loneliness: I imagine him falling like an abandoned astronaut, no longer tethered, his lifeline floating free as he sinks through dark galaxies and whirling fragments of comprehension that the world is disappearing far behind him. I wish I could have been there, to hold him and tell him how much I loved him, how much we all love him, how we would fight for him.

Ben and Charlie take us to the hospital. As we walk into the vast glass-and-concrete foyer of Innsbruck University Hospital I feel the air being sucked away from me. The floor rises in waves, the walls bulge in, I can't breathe; I have to get away. Disembodied, I look down from somewhere high above us all and watch myself talking calmly to Charlie as he leads our small group through the crowd of people towards the elevator, as though this were a perfectly ordinary thing to be doing this sunny morning.

WE ARE SITTING in a row in the waiting room, waiting. The room is silent, save for the dull hiss of oxygenated bubbles coming from the glass fish tank in front of us. Inside the tank tiny iridescent fish dart and swoop, up and down, backwards and forwards, their mouths gaping senselessly. The room is small and square, three walls painted a soft sea green and the fourth, adjoining the corridor alongside it, made of thick shatterproof glass. The fish tank sits on a plain black metal table pushed up against the wall and next to it there is a small wooden shelf with water jug, glasses, and a telephone for visitors to announce their arrival. There are some metal chairs, cold to the touch, and the long wooden bench on which we sit as well as a wooden coffee table with brightly colored Austrian magazines on it. At the end of the glass wall is a door with a small silver keypad next to the handle. It cannot be opened from our side without a code; we will have to be let out of this room when the time comes. Occasionally a doctor or a nurse passes by on the other side of the glass wearing cotton trousers and overshirts the same sea green as the walls. I notice they keep their eyes straight ahead, averting their gaze from us.

Only two people at a time can visit the ward, accompanied by a nurse. I go first with Will, down the corridor that we will come to know so well, stopping at the end to take out the plastic aprons and gloves from their dispensers on the walls. Even more disoriented in this new uniform, we then turn the corner to face the ward. It feels as though we have entered an underwater world: tinted green glass divides cubicles and nurses' stations, and everywhere is silent save for the rhythmic tidal swish of respirators and the soft sonic keening of machines, like whale calls in the deep. Nurses and doctors glide through the rooms, serious, intent on the silent bodies each beached on their high beds.

As we reach Miles's cubicle the dread of seeing him engulfs me. Will has his arm firmly around me as we enter what is—I sense it at once—a hallowed place, a shrine; there is an overwhelming impression of a warrior, wounded, suffering. Afterwards we discover that we all felt this same thing, felt the sense of spiritual power heavy in the room and that we were on the periphery of something beyond our mortal comprehension, as though Miles were absorbed in a conversation with Life and Death and we should not presume to interrupt.

He lies on his back on a high bed in the center of the room, perfectly still. The stillness is terrible. His strong face, the one we are so familiar with, that we know to be so expressive, humorous, animated, is closed from us in a way it would not be if he were asleep. After a week in the mountain sun his face and neck alone are tanned, a clear demarcation line where the top of his T-shirt would have been. He always tanned easily and it suited his dark looks; now that demarcation line breaks my heart. A sheet has been placed like a loincloth over his middle, but otherwise he is naked, his muscular young man's chest and arms and beautiful virile legs defying his injury. A multitude of wires and tubes connect his brain and body to the bank of machines and electronic charts behind him which are recording every tremor of his existence, tubes coming out of his nose, his mouth, the top of his head, his chest, his wrist; but his face, bruised down the right side only, is calm, his eyes closed, the violent new scar running serenely from his hairline up and over his partially shaven head and down to the base of his right ear.

He looks so *strong*, so healthy, in such fine physical condition. How can it be that only his brain is damaged, and quite so damaged? It is later we are told that he is known by the doctors and nurses on the ward as the Athlete; the nurses flirt coyly with the word. But it is not just his body that is powerful; something is radiating directly from him, the air is thick with his presence.

Will and I stand silently, on one side of the bed. On the other a male nurse is filling in a chart. He finishes and turns to us, apologizes for intruding at this moment but explains that because Miles is on a ventilator there must be a qualified person in the room at all times. His English is impeccable. A ventilator: I wonder what the word for it is in German. In whatever language it is a thing only ever glossed over, half imagined, in a fleeting glimpse of horror. An iron lung it was called when I was a girl and polio was the scourge of the age. I remember my childish incomprehension, seeing pictures of people encased in them, as though they were in an iron suitcase like a magician's accomplice, and the shock when told they could not breathe without it.

There is too much to take in. I bend down and kiss Miles's cheek, then the other cheek, his forehead, his nose, his neck, his chest, but it's no good, there are too many tubes in the way. I begin to speak, hesitantly, it seems difficult. We love you so very much, Miles. You know that. We adore you, we absolutely adore you. You know, don't you, that we are all here for you. We can feel your strong fighting spirit, you are with us as you always are. You will be all right, you're going to be all right, you are going to come back to us. I love you so very, very much, my extraordinary, precious, beloved son.

Who cares if I am gushing. Will bends to kiss Miles too. You're going to make it, dude, he says quietly, you'll be back. I love you, Miles. How gentle he is, this other precious son of mine, his gentleness intrinsic to his strength.

I need to ask the nurse some questions. The tube inserted into the top of his head, so dreadful to see, is monitoring the pressure in his brain and draining away the excess fluid to reduce the swelling. The tube in his mouth is intubation into the lungs from the ventilator; the one in his nose is intubation to his stomach from a bag of liquid food hanging on a hooked stand above his head. There are more tubes, for hydration, medication, monitoring the heart, a catheter draining dark yellow urine into a bag. The machines recording Miles's new state of limbo could be the controls of a spaceship, the flickering lines and lights on screens recording his dislocated journey into the future.

The first time I cry is in the bend of the corridor on the way back to the waiting room, out of sight of the ward. Crying in a way I don't know about, with great racked gasps. Will's arms are around me and I feel selfish; he must be feeling this too, it is his brother he has just seen, his closest friend and companion, but he is comforting me. We return to the waiting room and I'm conscious of composing myself to face the others, our eyes meeting first through the glass wall as they search our faces for information in a way that will become our twice-daily routine over the coming weeks. Holding hands, Claudia and Marina are now led by the nurse down the corridor to see their brother.

* * *

TUESDAY MORNING, THE second day. As I walk past the nurses' station a young doctor comes forward and asks me if I am Miles's mother. He hands me a copy of a letter received by fax that morning and tells me that the doctors and nurses have been reading it.

> For the attention of the Family of Miles Kemp
> We are thinking of Miles at this very tough time and wishing him the very speediest of recoveries.
> Miles has been playing a critical role in one of the BBC's most important projects. Throughout he has shown an intelligence, professionalism, commitment and charm.
> Please let me know if there is anything we can do for Miles or yourselves at this time.
>
> John Smith
> Chief Executive, BBC Worldwide

I can't control my tears. The letter gives Miles substance, a background, the importance of which we are only beginning to learn. In each new institution to which he will be admitted in the months to come he will simply be another TBI, another Traumatic Brain Injury. He'll have no history, no personality; all that defines him will be his sex, his age, and his injury. The medical staff cannot know that he is thoughtful, funny, brave, kind, impatient, and irascible. They can have no idea about his lived life, its failures and achievements, the way his energy and presence seem to contain some electrical force. The only story they will have in the notes that accompany him is that he once snowboarded, not that he likes boxing and playing poker, writing poetry and playing the fool.

Turning into Miles's room now, the shock of seeing him wired up and motionless on the bed makes a mockery of the letter in my hand. It was only ten days ago in the cosy sitting room at home with the fire lit and a glass of our favorite Rioja that we had a long discussion about his work and his plans for the future. After putting his fledgling company, K Tech, on ice two years ago he joined an international firm of management consultants and it was from there that he presented and won the account for them with the BBC. He had begun working at the BBC only a few months ago; he would be proud of this letter. Pulling up a chair next to his bed I read it aloud to him, and then I read it again, hopelessly searching his face for a reaction. Of course there is nothing, the softly flashing lights and the undulating lines on the screens above his bed the only proof that he is alive. He is there but not there, though a little part of me is certain he is listening and hearing me. I must hold on to this, my hope is tethered to it, a fragile skein of hope.

At the end of the morning visit we have our first appointment to meet Miles's doctors. We are back in the waiting room, waiting in silence, for fear that if we speak our dread will spill out. The fish continue to swim in their tank, the overhead strip light glares relentlessly. This room feels like an antechamber to horror, the air heavy with the distilled fear of all the people who have waited here before us.

I need to clear my mind for this meeting, but it's a scrambled mess of unfinished thoughts that keep sliding away, of questions I can't frame. With grim relief I see through the glass wall two men in green surgical uniforms walking towards us. Neither is what I expected of a neurosurgeon, the older man with his ruddy jovial face and thick blond mustache, the younger man tall, tanned and athletic-looking, both more like men with outdoor pursuits than doctors. I suppose this is the Alps, I think, but Miles's life is in their hands; I need to believe in them. When the older man introduces himself his voice is calm, authoritative, his expression no longer jovial as he looks around at each of us, one by one, taking us in. I am Dr. Stizer, he says. I operated on Miles on Sunday evening. He had suffered a severe brain injury and was unconscious on arrival here. We removed a large piece of bone from his skull to relieve the pressure on his brain. He is now in an induced coma and breathing by means of a ventilator. We do not know at this stage what the outcome will be. He lifts his eyes to the ceiling and raises his arms, hands upturned, a gesture of supplication. It is in God's hands, that gesture seems to say, and I think I don't want it to be in God's hands, look what's already happened in God's hands. He looks searchingly around at us once more and his expression is so concerned, so kind, that I can see he cares about the young man who is his new patient and he cares, too, about us. I understand the shock you are feeling, he says quietly. We will do our best for Miles. But now, please ask me any questions you may have.

Dr. Stizer is a good man. But what questions? All that matters is, will Miles live? He cannot answer that.

LEAVING THE HOSPITAL together we walk in silence, each isolated in our need to comprehend what has happened. Below us the river Inn flows busily, people stroll past or sit at pavement cafés chatting in the sunshine, the mountains continue to sparkle under a cloudless Alpine sky. The serenity is monstrous. Claudia starts to walk fiercely ahead of us, then stops and turns to me, her face wet with tears: I'm going to take the cable car up the mountain, I need to be on my own. I'll be back. She turns off to cross a bridge and disappears from sight. I look at Marina and her eyes are wide with pain as she says she will take a walk along the riverbank, giving me a quick kiss goodbye as she descends the steps leading down to the water's edge.

We all need to be on our own. The information just delivered to us by the two surgeons has become a broken jigsaw of meaning, splintered pieces that need to be reassembled somewhere, alone, in peace. Three of us are left behind standing on the edge of a bridge that leads into the cobbled streets of Innsbruck Old Town and I can see sunshine warming the ancient stone buildings. It looks peaceful; I want to go there. I turn to Will and he understands. He and his father will go back to the hotel and get some lunch.

I have no plan. I probably should have lunch, but I'm not hungry. The world has been put on hold and I'm drifting out beyond the edges. The aimlessness is soothing, a kind of willed deferral of all the jagged thoughts; I will face them, but for now I want to keep drifting. Across the bridge the scene looks comfortingly unreal: delicately ornate façades of buildings in the traditional Tyrolean style suggest a make-believe world far from the morning's reality. A sign hanging from one of the buildings draws my attention: "Goldener Adler" is inscribed in Gothic lettering and soon I find myself standing outside an old stone inn on the edge of a cobbled plaza. Entering the dim interior I see a chubby young woman at the reception desk who could be Heidi; her dirndl and shining golden plaits speak of mountain peaks and sunny pastures and innocence uncontaminated by pain. Can I help you? she says, and I hear myself replying that I need a room, some rooms. For which date, and for how many nights? she asks efficiently. I don't know, I answer. Indefinitely. She looks at me with concern. My son is in the hospital. I didn't want to say that, I haven't had to say it until now; it feels too private. She takes a key from the board behind her and says with such kindness I must fight back my tears, I hope you will be happy here. I think I have a room you will like.

She does. A corner room that looks out over the plaza, large windows on each wall and a sitting area with sofa, armchair, and desk, it is spacious and light. We could retreat here. The station hotel Ben and Charlie booked us into is perfectly suitable, closer to the hospital and with more amenities, but it is deadening. A businessman's hotel, its airless decor and efficiency leave nowhere in which to hide away and make private. I hadn't thought it out until this moment, but some primitive maternal instinct warns me that we could not hold ourselves together for long in such a place, and here we might. How ancient is this instinct to provide a refuge, a burrow, a nest, anything hidden away and safe from the dangers that lurk prowling and snarling in the dark outside? Stepping out of the Goldener Adler into the chill afternoon air I have a sense of having restored a kind of order, exerted some small control over the calamitous events that have overtaken us. Goldener Adler, golden eagle: light, strength. Miles would like that.

EARLY THAT TUESDAY evening Ron arrives from London. I have missed him; we've spoken on the phone but it is his presence I need. Now he is flying out to see Miles, and to see me. Watching him walk across the airport arrivals hall I think again how distinguished he looks, his integrity so obvious that it gives him his particular gravitas, but to know him is to know the ridiculous fun one can have in his company. When we meet I see the pain reflected in his eyes, complicated by his concern both for Miles and for me. How have you been? he says. How is the boy? He takes me in his arms and I feel stilted, different, I'm not the same as before; I am damaged. He was widowed two years before he met me when his wife died of cancer after many years of illness; theirs had been a long and stable marriage and for him and his two now adult daughters, Belinda and Amelia, it was a deeply painful time. I wish he did not have to suffer again on our behalf.

Ron had waited these two days before coming here out of respect for David, that at such a time it should be Miles's father who sees Miles first with all of us together, the original family. Such consideration is typical of him, though I know Miles would want him here from the beginning. All four children love Ron as a father as well as a friend and confidant; he is an integral part of our family now. David and I separated eight years ago and our lives have settled into their different ways. To be suddenly thrown together again is an unnatural and painful accretion to an already painful situation. To any curious fellow guests on the first morning before Ron arrives we look like just another family on holiday, father, mother, and children sharing a hotel breakfast and later setting off together for a walk through the town; that our group is anomalous and our walk leads to an intensive care unit does not show. The strangeness, the strain for us all, is subsumed by the horror of the situation that has brought us together and when in the evening the exuberant waiter in the Italian restaurant greets us as *la bella famiglia inglese* we don't put him straight. I worry that it is especially difficult for the children, but now Ron has arrived and I take comfort from the civility of his and David's relationship.

Ron and I take the airport bus into town and arrive at the hotel just in time to join the children and David setting off for the evening visit to the hospital. I can see the children's relief at his arrival, the sharing of our predicament, his understanding without explanation. Once at the hospital Ron and I go first, walking down the dreaded corridor before I show him where to put on his plastic apron and gloves and then leading him through the eerie silence of the ward to Miles's room. The machines are blinking, the ventilator soughs rhythmically, the nurse sits quietly in the corner reading. Miles lies alone on the high bed, so still he could be embalmed, a magnificent specimen of young manhood on display for whoever dares. Miles darling, Ron is here. Why do I say that? It's not for me to be the interpreter, their relationship so strong my intervention is not required. I wonder if Ron would prefer to be on his own with him; it is difficult finding the words, easier to be alone, I think. I kiss them both and leave the room.

The uncomprehending, raw pain on Ron's face when I return, this strong man rendered defenseless. I put my arms around him and we stand together in silence by Miles's bed. The nurse turns away and inspects the medical chart hanging behind her.

Embracing Ron, I think, I want Miles to be in love again, make love again.

A WEEK PASSES. Ron, Will, and David have gone back to London, to work, but they will continue to come and go. Still at university and now on their Easter vacation, Claudia and Marina have remained here with me. We visit Miles twice daily and are beginning to build our days into a routine. But this morning we must face our new reality afresh: the doctors are going to take Miles off his ventilator. They will "wean" him off it—that is the medical terminology.

The word *wean* is a singular euphemism here, though correct in its way. Miles has suffered a traumatic brain injury and, reduced to infantile dependency by the injury, he must now go through the hoops of developmental stages that are set out unconditionally in its wake. In the way that anxious new parents do, we follow the stages of his development intently and applaud each tiny sign of progress as though it were being achieved by a prodigy. The irony is not lost on us—Miles invariably succeeded, and when something wasn't easy he set his cap at it with unstoppable determination. How the tables have turned; determination is no longer available to him. The stakes are different: if he succeeds today he will breathe on his own; or he won't.

Our time with him is spent urgently, the three of us spurring him on in turn, goading him to success. Miles, we say, bending close to his ear, you have been breathing with the help of a ventilator for the past ten days since your accident. Today the doctors are going to take you off it—this is such a strong sign of your recovery. You are amazing, Miles. You are going to come back to us. You can do it, you can always do anything. You have so much life left to live, Miles, you must come back. You want to achieve great things and you will, you know that. You are so precious to us, we love you so very much . . . And so on, the urgency, once again, dissolving into an unabashed gush of feeling.

The afternoon shuts down; if I close my eyes I think I can feel the world rotating. When we finally arrive at the waiting room that evening and I pick up the phone to let the nurses' station know we are there, time stops altogether for that moment. And then within seconds it seems Dr. Stizer is walking down the corridor towards us and he is smiling, a huge beaming smile under his great mustache. The girls and I are gripping each other's hands so tightly mine hurts but yes, he unlocks the door and says to me, Your son is breathing on his own! He looks so genuinely happy and now with this kind foreign neurosurgeon in the little room we hug one another and hug him too and dance about like small children, crying the first and only tears of joy that we will know for Miles. He is alive! Breathing all by himself! The amazing boy! We can picture his recovery, we're euphoric. It feels as though Miles has won the most difficult race ever run, against the greatest odds.

We go out that evening to a Mexican bar we've come across that does excellent cocktails. We call the family and all the close friends to tell them the news and many mojitos later we dance down the street to the hotel, chanting as we go: He's-brea-thing-on-his-own! He's-brea-thing-on-his-own!

* * *

OUR EUPHORIA IS short-lived. The days sink back into their routine; each morning I wake in the hotel room with a stab of fear. I remember what it felt like to wake slowly and easily but now I am taut with foreboding at what the day might hold. I get up and fill the small hotel kettle to make tea for whoever is with me, either Ron or one of the children if Ron's not there.

Marina is with me today. She has just turned twenty, the youngest in the family and Miles's adored little sister. Looking at her small shape still asleep in the bed I am relieved to see her face peaceful for the moment. I switch on the kettle and sit down to wait for it to boil, leaning back in the armchair with my eyes closed. Miles is lying in a hospital bed just a few streets away from us; despite breathing on his own he is still in a coma. In the quiet of these cold mornings I have a new ritual: I go to him. I've never been able to meditate but this thing I can do, willing my mind to cut loose so that I can join him where he is. There is a list I repeat like a mantra when I reach him: please let him open his eyes and know us, please let him walk again, talk again, please, please let his brain heal so that he can come back and be the vital person he was. I want to use the concentrated force of furious love to make these things happen. I suppose this is the way that some people find prayer helpful; perhaps this is a prayer.

I wake Marina with a cup of tea and call Claudia, who is in the next door room, to join us before we go down to breakfast.

Breakfast has become an ordeal. I used to love hotel breakfasts like a childish treat, the anticipation of what new and exotic choice might be on offer in a foreign dining room, but now I find I can't eat anything. Walking into this Alpine dining room each morning I am repulsed at the sight of the serving tables set out with what seems a lavishly obscene spread of food: great bowls of gelatinous yogurt, muesli glistening with nuts and seeds, glass jars of dark sticky honey and blood-colored jams, fresh red raspberry, strawberry, dark blue fruits of the forest. There are platters of fat yellow cheeses or oozing creamy ones, slices of violent pink ham and salami, bowls of bald expressionless eggs and baskets piled high with voluptuous rolls. Around these tables the hotel guests circle intently, eyeing the food and jostling for position to load their plates, and I can only think of snouts and troughs. I find a table in the corner and sit down, and around me I'm aware of munching and swilling, a lifting of spoons and forks and cups to mouths that seem to open and close and chomp in a syncopated rhythm of mastication, all in time to the sickening jingle of hotel muzak playing on a loop in the background; it's like being in an orchestrated farmyard. I am trapped in a nightmare that has continued into the morning, a ludicrous object of grief crouched in the corner, pinched and thin and angry, hollow-eyed and foul.

It is a new thing, this anger, and it is taking unattractive and unexpected forms. It is mostly scattergun, undirected—above all I could machine-gun the moon and stars, but I also want to pepper with bullets anybody or anything that comes in the way of my private grief or, and especially, that may be a threat to Miles. For example, the nurse who seemed careless when taking his obs yesterday or the arrogant young doctor who told me that snow-boarding with a crash helmet causes more damage than doing it without one. Incomprehension is generating the anger I feel, we all feel—it is impossible to make sense of what has happened to Miles and our ignorance fuels resentment.

When the girls have eaten and I have drunk my coffee we escape upstairs to the privacy of our room, to think about the day. It will revolve around our visits to Miles, but visiting hours for the intensive care unit are strictly regulated. Two hours are allowed in the middle of the day, from twelve to two, and two again in the evening, from six to eight. We have some time to kill after breakfast and the girls try to study while I try to read. But reading eludes me now. I've lost the desire, the private pleasure; now when I pick a book up it feels flat, empty, extraneous. Fiction is impossible, as though my imagination has been depleted trying to comprehend my own story. The most I can manage is a newspaper, but even that is difficult; more than ever the papers seem filled with stories of disasters and tragedies. Miles's situation has opened a door onto the relentless, unstoppable suffering of other people, every day, everywhere; I feel viscerally aware that this terrible thing that has happened to him is only one drop in a vast cauldron of human suffering. Yesterday I read of a little girl at a fair nearby in Germany, who somehow got tangled in a giant helium balloon that broke its moorings. She was lifted up and away in front of her parents' eyes, her torn and battered body eventually recovered some kilometers away where the balloon had come to rest in a tree. How could you make sense of that? I feel an incoherent gathering of rage at the pain that has been endured by human beings since time began and that will continue, unabated and unresolved. Which god should be held accountable for this?

We all give up and go for a walk instead. Innsbruck is a gentle town and out on the quiet streets there is no visible pain. No homeless people, or indeed any sign of poverty, nobody who looks unwashed or distressed or intimidating, none of the enervated faces of big city life. The mountain air is healthy, the scenery from every angle calmly splendid, the streets and parks are clean and unhurried. Do we spoil the atmosphere, with our grief? But nobody would know if they looked at us; only rarely do we let our true feelings spill out in public, for that is not our way. I think about TV footage of men and women wailing and gesticulating with grief in the countries where this is their cultural norm and wonder if that helps them to bear the pain more easily.

Just before noon the girls and I turn the final corner of our walk and see the hospital once more like a glass fortress at the end of the street. We each feel the same tightening dread as we catch that first glimpse, the dread accompanied by a sudden surge of fearful hope—something may have happened overnight that we don't know about yet. We enter the hospital atrium and cross the light-filled space to the far corner where the elevator will take us up to the seventh floor, to Miles.

YESTERDAY, THOUGH, THE grief did spill. Marina and I had been out for a walk and passing a small church in a side street we entered it, in the hope that the place might lend us some peace.

After the glare of bright sunshine outside, the dim interior was instantly soothing, the air cool and fragrant with the scent from massed white lilies that gleamed from the chancel. It was empty and as the doors shut behind us a deep silence fell. Marina walked on along the aisle and I sat down in a pew at the back, to succumb to the silence and let the hope and faith of others with which the place was imbued envelop me. But as my eyes accustomed to the pale light coming through the high stained-glass windows and I looked across the rows of wooden pews, all I could see was the giant figure looming up above the bank of lilies at the far end. There he was, a beautiful young man, muscular limbs draped in a white cloth, hands and feet nailed through and coated in blood while his face looked down at me with an expression ghastly in its passive suffering. Instead of peace I felt a fury rising, I wanted to rage at the faith that allowed and venerated such a grotesquery. And then I began to hear a sound like the whimpering of an animal in distress, becoming louder and louder until it rose to a crescendo, an anguished howling of pain that reverberated round the once silent space. It was Marina, braced against the altar rail, her clear young face uplifted and fiercely streaming with tears.

We sat for a long time together at the front of the church. There could be no consoling, no words that could change the situation. We had already learned that comfort came from sharing the pain and waiting until its eruption had passed. When we emerged into the street some time later it was over, and we were just another mother and daughter out on a walk in the beautiful spring sunshine.

I NEED TO write and thank all the friends who have sent letters, cards, flowers to Miles and to us as a family. Grateful as I am, I can't find what it takes to write individual replies. So I compose a one-for-all response.

> Thank you for your wonderful supportive letter/card to Miles/me/us. It is a great comfort to know that you are thinking of Miles in the way that you do.
>
> There is so much and nothing to say. Miles is still in a coma and we wait. There is no respite from the anguish of waiting but he looks so strong and beautiful and seems so close that we feel very positive about his recovery. We just can't wait to have him back with us again.

That feels too close to the brink. For safety's sake I need to retreat:

> Innsbruck is ridiculously pretty and it snowed right down to the town last night, pure white from mountain tip to cobbled street. I wish Miles were awake to share the strangeness of it. The linguistic delights (*kieboschstrasse*, *crapfencake*), the delicate iced cake buildings and jolly Tyrolean men with their feathered hats and lederhosen, the elegant café where a Nazi

flag hangs proud above a meeting of bland young people and no one seems to notice (we complained and left, to their surprise), the pride, cleanliness and good manners of everyone, the comfortable conformity. Not one eccentric or homeless person to be seen—everybody looks healthy. Occasionally at night we hear drunken revellers but all they do is sing or yodel happily.

I've retreated behind some kind of glib façade. The truth is, I don't want to share the truth. I'm not ready yet.

I'M WORRIED ABOUT the children. Claudia is completing her MA in London, Marina is in her second year at Oxford, and Will travels backwards and forwards from London in the midst of trying to set up his design company. Their lives have been disrupted in a catastrophic way, disrupted but now in stasis. No one knows what will happen next, but we all want to be here with Miles when it happens. The future is held in abeyance.

The four children make up a unit. The boys seventeen months apart, first Miles then Will, a gap of five years and then Claudia and Marina, two and a half years apart. Together they are vibrant, warm, humorous, necessary; various, but one. It has been a constant marvel to me to watch them, know them, see how small frictions are resolved, the weight of their different personalities kept in balance. Now the balance has been upended. Miles, a heavyweight, is missing and the remaining three are having to realign the unit while united in their grief and their absolute commitment to him.

It's impossible to say whom it affects most. Will perhaps in the physical sense, because he has suddenly lost his lifelong companion. So close in age, attending the same schools one year apart and the same university, sharing many of the same interests and now sharing a flat, they are the best of friends despite their different characters. Miles is defined by his energy, vitality, determination, ambition; he is a natural leader. Will is equally strong-minded, but is happy to follow his own path alone, having no interest in shaping other people's lives. They share a similar intellect, but whereas Miles is a driver of ideas, Will is privately creative.

The girls' loss is different but as profound. Miles has been both their eldest brother, a self-appointed protector, and a friend and advisor, someone to have fun with and confide in. I see him now aged fifteen, an aspiringly tough, cool teenager, awful peroxided hair, standing at the kitchen window waiting nervously for the girls to return. They'd been allowed to walk on their own down to the shops at the bottom of our quiet residential road and Miles is reprimanding me. They're too young, Mum, you shouldn't have let them go down on their own. I'm going to go and find them. No, Miles, you must not, I tell him. You of all people! He laughs with me, acknowledging the double standards of an independent, experimental elder sibling not countenancing it in the younger.

As the girls grew up and the age gap between them and the boys became less pronounced, their relationships consolidated into the unit they have become. Now that all four are in their twenties their interests and many of their friends have converged, but Miles remains a powerful older brother and his absence has made a rift in their lives. Each one is in the middle of a defining process— university, setting up a business—that will suffer from being disrupted. The emotional impact of Miles's accident has been traumatic; we must not allow it to damage them practically as well.

Ron is in Innsbruck for the weekend and we talk about it together and with the children. Decisions are made. Claudia will return to London and ask to have her MA exams deferred from May to September, when rewrites are undertaken, so it should be a possibility. I will write to Marina's tutor at Oxford and explain the situation to him; the pastoral care there is excellent, I know. Will's situation is more complex, though in some ways easier; his time is not proscribed by terms and exams but by personal deadlines as his future career begins to take off. His business partner is understanding, but undoubtedly combining his work and being here for Miles is going to be a problem.

Traumatic brain injury is by definition sudden and unexpected. Shock and grief follow in its wake, but it is the unknownness, the complete lack of knowledge that compounds the horror. There is no known trajectory to illuminate the terrible blank thing one faces. Somebody you love is there but no longer there. Lack of consciousness is not comprehensible; the person looks the same and that is all. As a family we are adrift together in our ignorance and our craving for knowledge.

I HAVE BEEN talking to the athletic young neurosurgeon on the ward who is the same age as Miles and who, it transpires, is also a keen snowboarder. He is the one who tells me that he never wears a crash helmet when he snowboards. They may protect the skull, he says, the helmet will take the impact, but the sudden acceleration and deceleration can cause the brain to rotate within the skull. I don't want to hear this. *Rotate*—Miles's brain *rotated*? He continues, The medical term is diffuse axonal injury, or DAI for short. If that happens we do not yet know any way of reversing it.
I research DAI. Please let Miles not have suffered DAI. If he has, his brain will have sheared when he fell, or more precisely, the axons will have sheared. I learn that each of the billions of neurons, the nerve cells in the brain, has an axon, a long fiber that acts like a fiber-optic cable transmitting electrical impulses away from it, allowing one neuron to communicate with another. If the axons

are broken, the messaging system is broken. Apparently the brain is made up of tissues that vary in density and during that dreadful rotation the different tissues slide over one another, stretching and shearing the axons that connect them; they cascade. The words are surreal, beautiful: *rotate*, *shear*, *cascade*; it is a betrayal of language. The particular cruelty of DAI is that the areas of the brain stem involved with basic life functions, the cardiac and respiratory systems, may remain unaffected; the victim does not die but is left suspended between life and death. I read that 90 percent of people with DAI remain in a persistent vegetative state. Very few of the 10 percent who regain consciousness will return to near-normal neurological function, and of those who do, the improvement will have to take place within the first twelve months after injury. If there has been no progress by then the prognosis is bleak. It is only after a year from the time of the accident that a neurologist will be able to make a prognosis and even then it will be approximate; the brain does not yield its secrets easily.

Miles, do you remember my last words to you as you were leaving the house? Please don't do any dangerous jumps, my darling! It was my foolish, ritual request, a kind of game we played. I loved your daring and you enjoyed my mock protectiveness (although it wasn't really mock, I meant it but I had to say it lightly). I remember you hugged me with that crushing bear hug I love so much and you said, Don't worry, Ma, I'm older now. I promise I'll be responsible.

Miles bought his crash helmet that morning just before the jump. He would have died instantly without it. But perhaps without it he wouldn't have gone as fast, perhaps he would have been more cautious, perhaps it disoriented him.

Is it my fault he bought the helmet?

* * *

I COME ACROSS Dr. Stizer on the ward one day. He is in his scrubs, seeing his patients in a break from surgery. It's strange, he says, but I have connected with your son in a way I haven't done with a patient before. He could be my son. My greatest hope is that he will return here one day to speak to me himself.

I am profoundly touched by his words and we are both quiet for a moment. Then he says, May I give you some advice? Of course, I say. You saved my son's life! He looks at me quizzically. The first thing, he says, is that you must never reprimand him for doing that jump. It was a brave and wonderful thing to do. He is a young man and young men should all go out and grab life in the way he did. The second thing is that you should never feel guilty. It concerns me, he says, to see that you and your children come every day to visit Miles. I think it may be too much for you. You must not feel guilty if you go away and enjoy yourselves.

This is a surprise. Neither thing has occurred to me; certainly I would not reprimand Miles for doing that jump. As for feeling guilty, what I do feel is more complicated, not guilt but something stranger, whereby all physical and sensual enjoyment—eating, drinking, long hot baths, music, shopping, reading, making love, laughing—is shot through with a new awareness. It can no longer be simple untainted pleasure. Everywhere I go, everything I do, is suffused with, contaminated by, the image of Miles lying unconscious in his hospital room. The incomprehension at his plight has destabilized me; nothing makes its usual sense, nothing at all. Drinking a cup of tea reminds me he can't drink; seeing the sun set over the pale mountain peaks reminds me he can't see it.

Dr. Stizer is an unusual man and I am moved by his evident concern for Miles, on a personal level. Miles would like him, they would get on very well—I can imagine their mutual respect and the laughter their shared rumbustious humor would generate. A fifty-year-old neurosurgeon who snowboards and plays in an amateur rock band in his spare time—they could have a great time together.

FOR THE FIRST two weeks Miles remained in an induced coma; with a controlled dose of barbiturates, his brain had been artificially shut down to the baseline of function. By the time he had arrived at the hospital the right side of his face and neck were grotesquely swollen as the cerebral fluid found its only escape route out of the confines of the skull. When a brain is injured it swells and there is no space for it to swell to; the skull protects the brain but now the protector has become the instrument of destruction. As the swollen brain is compressed against the hard, bony helmet of the head, delicate brain tissue is being damaged in the process. If appropriate, the neurosurgeon will perform a craniotomy as they did on Miles, in which a "flap" of bone rather like a trapdoor is removed to make room for the swollen brain. Then, by inducing a coma, barbiturates will slow down the cerebral blood flow and the metabolic rate of brain tissue and so the blood vessels begin to narrow, allowing the swelling to decrease. The outcome for each person sustaining a brain injury will vary depending on the extent of the original trauma to the brain and, crucially, the time taken to reach a neurosurgeon and therefore the time the brain has to swell unattended. In Miles's case he had to get from where he had fallen, 2,000 meters high up on an Alpine mountainside, to a neurosurgery clinic 100 kilometers away. That journey took three hours and even the best efforts of a helicopter rescue team could not prevent secondary cerebral damage. There had been nowhere else his brain could swell to except against the skull or down into his brain stem. I have Miles's case history on admission to Innsbruck University Hospital in front of me. In a crude translation from the German it states the bald facts, as reported by the paramedics who attended to him on the ski slope and accompanied him in the rescue helicopter to the hospital:

State of conscious: unconscious

Breathing was still spontaneous, but he had an apnea soon

Ventilation with a mask was started immediately

Motor reaction: no reaction

Eye opening: no reaction

Verbal reasoning: no reaction

Pupil reaction: left, no reaction, wide

                 right, no reaction, wide

During transport they got unequal

Intubation was necessary immediately

Grade of injury: life-threatening

GCS: 3

GCS, the Glasgow Coma Scale. It would become our cruel yardstick, our unyielding beacon of hope, Miles's new star grading. First published in 1974 by two professors, Graham Teasdale and Bryan Jennett of the University of Glasgow's Institute of Neurological Sciences, it was devised as an attempt to put in place a reliable method of assessing levels of consciousness after brain injury. The scale is divided into three parts, E, M, and V—Eye Opening, Best Motor Response, and Best Verbal Response—15 points being the highest score and 3 the lowest.

Miles is rated 3. The minimal response a human being can have to life. What does that actually mean? What is happening in Miles's head? Can he dream? Can he feel pain? Can he *think*? How different would he be with a score of 4?

A year ago Miles crashed and wrote off his motorbike. I still have the London Hospital discharge report:

> Motorcyclist in RTA. Head on collision. Car at 35 mph, motor-
> cyclist at 20 mph. Over handle bars and rolled off bonnet.
> No loss of consciousness. Remembers entire event. GCS 15
> throughout. Patient discharged home with crutches.

GCS 15 throughout. That meant nothing to me at the time. How impatient and irritable he was, being on crutches. Instead of merely injuring his right leg as he did, I wish now that he had broken every bone in both his legs, crippled himself so completely he could never have snowboarded again.

EVERY DAY, MORNING and evening, we walk from our hotel to the hospital. We turn the final corner and there it looms, snowy mountains and serene blue sky unnervingly reflected on the elegant glass frontage. When we reach the seventh floor and I lift the phone to request admittance, I am as tense as if I were alone in a dark house and think I can hear an intruder: fear mixed with the hope that I may have imagined the danger, every nerve on full alert for this thing that is out there, unseen, unknown.

Claudia and Marina are with me this morning. Since the girls and I visit Miles every day the staff have waived the two-visitor rule, and as the three of us walk towards his room our combined fear and hope become tangible: dread that his incomprehensible stillness will be the same, nothing will have changed; hope that he will have woken from his coma, that the nightmare will be over. Dread and hope and incomprehension; it is the same every time. We turn in to his room and today something is different: Miles, inert, unconscious, still connected by multiple wires to those monstrous banks of machines behind him, has been strapped to his bed. The straps are thick brown leather, as I imagine the straps of a straitjacket must be, and they have been passed twice around his wrist and tied firmly to the metal rails each side of the bed. It is like unwittingly entering a room in preparation for torture. Pictures flash up in my mind, illustrations I have seen somewhere, Goya-esque sketches showing in finely etched detail the inmates of a madhouse cruelly restrained, shackled to great iron rings on the walls. What on earth is going on? I demand of the nurse on duty. Who did this? What has happened, what did Miles do that this is necessary? Oh, please don't worry, she says, this is normal. The doctors are planning to bring Miles out of the induced coma today and we often find that when patients are coming around they try to pull out their drips and feeding tubes. The straps are there for his protection.

After two weeks Miles is being brought out of his coma. This is momentous news. I wish they had prepared us; it seems a far greater test than his being taken off the ventilator. We no longer fear for his survival, but we have not yet addressed what comes next.

Dr. Stizer arrives but before I can say anything he apologizes. I'm so sorry, he says, I wanted to see you before you came to Miles but I was called away. You must be upset to see those, he says as he looks at the wrist straps, but I wanted you to know it is somehow good news.

His English is not perfect, but his kindness is all that matters.

We can see on the scan, he says, that the swelling on Miles's brain is coming down and it is better not to stay too long like this. He gestures towards the screens and monitors behind Miles.

We want our boy to wake up! Dr. Stizer smiles at me then, but the smile fades quickly as he speaks again, now serious. We do not know how he will be. We have to do this thing very slowly. Claudia and Marina are next to me and he looks at us all as he says carefully,

You must go away and you must not worry. We are taking care of him.

What Dr. Stizer does not know is the extraordinary rising, surging wave of hope that we cannot keep down for now; it has drowned out any worry we might possibly feel. When he leaves the room I tell the nurse that at all costs, no matter what time it is, even if it is the middle of the night, the nurse on duty must call me to tell me as soon as Miles begins to wake up. We will come to the hospital. I leave my mobile phone number and give her the number of the hotel in case it doesn't work. Then we stay on for a while with Miles and we tell him all over again how much we love him, that he is coming back to us and we will be with him every step of the way as he begins his recovery, that we are all here waiting for him.

We leave the hospital and return to the hotel and try to think what we can do to take our minds off this huge thing that is happening. The process is already under way in Miles's body, the drugs slowly ebbing out of him as in turn the Miles that has been shut down, the undamaged parts of the Miles we know, must surely be coming back to take their rightful place. Marina speaks for us all: this hope, she says, is like the beginning of a love affair, the intensity of it, the newness. She is right; there is the waiting and the tenderness in hoping, the absorption of all one's self into just this one encompassing fervent desire, and the dream, the beautiful dream, of fulfilment.

The evening comes, and the night, and there is no call from the hospital. Dr. Stizer said it would be a slow process. Walking towards the hospital in the morning we are walking to a scaffold where there may be a stay of execution. It is raining and the mountains ringing the town are hidden from view for the first time since we've been here. The streets are bleak; rain has put the city off kilter, it should be snow at this time of year and the ski slopes will be ruined.

Sitting once more in the waiting room, we watch the fish in their tank. There seem to be some new ones, none of us remembers seeing them before. They are black and larger than the decorative bright little fish that swoop so hopelessly through the seaweed. These new ones are purposeful, their sucker-like mouths fastened to the rocks as they clean off the pale green scum that has grown there, and two of them are fastened on the glass front of the tank, sucking and cleaning the glass. The movement of their mouths is repellent; I can't watch them, they're starting to make me feel nauseous.

The nurse is coming down the corridor to fetch us, her face impassive. She lets us out of the waiting room and we follow her in silence, still not able to speak as we go through the rigmarole of putting on plastic aprons and rubber gloves and then continuing to follow her past the nurses' station and through the ward to Miles's room. We enter and there he lies, in the same position as he was yesterday, on his back with his eyes calmly closed, the machines still blinking out their messages behind him. The straps have gone. It might have been a dream; reality seems very far away. But the dream has ended; the removal of those straps is the rejection we dreaded, the end of the affair. There was no need for them. He is still in a coma but it is his own.

A WEEK GOES by and there is no change. Then, suddenly, during our visit this morning Miles moves his arms. He pushes both arms downwards, stretches them down with his wrists bent back in the way one does sometimes, pleasurably, after sitting or lying too long in the same position. The shock of excitement—he's moving! he's starting to wake!—becomes tinged with alarm as he repeats the movements forcefully but his face remains blank, unchanged, his eyes closed, no flicker of expression. Such a powerful action, yet the rest of his body has remained inanimate. Even so, I can't help calling out to the nurse who is busy filling in forms behind his bed, Look, look, Miles is moving! She drops what she's doing and comes around to see and I'm deflated by her lack of enthusiasm. Surely she can't be so cynical or impervious to the significance of what happened—since Miles has been in a coma this is the first time he's made any movement of any kind. Later the young doctor comes in on his rounds and I tell him eagerly what happened, describing and imitating it to show him. Surely it has to mean something is changing? I ask him. It was such a strong action, does it mean Miles is beginning to surface? He is quiet for a moment. We don't really want him to do that, he says. I'm afraid I think it may just be a consequence of his injury. But it is still early, he adds quickly, don't worry, it will pass. He is being kind, trying to rescue me from my foolishness, my ignorant optimism. I've no idea how someone wakes from a coma, but every moment of watching Miles is geared to this end. I am consumed by the hope of it.

Now it is terrible to watch him make that movement. Each time I want to stop him, No, Miley, no, don't do that, please don't do that thing. The innocence of it, and the horror; his brain is in chaos and all the while he stretches out his arms as though he's just about to get out of bed after a long nap. *Decerebrate posturing* is the medical term, Dr. Stizer tells me later when I ask him; sympathetic storming, or just storming, is the more common description. Such a strange and beautiful word for it, I say to Dr. Stizer, and he looks at me quietly. It will pass, he says. What he doesn't tell me is that DAI may contribute to it, or brain stem injury, that doctors fear it because the action itself may suggest further injury is taking place in the brain. I don't know that yet and for the moment hope regains the upper hand—the doctors have said it will pass and, most important, it has shown us he is definitely not paralyzed.

I have a photo of Miles lying on a sun bed by the pool in France. It was taken from the lawn above the pool and he is looking up at the photographer wryly, caught off guard just as he was surfacing from a post-lunch snooze in the sun. His body is tanned and fit, his dark hair thick and ruffled from swimming. He is stretching both arms downwards, the wrists bent back, an enjoyable long, lazy stretch. It is a precise replica of storming.

AT FIRST IT was shocking to see how many tubes were tethering Miles to the world, but I have got used to them now. This morning when we visit, the nurse tells me that the doctors have decided to remove the one that passes through his mouth directly down into his airway, the endotracheal tube.

It was the first emergency tube used by the paramedics in that fearful helicopter journey. When he collapsed on the mountain slope they had to ensure he was getting enough oxygen, and the initial procedure would have been to administer it through a mask fitted over his nose and mouth. But when his pupils registered as unequal it signified a further emergency. The endotracheal tube would have been inserted, jammed down, I imagine, in the rush to save his life, before being connected to a portable ventilator to keep him breathing.

The nurse tells me now that prolonged use can damage the vocal cords over which the tube passes and since it has been in place for three weeks the doctors consider it time for removal. Please let his voice not be damaged, that warm, humorous voice I know so well. In place of the tube Miles will be fitted with a tracheostomy, she says. I have no idea what a tracheostomy is and so the nurse describes it to me. Involving a minor operation, a curved plastic or silicone tube will be inserted into a hole made in Miles's neck and windpipe just below the larynx, bypassing the vocal cords and leading directly into his airway. It is necessary to keep his airway open and accessible, so that it can be cleared mechanically if necessary or used to administer extra oxygen when needed.

The young doctor on duty today has been deputed to discuss this with me and ask for my permission to perform the operation. He tells me that it is a simple procedure and there is very little risk of complication, that once the tracheostomy, or trachie as he calls it, is no longer necessary it can easily be removed leaving only the smallest scar. Having discussed it with the rest of the family I give the go-ahead. The most important consideration for us, all we can really think of, is that Miles's voice should be saved; our sweetest dream is to hear him speak again in the particular vivid, engaged way that he does.

Will and I are the first to visit Miles after the operation has been performed. I don't know what to expect but the shock of seeing the tracheostomy in place undoes me completely. I am not at all prepared for the collapse of misery it brings me to; I can only sit down and bury my head on Miles's chest, pressing my face into his inert body to try to staunch the torrent of pain that, if I let it go, is threatening to bring this precarious thing I hold inside myself to its destruction. Will's hand is resting gently on my back, he is talking to me. It's okay, Mum, it's the best thing for him now, he says, we have to try and remember it's only temporary and the doctors say there won't be a scar. Lifting my head from Miles's chest I am on a level with the trachie and however right it is for him now I hate it, I loathe its monstrous, domineering protuberance. It looks predatory, fixed, foreign; it has claimed him, branded him. A hole has been cut in this strong young man's throat. I remember the Adam's apple that appeared in adolescence, the strange ambulations in his voice as it began to break; I remember his smooth vulnerable teenage throat. Imagine the cutting that has had to take place—surely the windpipe is cartilaginous. I stand up with Will's arm supporting me and look down at Miles. He lies unmoved and unmoving, his face serene, the hard plastic ugly thing with its crude white rim standing proud from his throat. There is this one comfort: that of us all, Miles in his coma is at least not suffering.

GOOD FRIDAY MORNING, and I am surprised to learn that Dr. Stizer will be performing a cranioplasty on Miles this afternoon. I would have thought that being a public holiday there would be no surgery today, but he says they will be working as usual. He has come to see me in Miles's room, and Claudia and I listen as he tells us that the piece of skull, the "flap" that was removed to make space for Miles's swollen brain when he was first admitted, is going to be replaced by a piece of titanium. The original piece of bone, frozen in a solution to prevent infection, was kept so that it could be copied precisely to make the titanium replacement that would eventually be inserted to protect the brain. I ask him what the procedure will involve. The titanium piece will be fixed to Miles's skull, he says, and then stops. Looking at me closely, he continues. Are you sure you want to know the details?

Perhaps it's unusual, but I do. I would like to be present during the operation, see it taking place, see the area of unprotected brain before it is covered, just as I wished I had been with Miles at the time of his accident. I want to understand every element of what is happening to him. I don't want to be protected from it—why should I be? It doesn't make me feel squeamish, nor does knowledge make the situation any more painful.

Well, Dr. Stizer says, and I can see he is choosing his words with care, I will use screws to fix the titanium plate to Miles's skull. You mustn't worry, he adds quickly, the screws are very short, they won't damage his brain. They are self-drilling. When his hair grows again you won't know it's there.

Miles's body, it seems, is being adapted to survive his new life. First the PEG, or percutaneous endoscopic gastronomy, a feeding tube, was surgically inserted directly into his stomach, then the tracheostomy was fitted, and now this, his skull fixed with self-drilling screws; it is as though he is being armed for survival.

EASTER SUNDAY IS four weeks to the day since Miles's accident. I can't help it, but the combination of four precise weeks falling at Easter feels imbued with significance, though of what exactly I'm not sure. Perhaps some atavistic stirring, that Easter is a day of hope, of a rising from the dead, of new life beginning. Lying in bed in the hotel room with Ron next to me, here for the weekend, I try to suppress the strange excitement that something is going to happen today. It feels like a private premonition that I will ruin if I speak it out loud, so I don't mention it to Ron, and instead we talk about our plans for the day. He thinks perhaps it would do us all good to go out for lunch after visiting Miles. I can see how exhausted you are. It's Easter, and everyone's here; it'll do you good to have a treat. He plans to take us to the restaurant with a sheltered garden near the Hofgarten, the beautiful Imperial Court park on the edge of the Old Town that we have often passed on our walks through the town. We can sit outside and enjoy the sunshine, he says. I'll book a table. In my superstitious state even his suggestion seems significant; he is attuned to Miles, maybe he, too, senses that something is different today, that finally there may be something to celebrate. Spring has arrived in Innsbruck and the town has come to life, window boxes now blooming with color and the trees in the somber winter parks alight with new growth. Everything suggests renewal; surely Miles will be part of it.

As we gather together in the hotel foyer after breakfast I try to gauge if anyone else is sharing this feeling I can't shut down. Maybe I am oversusceptible, but somehow the atmosphere feels heightened. Perhaps it's just that Ron is right, I'm exhausted. Stepping out all together from the dim interior of the hotel into the bright spring sunshine I wonder if it's visible to others, how fragile a group we are, how taut with uncertainty. Reality feels fluid; nothing is fixed anymore.

Turning the corner into the plaza for a moment I think I have truly lost my senses. Huge white rabbits are dancing in the sunlight to music played by three wizened old men dressed in Tyrolean costume playing squeeze boxes, their short leather trousers, long white socks, and feathered hats making them look like ancient schoolboys. The normally sedate cobbled space is a riot of noise and color, small children racing through stalls laden with elaborate breads and cakes, bright marzipan sweets, painted eggs, colorful wooden toys, and all the while the stout men and women dressed in their rabbit costumes are, I now realize with even more bewilderment, selling loops of giant sausages as they regale the crowd. We wend our way through the surreal scene, smiling politely at the stallholders as they offer their wares and dodging the happy children as they run around us.

Our destination, when we reach it, seems just as surreal. My superstitious hope is irrelevant to Miles as he continues to lie, oblivious, on his high hospital bed.

THE SENIOR CONSULTANT on the neurosurgery ward is Professor Benir. He introduces himself and explains that he has been in America at a medical conference, which is why we have not met before. His manner is quiet and thoughtful, his dark Middle Eastern features severe against the crisp white of his doctor's coat.

We are standing by Miles's bed and he looks down at him, studying him silently for some time before he turns back to me.

I would like to know about your son, he says.

And so I tell him about Miles. That he has been a joyful son to have, my firstborn child. That from the beginning he has been quick and bright, an adventurer, a risk-taker. That one of the things that has defined him has been his brain. After academic success throughout school he got a first-class degree from Oxford. He started his own company at twenty-four. At twenty-five he was selected as one of five young people to represent Britain during Giscard d'Estaing's European Youth Convention. At present he is a management consultant for a large international company based in London but will take his own company further when he has gathered more experience. He is writing a book in his spare time. He likes to keep fit and enjoys white-collar boxing. He skydives, he dives with sharks. He practices qigong. He makes electronic music. He writes poetry. He is funny. He is kind. He loves life, attacks it head on, dangerously, seeking adrenaline, sometimes foolhardy, learning from his flaws while exploring, always, his spiritual resources. He is full-blooded, down to earth, but at the same time he is an intellectual.

I'm boasting about my son. But what seems important is that Professor Benir should know about Miles's brain, the brain that he and his team are now responsible for. He must know that it is exceptional.

I apologize for boasting, I say to the professor, but what I have told you is true and it is breaking my heart that one of the things defining Miles was that he was an intellectual and now he is brain damaged. I find that the most difficult thing to come to terms with. I wouldn't mind anything else, his legs, his arms, anything, but not his brain. He used it with such vitality, it was crucial to his enjoyment of life, right down to his particular wit and sense of humor.

Can I ask you for the truth, Professor Benir: what form is this brain damage going to take?

He waits some time before answering. Miles lies quite still next to us, only the faintest movement visible as his chest rises and falls with the intake of each breath. Now that the swelling in his brain has subsided, the shunt that was draining off the excess fluid has been removed. There are no longer any tubes coming out of his nose or mouth; the tracheostomy and PEG have taken care of those. Void of expression, his strong, closed face is intimidating in the stillness of its silence.

Professor Benir looks back up from Miles to me. The damage is not to his intellect, he says. That is not the area of the brain that is damaged. But he has suffered a very serious trauma to his brain. What is crucial now is that he begins intensive rehabilitation. We have done our work here, the surgery is complete; the important thing now is for you to arrange the next stage for him. We could move him to our neuro-rehab clinic forty kilometers from Innsbruck but I think it would be best for him to return to England, where you and he will be at home. I would recommend the Acute Brain Injury Unit at Queen Square in London, the National Hospital for Neurology and Neurosurgery, which has an excellent reputation for neuro-rehabilitation. And please, he says, gently laying his hand on my arm, don't worry about boasting. I asked you to tell me. I wanted to know about him. I am very sorry that this has happened to your son. I wish him, and all your family, very well.

Now we must get Miles home—how, and where to, such obvious and crucial questions that we have deferred facing for the past five weeks. Such a lapse seems extraordinary, though for a time we had talked of staying in Austria until he was well enough to leave. We know better now. And so we get to work, David, Ron, and I researching London hospitals that offer neuro-rehabilitation, contacting anybody we know who might be able to help or advise us. Friends who are doctors are invaluable, generous and patient with their time.

It takes a week of intense negotiation. After a flurry of telephone calls to London hospitals Miles is finally offered a bed in the Intensive Care Unit at University College Hospital, to be reviewed and assessed before being moved to the Acute Brain Injury Unit at Queen Square, the ABIU. Our twin goals have been the ABIU and the rehabilitation ward at the Wellington Hospital, both centers of excellence specialising in neuro-rehabilitation following traumatic brain injury. The Wellington is private, however, and the costs are prohibitive. Receiving the news that Miles is to be admitted to the ABIU feels like winning the lottery.

The logistics of flying home are daunting. To return on a stretcher with a commercial airline would require the space and cost of nine seats, but patients with tracheostomies are not accepted so that is ruled out anyway. There are companies that specialize in repatriation by air ambulance, small jets that have the intensive care equipment to cover every eventuality, but talking to their representatives I get a chilling sense of impersonal service at great cost, that the payment is more important than the patient. Dr. Stizer recommends a friend of his, a doctor who flies a private air ambulance, and the decision is made.

TODAY MILES AND I are flying back to England. On the runway our plane is dwarfed by everything around it. Tiny but purposeful, it looks like a hornet waiting for takeoff, fragile, thread-thin legs and delicate wings outstretched. The airport is closely ringed by high mountains, snow-covered, jagged and implacable, and I cannot imagine how this tiny thing will lift us over them. Once inside the plane you cannot stand upright yet unbelievably there will be six people on board. The pilot, Dr. Stizer's friend, is a handsome, swashbuckling neurosurgeon who flies for a hobby and often ferries his own or other intensive-care patients. His exuberance makes me realize how brittle I am, how taut and isolated is the space I've come to inhabit. His co-pilot looks reassuringly serious, a young man who shows great concern for Miles as he is being lifted into the plane. There is a male nurse from the hospital, and he and I sit belted in with our backs to the pilot and co-pilot, our shoulders almost touching theirs. Relaxed and friendly, the nurse tells me that he is now studying to be a doctor but takes on this work when he can to earn the money and for the ride, and, I can tell, this outing to England will be fun for him. In front of me, almost taking up the body of the plane, Miles lies on his back on a stretcher and I can just about reach across and touch his head to reassure him, or reassure myself. Next to him, at the other end of his stretcher and facing us, sits a young woman doctor; throughout the journey she monitors Miles and fills in the clipboard chart she keeps on her lap. Beside her is a bank of resuscitation equipment and a portable suction machine. Once the plane has taken off we can't talk, because the noise of the engines is deafening; this air ambulance has no luxury trimmings.

I don't like flying at the best of times and I especially don't like flying in small airplanes. This is the most physically frightened I have ever been. I fear the laid-back pilot, the tinny fragility of the plane, the grinding noise of the engines, the low altitude and proximity to the snow-covered mountains below us; above all I fear the effect of the rarefied cabin air pressure on what little oxygen is still being supplied to Miles's brain. Half an hour into the flight I begin to detect an unmistakeable smell of burning; yes, there is undoubtedly something burning in this airplane. I lean over to the nurse and he leans towards me. I shout in his ear, Can you smell burning? Mmm, he says, and turns to tap the co-pilot on the shoulder. They talk closely and then the nurse undoes his seat belt and crawls, bent double, down to the back of the aircraft. I can't see what he is doing as he crouches down but he returns calmly and now shouts in my ear, Heating, the heating, better it's off, okay?

I nod but I'm not okay. Miles has begun to judder, his body jerking, his head shaking terribly from side to side. The doctor leans forward to take his pulse and check his oxygen saturation level, then sits back in her seat. He continues to judder and I think he must be sensing something through his comatose state, that his unconscious registering of the change in his environment is triggering these severe spasms. I can do nothing to soothe him, except let my hand linger on the top of his head and try to will my love through to him, to enfold him and cocoon him with all the force of my love.

Ridiculously the plane lands at Biggin Hill, with its connotations of Biggles, the adventurous pilot of the vintage schoolboy comics; how Miles and Will would have loved that as small boys. It's a beautiful day, and as Miles is lifted out of the plane and on to the runway I realize it is the first time the sun has shone on him for six weeks. His skin has a ghostly sheen, his immobile eyebrows and closed, thick eyelashes unsettlingly dark in comparison. I can see that the two young men wheeling his stretcher try not to look at him too obviously, but it is unusual to see someone in a coma at close hand and they are both fascinated and repelled. Miles is still a handsome, powerful, athletic-looking young man in spite of his pallor; his rigid unconsciousness shocks. An ambulance is waiting outside the small airport and the cheerful driver helps me in. You sit next to me, love, in the comfortable seat, he says. You must be a bit out of sorts after that flight. The medics can go in the back with him. He'll be all right, don't you worry, love.

He talks all the way to London, turning on the siren whenever the traffic looks bad ahead. That's the joy of these things, he says, gets you where you want to in no time.

II

The ambulance drop-off point is in a small street at the back of University College Hospital, one of London's great flagship modern hospitals. Two porters wheel Miles on his stretcher up to the third-floor intensive care unit. I follow with the Austrian doctor and nurse, and entering the unit we are met by a young man with a harassed expression and a junior doctor's badge pinned to his white coat. Take the patient into this room, he says, pointing it out to the Austrians, and then to me, Please wait in the reception area while I examine your son. I have time to see Miles handed over to two nurses waiting in his empty room, to see him being slung, rigid, from the slightly higher Austrian gurney onto his new bed so that he lands awkwardly with a jarring thump. I register the first inkling that something is different here. For the past six weeks the Austrian doctors and nurses have done what they had to do with a kind efficiency that I assumed to be the norm.

Waiting as instructed in the empty reception area, I close my eyes and feel myself falling exhaustedly through deepening layers of incomprehension. But I'm back in England, I tell myself, and things will be easier now, things should become clearer. Eventually the young doctor reappears, and as I instinctively search his expression for any glimmer of hope, there is nothing. I'm afraid the Austrians seem to have got it wrong, he says, without preamble. I don't understand why they appear to have increased your son's score to four on the Glasgow Coma Scale whereas in fact he's only three. It's not a very clear report, he says (the Innsbruck doctors had taken the trouble to translate it into English). And I'm afraid too, he adds, that since he's arrived on a Sunday the on-duty neurologist will have to be called, which may take some time.

As I wait for the neurologist in Miles's room, I stand at the window and stare out over the teeming Euston Road below, cars streaming in both directions, hundreds of people going about their Sunday oblivious to the crises of lives they are passing by. Each time I close my eyes the sensation of falling returns. The neurologist finally arrives, flustered; I realize it must be irritating to have been called away from her Sunday especially to see Miles. There is barrier nursing on intensive care units; everybody, staff included, must wear plastic aprons and rubber gloves when handling the patients but this doctor does not. Are you the mother? she says to me. Yes, I reply. I am going to examine your son, she tells me, and then asks the nurse with a hint of exasperation to pass her the small torch that is quite easily within her reach. Pushing back Miles's eyelids in turn she shines the torch close up to see whether his pupils contract with the light and then hands it back to the nurse with a grimace: hopeless, it implies.

I watch her as she continues her examination. Miles is still in a coma after six weeks, he is evidently severely brain-damaged, what is the point of her or him being here—she makes this all very clear. Then, looking at me directly for the first time, she says, I'm afraid I don't think it's worth sending him to the Acute Brain Injury Unit at Queen Square. I think he should just go straight to Putney. Perhaps she meant to use the word *appropriate* instead of *worth*, but *worth* just slipped out. Nothing else is said; she leaves the room.

Putney: I know the hospital. Formerly the Royal Hospital for Incurables—a large billboard at the side of the road proclaimed its ominous presence on the A3, the route I took every time I drove Miles and Will to school in Winchester; it was a shock each time to read it. How terrible, we would say every time we passed. How chilling the name was: Hospital for Incurables. Then one day when we drove past the sign had been replaced with the grander and more politically correct Royal Hospital for Neuro-disability. I remember we talked about the change, about how words can influence attitudes, that *moron* and *spastic* and *mongol* are no longer usable. I can only think now of the unknown future that was crouching so mockingly, viciously, ahead of us as we drove blithely by. What else might still be waiting there?

Before leaving I meet with the young clinical director of the ICU with whom I had spoken from Innsbruck. He had been helpful and reassuring throughout and all the arrangements for Miles's admittance to UCH had been made by him with the expressed intention that after examination and assessment Miles would be transferred to the Acute Brain Injury Unit at Queen Square. I wonder if he has already spoken to the neurologist or to the junior doctor who saw Miles on arrival, but his assurance no longer seems as certain. I am alerted to something going on that concerns Miles and to which I am not party. But with relief I find the sensation of falling has disappeared and instead I have landed with an invigorating shock. If I'm to be at war here, I think to myself, I will fight them to the last.

* * *

I HAVE COME home for the first time in six weeks. Inside, the house looks strangely distant, as though I am seeing it through the wrong end of a telescope. Everything is the same and not the same, it has been recalibrated by this thing that, last time I stood right here, was in the future, and now it has happened and nothing can be the same again. The house is old; it knows more of life than I do. Built in 1780, solid and Georgian, it is a house confident of its place. How many people have come home to it, opened the familiar front door under its delicate tracery of glass fanlight and stepped into the wide hall with this same mixture of feelings? Relief to be safely home, mixed with new and terrible knowledge? Soldiers have returned here from the horror of trenches and gas; what has happened to Miles simply adds another layer to its accumulated history. Life will go on, it says. Here, for the time being, you are safe.

There is an antique painted Vietnamese cabinet in the hall, which had been due to be delivered the day after Miles's accident. It seems to hold a special significance, straddling the break in my life; how innocent Ron and I were when we saw it and decided to buy it, and when I arranged for it to be delivered that particular Monday morning. Miles has never seen it; he will be pleased that it has replaced the carved wooden African drum he disliked so much. In fact it wasn't a large drum but the suitcase of a former queen of the Cameroons, packed and carried by her slaves, intricately carved out of some exotic black wood that gleamed even in the dark. Miles thought it had bad karma, that it filled the air with sinister intent. Please get rid of it, Mum, he said, it's malign, it's not right here, it isn't meant for this house. It's as though it holds a curse, he said. Too painful to think about that now. I walk through to the kitchen and open the fridge and find a glass bowl full of sliced oranges in caramel syrup—they would have been served with my homemade cardamom ice cream at the lunch party that was interrupted six weeks ago, but Ron saw the guests out after I'd taken the call. How strange that the oranges have lasted; I suppose the caramel syrup preserves them. The ice cream is in the freezer untouched, a family favorite and certainly still edible, but I scoop both oranges and ice cream into the bin. I don't want them in the house.

Outside, the garden has changed from the last bleak bare bones of mid-March to freshest early summer. Everything has come into leaf, a wild palette of greens touched here and there by late-flowering tulips and the earliest roses just beginning to bloom. Will, Claudia, and Marina are here, Ron has put champagne on ice for us all, and as we sit outside in the cool scented evening we drink a toast for Miles. His absence is ringing through the house and we each have the same urgent need to include him, keep him here with us, not let him go. There is so much to talk about, not least the events of the day, but I am wondering why Ron isn't having a whisky—I know he prefers it to champagne but he has poured himself a glass of wine instead. Miles enjoys whisky as much as Ron does and a ritual has evolved whereby he gives Ron a special bottle to try out every Christmas and whenever he is home they sit down to a glass or two together and put the world to rights. I ask Ron if he wouldn't prefer a whisky and he says, No, I don't feel like one. He looks away down the garden, lost for a moment, then turns back to me and says, I don't think I'm going to have another whisky until I can drink it with Miles. I reach across and hold his hand; for such a powerful and complex man Ron can be as transparent as a child. We fall to silence. The garden walls are high, the world shut out beyond them; this place will be a retreat for us all.

* * *

DESPITE THE HORROR of those weeks in Innsbruck, the dread-filled walks to the hospital twice a day and the inert, profoundly damaged Miles we encountered every time, I had guessed they might be halcyon days. While different members of the family came and went and I remained in the quiet town with its clean cobbled streets and Tyrolean propriety, we were a family together in a bubble of privacy, isolated by our shared grief and protected by our anonymity. We had no need to present ourselves or explain our situation.

Back in London we are a family that has been visited by disaster, marked out, different. I could be a foul black crow. Limping with my scabbed feet, dragging a broken wing behind me, eyes glittering, my wound an open gash; I leave a trail. I go out to parties, meet my friends, and that is what I am. They see me coming and part silently, afraid. What can they say?

Grief, I discover, changes you. I have become different, outside and inside: outside, because I am now an object of pity and horror, no longer safe; inside, because my terrible new sensitivity has destroyed tolerance—there is no room left for it. Friendship is put to the most severe of tests. I cannot bear to think how often I may have failed my friends in the way some fail me now, so often unwittingly, I know.

I don't like my new self.

AT THE TIME of his accident Miles was in St. Anton with work colleagues on an office-sponsored break, but it has not occurred to me to connect his employers in any way with the tragedy that has befallen him. So I am surprised to receive a call from a senior partner at the firm with an offer to cover the cost of the air ambulance home, and asking whether there is any other help they can provide. I am touched by his evident concern for Miles and we arrange to meet. We sit in a coffee bar in the City and talk about Miles, and this obviously successful and impressive older man tells me that it was difficult having Miles working for him. The difficulty, he says, was that I knew in many ways he was already better able than I am to do my job. But he was nevertheless junior to me and so that could be a problem. I wish Miles could have heard these words; I know, from what he has told me, that their working relationship was not easy, but I wish he could be here. I know he would share my admiration and respect for this man's honesty and graciousness.

After the meeting I receive a letter from the company's HR department, informing me that Miles will continue to receive two thirds of his salary until a clear prognosis is made. Later on he will receive a lump sum in an insurance payout. I could not be more grateful for this extraordinary generosity and support from what, from the outside, might appear to be another large faceless corporation. I am just beginning to realize, too, how much this financial support will be needed in the months to come.

DURING THE NEXT two weeks Miles is seen by a procession of doctors, to assess his condition before transferral to Queen Square. I listen with bewilderment as one after the other is dismissive of his chances of recovery and is against sending him to the Acute Brain Injury Unit. We had understood that he'd returned to London on the assurance of a place there, and after the professional and ambitious approach to Miles's treatment by the Innsbruck medical team I am shocked. I am given a range of reasons why Miles cannot go to the ABIU: there are no beds available, the ABIU does not admit tracheostomies (this is patent nonsense, as a friend who is a speech therapist at Queen Square confirms), Miles lives in the wrong postal district for admittance, there are only limited resources for neuro-rehab, unlike Putney. There seems to be a strange game being played where the rules have been intentionally withheld from the family, and it begins to take on the dimensions of a blood sport with Miles as the quarry. We feel as though we are being treated with contempt for not knowing the rules and for blindly playing on, ridiculously keeping up a fight for Miles to have a chance. It is as if the medical establishment is amassing its ranks against an irritant intruder. A mistake was made in accepting him into this hospital and he is not wanted here. He is transgressing the norms of admission and hospital spending, particularly, it seems, since his injury did not take place within the right postal code for admission. It could be a farce, but I discern the unmentionable truth: he is too damaged to warrant time and money being spent on him.

It is a matter of medical politics and budgets, and my confusion begins to turn to disillusionment. I had not thought doctors operated, as a banker or a businessman must do, in monetary terms. But suddenly here it appears to be the case; the concern is above all for keeping to the rules of the budget. Naïvely, I see now, I had believed in the humanity of doctors, but even more disillusioning is their comprehensive dismissal of Miles as a person; the human story is irrelevant and he is just another traumatic brain injury, a TBI, a bed blocker. I long for Dr. Stizer and Professor Benir and bitterly regret our decision to come back to England.

As a family, we understand Miles may never recover, but how can we be asked to abandon him at this early stage without trying everything in our power to give him a chance? We know the first twelve months are the most vital and at this point it is only six weeks since his accident. Miles is still in a coma; to give up now would be unimaginable. We exist on a taut wire of hope and despair, and hope is not synonymous with optimism. Optimism is to believe that things will always turn out for the best; true hope is clear-eyed, knowing the negative but desiring the positive. For Miles's sake we must retain hope; if we let despair tip the balance we are all lost.

TEN DAYS HAVE passed when I am told Dr. Stephenson is coming to see Miles. This is extraordinary, and our last chance, since as a consultant on the Acute Brain Injury Unit he may have the power to overturn the other doctors' decisions. I wait for him in Miles's room, sitting by the bed and explaining to Miles that an internationally acclaimed expert in brain injury is coming to see him. I want him to find this reassuring but I want him to perform, too, to impress the doctor, to rise to the occasion. He has always risen to a challenge, but how can he now? I'm sickened by my desperation.

The door opens and Dr. Stephenson greets me briefly before continuing straight over to Miles's bed. He is an imposing-looking man, tall, dark, the impression austere. He acknowledges the nurse but appears to have no need to assert his position with either of us. He introduces himself by name to Miles and then watches him silently for some time before he begins to examine him. He might be a pediatrician examining a newborn baby, so gentle is his handling of Miles, his quiet, serious manner conveying a sense of profound respect for this mute, damaged young man under his care.

When he has finished he looks across at me for the first time; it is as though he had forgotten I was there. Could you tell me how you find Miles at the moment? he asks me. I am taken aback—this is the first time since arriving back in London that anyone has asked me for my opinion. I tell him I am surprised to be asked this, that I have not been asked before, and he says, It's very important. He seems surprised and disapproving, I don't know whether with me or the doctors who omitted to ask the question. Then he adds firmly that the close relatives of a person in this situation have the best understanding of the patient and the clearest idea of whether there is any response, or any change in response. It is a question I always ask, he says sharply, and I see the intimidating professor rebuking a student with one peremptory aside.

I tell him that in truth I don't know how Miles is, but that in the last few days the other children and I have independently thought that he seems closer to the surface of consciousness, that there are small, barely perceptible signs of awareness. When we greet him each day there is now a slight flicker of movement across his face; for the first time we are seeing a glimpse of some dimly felt expression, as though he were trying to reach through to the surface. I imagine a sea of unconsciousness and tiny islands of awareness; some are too far away to make out clearly but others are closer, gradually coming into focus as we watch. It feels an intimate thing to be telling this reserved and clearly cerebral man, but then I narrate everything that has happened; his respect for Miles and his inclusion rather than dismissal of me have breached my defenses. I tell him that from the moment of Miles's arrival here we feel no one has taken responsibility for him, or given us any constructive information, and that, crucially, he has not been receiving the regular physiotherapy I understand to be so important for his rehabilitation. At different times we have been given completely different reasons why he cannot go to Queen Square. I also tell him that if Miles hadn't returned from Innsbruck they would have been starting him immediately on a comprehensive rehab course; the professor there believed it was imperative at this stage if he was to have any chance of recovery.

Dr. Stephenson listens intently without intervening. When I finish he turns from me and looks at Miles, then back to me. In my view, he says, your son is suitable for, and would benefit from, immediate admittance for acute treatment. He needs concentrated, appropriate neuro-rehabilitation. It will have taken at least a week for him to settle down after the journey back from Austria. I am afraid, he adds, that because he arrived at UCH from Austria and therefore without the normal process of admittance, it has become a political matter. The question is whether or not this can be overcome.

He gets up to leave and I thank him for coming, trying to remain calm as I say that I hope it will be possible for him to admit Miles to the ABIU under his care. As the door closes behind him I run straight to Miles's bedside and lift his shoulders and head up from the pillows, cradling him in my arms as I hug him, tears wetting his face. I realize I'm crying in front of the nurse but I don't care, I think Miles can hear me: I love you so much, my precious, precious darling, you *will* come through this.

In a Sunday magazine I read the story of Karen, a teenage girl who died suddenly without warning from meningitis. The father recounts the aftermath, how the family was diminished by her death. His wife ceased speaking, would stand at the kitchen sink washing the dishes or gazing out into the garden, silently weeping. The two teenage brothers no longer slept upstairs, where their sister had died in the bedroom next to theirs, but instead carried their duvets down and slept on the living room sofas. One of the brothers grew his hair so long that his fringe fell over his eyes, blocking out the world. The father stayed up late into the night, writing a journal in the form of a letter to his daughter in which he described the passing of each day, of the familial keening for her. The mother could no longer go to work as a school receptionist, the father lost his job as a university lecturer because he had to stay at home to look after his wife. The mortgage payments could no longer be met. Their house was repossessed. This second shock, the father recounts, the forced move out of the grief-locked stasis of their lives, led eventually to their recovery; obliged to confront their loss and the unavoidable continuation of life without Karen, they found a resolution of sorts.

It is a tragic story and I understand their retreat into grief. They lost Karen. But it also galvanizes me; we have not lost Miles and so we must continue functioning fully, for him. The story feels like a warning—I realize I have begun to let things go at home. Coming back late from the hospital I can see the children have been foraging in the kitchen, open cereal packets and the remnants of toast and Marmite on the worktop. Supper is a thrown-together affair. I don't feel hungry, in fact all I really want to do is to sit down with Ron and whichever of the children is at home over a large glass of wine and talk about our continuing strategy for Miles's recovery. There is a subtle sense of abandonment through the house, as though only the kitchen is inhabited now, precariously, the dining table a mess of old newspapers and my unopened mail. There are no flowers in the hall. I must take stock.

THE NEXT MORNING Will visits Miles and is told by the nurse that a Dr. Mosley would like to see him. At midday Will calls me. His anger rings down the line like an unearthed electric current.

Dr. Mosley is the eighth doctor to see Miles; none of us has met him before. He does not introduce himself to Will. He begins: Miles's prospects are extremely bleak. He is going to be severely disabled and it is my opinion that treatment for him at Queen Square would at best only make him slightly less disabled.

Will is taken aback at his abruptness. He replies, Then surely we need to give him that chance?

It would only mean the difference between his future being grim or not quite so grim, says Dr. Mosley. Treatment would not serve any useful purpose.

Any useful purpose! How can a doctor have become so inured to the hopes and fears of the person behind the patient, or of the patient's family? At this early stage hope is still precarious. Will is facing the loss of his brother.

Will answers: Miles has not yet come out of his coma. We want him to have the best possible chance of recovery with the best possible treatment.

The doctor continues undeterred: Many people, if faced with the prospect of being kept alive artificially, would rather be allowed to die if being kept alive involved great discomfort, intensive nursing, and severe disablement. Many families decide, on reflection, that their loved ones would want not to be kept alive like this.

We as a family are not being blindly optimistic, says Will, with furious calm. We are prepared to accept whatever happens to Miles. But we are not prepared to assume that he has no future without giving him the best possible treatment now, at this early stage, and thus the best chance of recovery. Miles is a fighter—he is incredibly determined and motivated and I can pretty categorically state that he would want the best and most ambitious treatment possible.

Would he? replies the doctor.

Who is this man? How can he talk like this to Will? Miles is not on a ventilator. He is breathing on his own. There is no machine to turn off. The issue in question is not whether Miles lives or dies. It is about whether he goes to the ABIU or is left to languish on a general ward without any dedicated neuro-rehabilitation. It is only eight weeks since his accident. Our hope may be fragile, but how can he possibly think we could abandon Miles?

If this conversation had to take place, it should not have been now and not with Will. He is not the official next of kin. He is Miles's younger brother who has lost his closest friend and confidant. Afterwards, when I take the matter up with the head of the ICU, it transpires that Dr. Mosley is not a neurologist with expertise in brain injury, but a pain consultant.

THE TALL AUSTRALIAN nurse we all dislike is on duty when I visit Miles late that afternoon. There is a prickle of menace about the nurse, his manner supercilious and his handling of Miles curt and dismissive, as though his vulnerability were a cause for derision. He looks up as I come into the room and then with a sweep of his arm towards Miles he makes a mock bow. There he sits, he says, King and Lord of all he surveys.

Miles has been placed into a large high-backed armchair covered with the ubiquitous green plastic of hospital mattresses, his body slumped forward awkwardly against the canvas straps that are holding him upright. Across his forehead the strap is thicker and softer, padded on the underside with sheepskin, but I can see the edge of the red weal it is going to leave when removed.

I want to throttle this nurse, gouge out his eyes, beat him until he whimpers for mercy. I want to see him cowering and gibbering with fear while I beat him until I can beat him no more. Miles is still in a coma; not only are his eyes closed but the one certain evidence of brain damage is to his right occipital lobe, so that half his vision, if he is ever to open his eyes, is irrevocably damaged.

He could be a young man in the aftermath of Death Row, his body slack and quiet after the juddering; an image of horror. King and Lord of all he surveys!

* * *

THAT EVENING I receive a call from the head injury nurse at Queen Square. A bed has become available and Miles is to be admitted. Arrangements are already being made to have him brought to the ABIU by ambulance the following day.

How bittersweet the pleasure I feel. The revenge on Dr. Mosley; on the Australian nurse; on all the doctors who have dismissed him; and then the fact that we are *relieved* Miles will be in an acute brain injury unit. He might as well have won a place at the most prestigious institution in the world against the greatest competition.

III

How different is the arrival at Queen Square. On entering the ward I am greeted warmly by the head injury nurse, who is expecting me. Miles's journey went smoothly, she says. The ambulance arrived about half an hour ago and he is now settled in. She is efficient and friendly, and with relief I think, Here perhaps I might be able to let down my defenses. Here Miles is not going to be considered a nuisance, and nor, it seems, am I.

IT IS TWO days after Miles's admittance to Queen Square; he is still in a coma. His friend Jasper is visiting him and I have left them on their own and gone to sit and read in the vestibule outside the ward. Friends are finding it difficult seeing him for the first time. I watch them trying to suppress their shock, then finding themselves at a loss as to what to say to him, feeling awkward in the face of his intimidating blankness and embarrassed in front of me. It is difficult to know how to speak to him; we all find it impossible to sustain a flow of one-sided conversation that sounds in any way normal. Each word echoes in the silence. It is easier to try to bolster our own morale and his by reminding him of all that he has still to do and to look forward to—completing his project with the BBC, writing his book, dreaming up more entrepreneurial schemes, making his fortune, getting his ranch in America, finding a beautiful girl. But as another friend, Simon, said, Miles is a person you can never bullshit. Not only do I feel a fool rabbiting on about my life when he is trapped there in front of me, he said, but everything I say sounds hollow and futile.

Suddenly a nurse comes running out of the double doors from the ward. Miles's mum, come quick, come quick! she says, Miles has just opened his eyes! I fly through the ward and yes, there he is, sitting in his wheelchair facing Jasper with his deep green eyes open for the first time in eight weeks. Miles is back! He has emerged from his coma! He's going to be all right. Every moment of the past eight weeks has been geared to this one longed-for moment, the fragile dream come true. I'm overwhelmed, perilous with relief, as though I have become too frail to be able to contain such intense happiness, such pure fulfilment of hope—that Miles is back and the horror is over. His life can resume. All I can do is repeat his name, Miles, Miles, oh my god Miles, you're back, you're awake, I must call the family, you're back my darling Miles . . . As I search in my handbag for my phone Jasper remains quiet, I'm sure he is too moved to speak, that this momentous thing should have happened during his first, shocked visit. The nurse has gone quiet too and then I realize everything around us has gone quiet. Something's wrong. I look up and in the awful silence I watch Miles's eyes drift slowly from right to left and back again, unaligned and empty. He sits, strapped in his high-backed wheelchair, his head also strapped and held upright in the curved and padded headrest, and slowly, very slowly, his eyes close. A faint but unambiguous expression of the purest, deepest misery begins to disturb the set of this face that has not moved for eight weeks. It is detectable only by the minute tightening pull at the sides of his mouth that freezes into a rictus of pain. If magnified, it would outdo Munch's *Scream*.

That night all the children are home for dinner. It should be a joy-filled occasion—Miles has opened his eyes and that, as we understand it, means he is officially out of his coma. For eight weeks we have been dreaming of this moment. But he cannot see properly, and he did not speak. Although we know now not to expect the Hollywood awakening from coma, nevertheless we had dared to hope for it to mean the return of *Miles*; that even if gravely damaged we would have him back in some recognizable way, that son and brother we know so intimately and miss so painfully. Our excitement at his awakening is freighted with fear, but as we talk together hope begins to rise once more: even if his sight is damaged it may not be complete; at least now his eyes are open the neurologists can explore the extent of the damage; maybe all he needs is special glasses; and of course it would take some time to recover his speech. The sensation is precariously sweet, like holding a wounded bird in your hand that is just beginning to flutter its wings.

Driving in to visit Miles the next morning, I think about how proactive and determined he is, how impatient when things move slowly, when he can't solve a problem. How will he be when I see him? How will I know, if he can't tell me and I can't read his eyes? Waiting at a traffic light I watch a young man walking from car to car. I notice that in between cars his face in repose is sly and confident, but as he approaches the drivers he tilts his head to one side and adopts a meek, ingratiating smile, his hand outstretched. As he comes up to my window I'm shocked to hear myself shouting, Get away from me! How dare you do this—you can talk and see, you're lucky, you've got a brain, for god's sake! It's undamaged! Use it! Go away and *do* something.

MILES OCCUPIES THE first cubicle in the ABIU and is the first person you see as you come through the doors of the ward. As I arrive I notice he is still in bed, propped up, the pillow end of the bed raised high so that his face is clearly visible, and I have to cry out, Miles, what on earth is it? There is a look of such agony on his face that I drop my bags and run straight to his bedside, I'm crying, bending over him and hugging him, what's wrong, my darling? His eyes are screwed shut, his face hunched and frozen in a sound-less howl of pain. And then as he hears my voice his face begins to soften, his eyes open wide and the sweetest expression of love and relief comes over it, trusting, childlike, as though to say: It's Mum! It's okay, I'm not in hell, I'm coming out of this, and I can see him trying to raise himself up from the pillow towards me. But nothing happens. Only his head and neck move forward a centimeter or two with what is clearly the greatest effort, the veins on his neck are bulging out. He stops, and then there is a long moment of shared horror as he realizes the truth, that I make no difference: he can't move, he can't speak, he can't see, he is in hell. Slowly he lets go and I can feel, I can see him sinking away from me into the depths of the abyss that is his new world.

THE HORROR OF imagining his world. My mind batters against invisible walls, I am in the blackest dungeon of incomprehension. I want to be with him. Closing my eyes, I try to dissolve into the darkness...

    There are voices.   *The darkness*   *this darkness*   *a faint light flickered.*   *It's gone.*   *They're searching they're looking*   *they must be looking*   *they're close*   *they'll find me.*   *I can't move. How.*   *Too heavy   I'm tied down, my weight shifts   and then.   Nothing.   I feel nothing anywhere   just heavy   How can   I can't   make any sound. The light   it's   nearer   they're coming   Mum's voice   it's right up close I can feel her breath on me   the smell of her perfume   can't she see me can't she   Why   I'm in a nightmare   wake WAKE I've got to wake. Wake out of this get out of it.   That's Mum   she will she   must   do something   why   telling me she loves me   and again, I KNOW   just do something   for fuck's sake please SOMEONE HELP ME*

I fail. It is impossible.

MILES IS GOING to have his first working session with the occupational therapist and she has asked for one of us to be present. I am glad Will is with me; it's a date I have been both longing for and dreading in equal measure, living on the eternal seesaw of hope and despair: in this case either the unimaginable ecstasy of finding a tangible connection or the dread of nothingness, a chasm, not even an echo where Miles should be. It is apparently the occupational therapist who holds the key but I wonder how in this context, how exactly they work with people who are unable to interact. I have a vague idea of occupational therapy through pictures I've seen of blind people in workshops making baskets or prisoners embroidering cushions, but I will come to learn and appreciate the subtle, painstaking work undertaken by neurological occupational therapists treating people who are brain damaged by TBI or stroke or disease. Like an air crash investigator, they must first locate their patient's internal equivalent of the black box, an often long and arduous process, and if they are successful in locating it they have then to piece together and interpret, if they can, the information it reveals.

When we arrive the therapist is already with Miles. She has drawn up a chair next to his wheelchair and with relief I see she has managed to engage him. He is facing her and listening intently, his eyes, though unfocused, directed at her, his body quite still. She has been introducing herself to him, she tells us, and explaining her goals. Her voice is calm and devoid of the ubiquitous singsong tone that so many people adopt now in talking to Miles, as though he were a small child, that tone which is for us, as it must surely be for all relatives in this situation, one of the most painful and infuriating side effects. She sets up her first, basic piece of equipment, which is a large flat round button placed in front of Miles on the tray of his wheelchair. A bell rings if it is fully suppressed and she presses it to show him, explaining that he should press it for yes and do nothing for no and apologizing in advance for the infantilizing questions with which she will have to begin. Is your name Miles? Watching silently we are as tense as NASA scientists waiting for confirmation that an astronaut has survived a moon landing. With excruciating slowness Miles's thumb begins to move over the button but then stops. We have been asked not to make a sound and the effort of holding back encouragement is agonizing—Come ON, we want to shout, keep going, keep going, keep going, push DOWN . . . His thumb starts to quiver and move again and then I realize: this is as difficult for him as rolling a giant boulder away from the mouth of a cave, that a gigantic physical effort is required for this one tiny movement. Now the quivering is growing in intensity, the whole hand is shaking and then his thumb goes down and the bell rings and we can't help shouting out, Yes! You did it! You did it! Brilliant, Miles! He understands. There is no doubt.

By the end of this first short session he has managed to press the bell correctly six out of ten times. When the answer to a question should be yes and there is no movement our silence is now an agony of vicarious effort. However difficult the movement is for him, in order to lift him out of the diagnosis of no hope there needs to be evidence that he can *consistently* respond. But today is only the beginning and we have the hard proof that he understands; we have felt it intuitively but, most important now, the therapists have proof.

The session ends and we stay on. You were amazing, Miles, Will says to him. You're the most determined person I know and if anyone can do this, you will. You were incredible, dude. Miles slowly closes his eyes. I take his hand and tell him how proud I am of him too. We could see how difficult it was for you, but you did it, as you always do. Our words fade into the silence. What is he feeling? Are we saying the right thing? It's time to leave, and as we say goodbye and leave the hospital I link my arm through Will's in a confusion of tears. This is like being drunk with hope, I say, and Will agrees. He really did it, Mum. It was quite clear—he's there, he showed them.

We do not know it yet, but this sets a pattern that will continue. Miles undoubtedly is conscious and sometimes understands, but how aware he is and to what degree he understands, nobody can be absolutely certain. We must learn to calibrate the meaning of his moods, expressions, body movements, learn to read the new language that is all we now have. It is difficult to explain how we interpret these signals, for it is a mixture of our knowledge of, and familiarity with, Miles and our intuitive reading of his expressions and movements. Added to this are the normal interpretative skills used in any social situation, discerning whether someone is friendly or hostile, sad or happy, comfortable or in pain, social skills that are taken for granted. We know we face the skepticism of some doctors and therapists, and the anger this generates is so wounding that we take the decision never to discuss our interpretation of Miles's awareness unless it is with someone trusted. When we encounter those few who look past Miles's brain injury and read the person behind it our gratitude is overwhelming.

TWICE A WEEK Miles is put on the tilt table. I remember reading Jean-Dominique Bauby's description of himself in *The Diving Bell and the Butterfly* as, immobile and tethered to the inclined board, he evoked the appearance of the Commendatore's statue in Mozart's *Don Giovanni*; I remember, too, finding the idea painfully moving, that a grown man should have to be tied to a board in order to be held upright. Now I watch as two physiotherapists start by sliding a strong nylon sheet under Miles, like the waterproof ground sheet you might use in a tent when camping, and then together they pull it to ease him across from his bed onto a large board on wheels aligned horizontally with it. Once there, he is strapped to the board before it is slowly raised to a more or less vertical position, the angle of upright tilt that he can support being carefully monitored by the physiotherapists. The goal is for him to stand at 90 degrees for a period of time, but the angle will vary depending on his heart rate, oxygen levels, and general level of comfort. Apparently being upright is good for his circulation and for his lungs, and as the tilt table is weight-bearing it helps, I am told, to loosen his joints and break up the rigid muscle tone. I just think it must be good for the soul, to be held up and out of the perpetual confines of his bed or chair.

The first time he used the tilt table I worried that he might feel faint or giddy but he appeared to enjoy it, his face relaxed and his eyes wide open. Standing next to him today he is, wonderfully, once again as he should be, taller than me, and the physio takes his hand and says, Miles, I'm going to place this on your mum's head so you can feel her hair. She moves his hand slowly up and down through my hair and then rests it on my cheek and we all see it, the faintest lift on one side of his face to a look of such sweetness I must hold back the tears. I don't want him to feel them run down over his fingers.

As PART OF his research into the book he was writing, Miles had been attending the classes of a Chinese teacher of qigong, the Chinese martial art. The teacher, Li Hu, also practices a form of Chinese healing, and he has asked if he may visit Miles. I know from Miles that the work he does is serious and that he returns to Tibet frequently to a Buddhist retreat where he also practices.

We arrange to meet in the hospital entrance. I could not have mistaken him, his manner and his bearing as he crosses the hall towards me one of extreme self-containment and reserve; he could be a Buddhist monk. His face is expressionless as he greets me with a bow of his head. I will follow you to Miles, he says. We walk in silence along the corridor to the elevator and wait in silence until it arrives. I'm slightly apprehensive now and feel I need to explain something of Miles's situation, to prepare him. He listens as I speak and then says, When Miles came to me as a new student I did not need to teach him. He understood already. His soul is old. Nothing more; he doesn't commiserate or refer to what I have been telling him.

Miles is asleep when we arrive, seated in a wheelchair next to his bed. Do you need me to wake him? I ask Li Hu, but he says no, it is enough that he is here with him. Drawing the curtains around the bed, I tell him I'll be back in ten minutes or so and leave. As I walk down to the canteen for a cup of coffee I'm trying to contain the vivid, rising excitement that has drowned out my earlier apprehension. Li Hu is a healer. Miles respected him. Maybe he is the person who will be able to reach through to him. Maybe he *can* perform a miracle. Maybe . . .

Returning to the ward I tentatively enter the curtained cubicle of Miles's bed. Li Hu is standing facing him and Miles is staring back, his eyes burning with a strange fierce light while his whole body is trembling and juddering uncontrollably, his head jerking from side to side. I'm horrified and bend over him, Miles, are you all right? What's happening? It is his chi fighting to stay here, Li Hu replies calmly. Miles wishes to stay. He is very strong, but his chi has been damaged. We must wait for the outcome. I take Miles's hand and try to soothe him; I'm so frightened by this state he is in, but I feel as though I'm intervening in something beyond my comprehension, that I should leave this to Miles. I have seen him in this state once before, though with his eyes still closed, some weeks after his accident. He had come out of an MRI while he was still in the coma and had just experienced the dramatic electronic thudding of the apparatus imaging his brain. Miles, you *are* going to come through this. You *will* stay with us. Li Hu watches me. We wait in silence as Miles's trembling gradually begins to subside until finally, exhaustedly, he closes his eyes.

Li Hu gives me some sheets of paper that he has drawn on and tells me to place them above Miles's bed. They are to strengthen his chi, he says. Weird shapes and swirls that mean nothing to me, but I will put them up. Something powerful has taken place here today even if I don't understand it, and Miles respected this man.

I AM CONSCIOUS that my days now revolve around seeing Miles. Although Ron has not referred to this in any way, I don't want it to compromise the time I have with him. Miles is settled at Queen Square, and when I suggest that Ron and I take some time away, a long weekend, the children are encouraging. You need time on your own together, they say, we can take care of Miles, and they immediately arrange a rota of seeing him so that there won't be any day when he doesn't have a visitor.

We will go to Paris. Friends have kindly offered to lend us their apartment there, which means we will be on our own and self-sufficient, easier than having to face the other guests in a hotel. Leaving Miles behind is more painful than I imagined. The idea that a sea lies between us fills me with fear, the sense of sheer physical distance and of my helplessness. I feel I *need* to be there with him, to oversee his care, though in truth I know the children will give him just as much comfort. I don't want to discuss the strange sense I have of dislocation, of homesickness, with Ron; I know I must not let Miles intrude on this time we have on our own.

And now we are here, in this tiny apartment on the Île St-Louis. The bells in the church across the road are tolling the 6:00 p.m. mass. Next to the graceful seventeenth-century church, the only one on the island, there is an infant school and the children have just been released for the day, so that the sound of pealing bells is accompanied by the tinkling cries of children. Parents are assembled in the street to collect their children and from my windowsill up on the fourth floor I watch a young mother waiting with stylish nonchalance astride her bicycle, one foot on the ground, slim jeans rolled up, long dark hair tied back casually, a small blond child in a bucket seat behind her. As her elder son comes out of the gates she waves and sets off on her bike and he runs alongside her down the street, passing her one of his satchels which she takes from him and slings over her shoulder, one hand resting on the handlebars. I think of Miles at that age, for it seems to me he ran just like this boy, purposeful and energetic.

I lived in this city a long time ago as a girl of twenty and it is where I began and lost my other first child. Never a real one to me, a child shared with my gentle French boyfriend, Serge, and aborted clandestinely at seven weeks by an off-duty nurse in her home in the suburbs of Paris. I wasn't curious or confident enough to ask whether she did it for money or on principle, abortion being illegal in France and other Catholic countries at that time. Serge was an art student and it was inconceivable that we could support a baby; I was certain it was kinder not to bring it into the world.

We traveled by train early one evening to the end of the line and walked down the gray streets to her house, where she was expecting us despite holding a cocktail party. We rang the doorbell and were let in by her husband, who looked knowing and asked us to wait in the hall. As we waited we listened to the guests getting into their swing until a small woman in a tight black dress appeared and asked me to follow her down the corridor. I lay on a bed as she performed her rudimentary procedure. Wait a few days, she said, and the baby will pass. We paid her and she waved us off briskly at the door. Returning to her party, her absence would have been so fleeting it probably went unnoticed.

The baby never did pass and eventually I had to go to a doctor. Living as I did in the *haut bourgeois* arrondissement of Passy, albeit in a bedsit, the doctor was elderly and aristocratic and shocked by my naïveté. Did I not know how dangerous and unscrupulous backstreet abortionists were? Had I not used a contraceptive (I was so foolishly naïve it hadn't crossed my mind)? It was impossible, this overlap of the new sexual liberation in a secular state with laws that were still framed by Catholicism. Medicine should be intended to take care of people, not prescribe morality. He admitted me straight into hospital on the grounds that my health was at risk and performed a curettage. I have only two clear memories of this part of the story, one being the softly bearded, sympathetic male nurse who wheeled me down to the operating theater and commiserated with me about how difficult it must be to lose a baby—until I told him I didn't want it and the disgust in his face shocked me. The other memory is of unfathomable misery after I came round from the operation, which I put down at the time to the aftereffects of the anesthetic.

Nine years later and married, I gave birth to my first, much-wanted child in London. I was twenty-nine years old, on the threshold of the unknown, deeply lived new phase of family life of which Miles was the joyful beginning. Twenty-nine years have passed since then. I've lived a full life, have had four children, and am now married to a husband whom I love with the particular, intense fulfilment and intimacy that a happy second marriage can bring. Is twenty-nine years of conscious life all that Miles will ever know?

The church bells have ceased their tolling. Stepping down from the windowsill I realize Ron has been sitting across the room watching me quietly. Why don't you tell me what you've been thinking about? he says. And so I do and when I finish I apologize. I'm so sorry, Ron, I really wanted Miles not to intrude into these few days. It's not possible and it doesn't matter, Ron says. What matters is how much I love you—nothing can intrude on that. He stands up and comes over to me and he takes me in his arms. I know, he says, I think of him all the time too. We can do this thing together. I am not alone; Ron understands even this. I'm aware of sounds drifting up from the street, the hum of people talking, a car door shutting, the soft, quick stutter and thrum of an engine starting. They are some of the everyday sounds of life in the city and we must go down and take part, we must celebrate these few days here on our own. Miles would want us to do that, I know.

I AM CONSUMED by the need to understand what has happened inside Miles's brain. Dr. Stephenson is generous about this and one afternoon he takes the time to show Will and me the MRI that has recently been done. He talks us through what it tells him, reading the black and gray images on the screen as though they were text. It remains inscrutable to me, a pottage of shapes, but I can see the slight gap he points out between the brain and the skull. That gap reveals that the brain is already beginning to atrophy, he says, which happens following brain damage as it does in old age. The sight of Miles's young, quick, sharp brain already beginning to shrink is so shocking and so harrowing a piece of news that I can feel my mind sliding away, I can't retain it. Instead what I take away from the meeting is the reminder that no definitive prognosis can be made until a year has passed from the time of injury, which means there are nine more months in which he can recover, start to speak, return to us. Dr. Stephenson says that if he does recover we should not expect him to be able to go back to work in the way he did before. But that doesn't matter anymore; all that matters is that it's still possible he will come back to us.

Dr. Stephenson also tells us that Miles will have no recollection of his accident or of the minutes preceding it. Of course, I have heard this before. How dreadful, how confusing, for Miles. Why didn't I think of it? What possible sense can he make of where he is if he doesn't know what happened to him on that mountain slope?

THE NEXT MORNING Claudia comes with me to the hospital. Miles is in his chair, having already had a session of physio, and he is awake and alert; we have arrived on one of his clear islands of consciousness. The physical signs for this are subtle and we read them today just as a hunter might, observing a deer that has suddenly become aware of his presence. A slight movement of the head, body held stilled, eyes turned towards you but holding their gaze somewhere in the far distance, on full alert, as though not seeing but listening is all. We read it subliminally; attuned to him as we are, the signs are clear.

I tell Miles what Dr. Stephenson has told me about brain injury and memory, and that I'm concerned that if he does not remember what happened to him he might not understand why he is here. It feels crucially important to stress that this is normal, my ever-present fear of alarming him or patronizing him, that if I get it wrong he might fear he has lost his mind. Would that be worse than brain damage? For the moment it seems so.

Claudia and I take turns telling him the story. As we mention St. Anton and his friends setting off on the last day for the snowboard park we both see the shift of expression on his face, tense, as though he is straining to hear, not wanting to miss a word. Are we reawakening the earlier memories now? Suddenly I feel fearful. What effect will describing the accident have on him? If he cannot lay down new memories, is there any point? But surely worse still is never to know why he is in this state. Knowing Miles, he would always want to know the truth. As I begin to speak, describing the moment his snowboard clipped the edge of the jump, he slowly closes his eyes. I must reassure him. Miles, please, please don't worry. You are in one of the best neurological hospitals in the world under the care of one of the best brain injury specialists. You will recover. Everything is being done to help you. You will come back to us and we are all going to be with you, every inch of the way. All your friends are rooting for you. You are our formidable, determined, amazing Miles and you will do it. He opens his eyes again and neither Claudia nor I can bear to see the pain that is refracted in the unaligned green depths. We're sitting either side of him and we both lean over to put our arms around him and we stay there like that for a long time.

* * *

THERE ARE TWELVE beds on the ward and the patients come and go. Patrick arrives on the hottest day in mid-July and in the badly ventilated room the smell of him is shocking. He lies on his back unconscious on the bed, a delicately built man with a mass of wild, matted curls framing something terrible and purple that was his face. We call him Panda Man because of the huge black circles where his eyes should be, but really he looks more like a little elf that has been in a violent punch-up. It turns out he *has* been in a punch-up of sorts, having been picked on by a group of young men who knocked him down and kicked his body repeatedly for that Saturday night's entertainment. Apart from the broken bones so much of his brain was damaged that he is here now, in this acute brain injury ward. Over the next few days he regains consciousness and his face pales into beautiful shades of lilac and violet as the bruising subsides. He speaks in a surprising, mellifluously precise voice, choosing his words with great care as he refuses to cooperate with the nurses' attempts to wash him or clean his teeth, change his pajamas or brush his hair. He will not endure any attempt at personal hygiene, and his cracked and blackened feet and ragged yellow toenails reveal years of neglect. His meal tray is still untouched when the carer comes to collect it, because he will eat only when he feels like it. Often he's nowhere to be seen, until we realize he is asleep on the floor under his bed; sometimes he will squirrel around and around and around into position on the chair next to his bed before going to sleep there instead. He doesn't like beds, he says, they're too soft, he isn't used to them, and tells the social worker he preferred his cardboard box. A nurse bends down to coax him out from under the bed, in the patronizing singsong voice reserved for brain-damaged patients. Oh gracious, Patrick,

I can see we're under our bed again. You're very clever at hiding, aren't you? I'm sure it must be awfully nice and quiet down there but perhaps you'd like to come out and join us this morning? There is silence from under the bed and the nurse bends down even further, peering under the bed as she tries again with exasperation now overlaying her coaxing tone. Come out now, Patrick. Maybe there is something I can get for you? Slowly Patrick emerges and sits up on the floor. Thank you, how very kind, he says. I would very much like some roasted peanuts and a glass of dry white wine.

Some days later he disappears and this time is not to be found. Still under treatment, badly bruised and in obvious pain, he had gathered his few bits of clothing and walked out of the hospital, back to his life on the streets where he wanted to be. I hear later from the social worker that he was a highly educated man from a cultivated background who had chosen to become a tramp—it was the result of a clear decision. He had no contacts and no official support. He did not draw the dole or claim any benefits, and when pressed to do so he retorted that he considered it immoral to accept help when it had been his choice.

MILES HAS BEEN out for the evening with friends from work. They went straight from the office to a bar and then on to dinner, and now he is waiting for the bus to take him home. It was a good evening and he has had more than a few drinks. There are two other young men waiting at the bus stop who are very drunk; it appears from their conversation that they have been drinking together for most of the day. One is small and sharp-faced, his movements a little too jittery for comfort, his friend larger and slower but not unmenacing. They've ended their evening with takeaway pizzas and the smaller man is enjoying kicking the empty pizza boxes around the bus stop. It is bothering him that Miles is standing there in his suit. Miles knows he must look a prat in a suit at this hour and has been on the phone to his girlfriend, trying to ignore the comments and the clearly provocative kicking of pizza boxes. The small man can't contain himself any longer. Hey you, are you looking at me? he sneers, lurching up to Miles, who ignores him and turns away, continuing his conversation with Annabel. The man is even more insulted and he persists. Did you hear me? I said, you wanker, are you looking at me? Still Miles ignores him, but after a few more taunts the irritant hits its target. Okay, says Miles, putting away his phone. Yes, I was looking at you. And I was looking at my phone, and at this bus stop, and at a load of other shit all around the place. He has given Jittery Man just what he wanted; he could have ignored him or given the pacifist's reply but he hasn't and he has hit home. You can fucking piss off, you fucking posh twat. Been at the office today, have we? Fucking wanker with your fucking bonuses, and he comes closer, weaving in for a fight. Hey, hey, calm down, boys, says the larger man, restraining his friend with his left hand, but as Miles steps back the large man uses his free right hand to deliver a surprise punch hard in Miles's left eye. Miles reels back as his eye immediately puffs up and closes but he recognizes with a surge of pleasurable adrenaline that his boxing training can finally be put to use. One right hook removes the large man's front teeth and his second punch knocks the smaller man to the ground. He walks down the road and hails a cab.

When he tells us the story he makes it wryly funny. He is ashamed, but a part of him is pleased. Only one eye and he still knocked the bastards out, even though he'd been fool enough not to keep a look out for the second man. But I know I was an idiot, he says. I should have walked away.

* * *

THE PHYSIOTHERAPISTS ARE fighting a losing battle against spasticity, one of the most common side effects of brain damage. Miles's feet are beginning to turn inward, arched like a dancer on pointe. As a consequence of the initial injury having been to the right side of his brain, his left foot is the most affected; his left hand, too, is beginning to stiffen inwards, the fingers becoming clawed and difficult to stretch out fully. The physiotherapist makes splints to support his feet and hands and to hold them in an open position, and his antispasticity medication is increased.

I remember being surprised when the physiotherapist at Innsbruck asked if I could bring in a pair of Miles's shoes. Will found a pair of his trainers but they wouldn't do—stiff leather shoes were required, she said, they needed to support his feet when he was sitting up in a chair. I didn't understand, and found the incongruity distressing, seeing him sitting up strapped into his chair, eyes closed, in a coma, with his black leather office shoes on. Now I understand.

I wish it wasn't called spasticity. I had not heard the word before Miles's accident, only knowing *spastic* as a term used to describe cerebral palsy before it became a term of abuse. I had a friend who worked for the Spastics Society when the name was changed to its present name, Scope; the word *spastic* had been an issue for some time with its members and finally research was undertaken to ascertain its effect on the charity. Parents were not contacting the society for help because they feared their children being branded as spastic, and business corporations were not supporting it because they did not want to be associated with the derogatory image. In 1994 it was relaunched as Scope. I remember the public relations exercise, the billboards: *Pillock, Nerd, Spastic, Moron: which is the odd word out?*

Now I learn that spasticity can follow from traumatic brain injury, stroke, or disease and that it is damage to the upper motor neuron that causes the stiffness and involuntary, uncontrollable muscle spasms. Even though I'm not sure exactly what the upper motor neuron is, I know that spasticity is a chronic, debilitating, painful condition, prevention of which is key to acute neurological rehab. If Miles's spasticity is left untreated, his limbs will continue to stiffen as the muscles contract and his joints will lock, eventually becoming immobilized. I see pictures of untreated brain-damaged patients curled up into the fetus position. If unhalted he will be in severe cramp-like pain from the contractures, which will further exacerbate his spasticity, and the immobility means he will be more liable to develop bedsores. I understand it is a race against time.

Queen Square leads the field in the treatment of spasticity. Alongside conventional treatment, homeopathy is offered, and I meet a therapist on the ward one day who works at the National Homeopathic Hospital next door. He has just given Miles a massage and Miles looks so peaceful I ask him to show me how to do it. He does so, and suggests I bring in some essential oil to massage him myself. It seems a good idea.

The next day I tell Miles what I am about to do. He is seated in his chair, eyes closed, possibly asleep. As I begin to massage in the pungently scented lavender oil I've brought I'm uncomfortable, it feels somehow presumptuous, assuming that he will enjoy my doing this. We are a tactile family and my relationship with Miles is a close one. But I am sitting at his feet, anointing them with oil in public; what does that signify to him? I try to remember the movements the homeopath used, slowly pressing down on each toe to lengthen it, kneading the arch of the foot with my thumb. Slowly Miles's face changes, a slight twisting of his mouth and a movement of his forehead that could almost be a frown, and I can't tell whether it is an expression of embarrassment or disgust or simply that I'm not doing it properly. Does he find this demeaning, for himself and for me? I stop and rest my head on his knees and cry with bitter shame and disappointment at failing to get this right, to bring him some little pleasure at least.

A FRIEND HAS come to visit Miles whom I have not met before, though Miles has often spoken of him. Mitran is a photographer, at present helping children in Afghanistan by teaching them to skateboard and have fun despite the war they are living through. He looks striking in the orderliness of the hospital ward, his wild hair and laid-back appearance a refreshing contrast. Ron and I like him instantly on meeting him and I can see his warmth and unaffected charm is attracting the nurses, too, who seem to have converged around us. He is in London for a short visit and he has brought a photograph with him that he took on holiday with Miles. It is extraordinary—not only is it perfect as a composition, but he has managed in the split second it took to capture the essence of Miles's particular vitality, of his energy and his joyfulness. Oh wow, the nurses are saying as they look at it too, that explains so much about Miles. What an amazing picture! As it is passed around I think I must frame this photograph and leave it next to Miles's bed. Anybody treating him will understand him better when they've seen this.

Miles had invited a group of friends out to our house in France for a week of sunshine and poker. We had a brilliant time, Mitran says. We swam and messed about in the day and in the evenings we barbecued and drank that sweet fortified wine you have down there and played poker into the early hours. His photograph catches Miles "messing about" with another friend: there is a short lawn which ends in a two-meter drop to the stone-paved poolside, and Miles and his friend are leaping over the gap with flying kung fu kicks into the pool beyond. It was a particularly dangerous drop, one we worried about when we bought the house. We had expressly asked that no one attempt to jump into the pool, half-knowing that the challenge would be irresistible. Now I'm glad that Miles did it— Mitran has caught them in midair and the expression on Miles's face is one of pure exhilaration, vividly alive. It is a powerful affirmation of his vitality and his daring, but now it reveals something else to me too—fragile, existential, of life and living, our dreams and hopes and eventual isolation and loss.

PEOPLE SO OFTEN say to me now, when the subject of Miles arises: I don't know how you manage. I have no option, I tell them. But it sets me thinking. In the end I suspect it is the small, routine pleasures in life that make the best building blocks for survival. The things that have to be continued with, the unavoidable humdrum facts of just living: I try to engage in those moments and make them, at least *them*, enjoyable. What to have on my toast in the morning, tart marmalade or sweet honey, making sure the toast is still hot while I butter it. Getting the ratio of milk to coffee just right. Putting together clothes that please, then finding the earrings to lift my mood. In the evening time to sit down with Ron and whichever of the children is at home, to have a glass of wine the color for the day, warming red or a cool white. Time to sit over dinner, even if I don't have time to cook anymore and it's another Tesco's fish pie.

The final treat, an unhurried bath to end the day.

Though not infallible, these are the everyday things that, made pleasurable, help for that particular moment to keep reality at bay. My evening bath is a case in point: with deliberate care I will set about to run myself the perfect one, testing the water from the mixer taps for the right proportion of just too hot to cold, adding a few drops of a favorite bath oil to scent the water, rose geranium or lime and basil, placing a large, clean towel within reach on the floor, and fetching a book to place it safely on the edge of the bath in case I feel like reading. When the bath is run I undress and slide into the water, letting my skin register with a delicious shock each slow second of not quite scalding immersion. Then, taking a deep breath and exhaling the day with relief, I can finally rest my head on the bath's edge behind me. As the water stills around my submerged body I luxuriate in this fleeting, scented interlude of peace. For the moment physical sensation takes over to soothe away the clamoring thoughts.

Cushioning reality, distracting the mind through the small pleasures of living. Although not entirely unmuffled by grief, they offer a small coating of armor against the day. Sometimes, though, reality intrudes. I may be buttering my toast at breakfast when suddenly Miles is there across the table, reading the paper with uninterruptable concentration over great piles of toast and peel-thick marmalade, his coffee cooling to the temperature he likes it. Or at the supermarket, absorbed by the choices in the cold meat counter, I'm suddenly aware of the music overhead, a song Miles discovered as a teenager and played over and over in the car on our long journeys to and from school. Standing there, holding a packet of smoked ham and feeling the cold air drifting out from the counter, I see Miles as though in technicolor beside me, his face just beginning to elongate into adolescence, the first few spots broken out, his strong, decisive hands as he slips the Cure CD into the player; then, for a moment, I am lost in the joy of his company, the way our conversation covered everything that mattered, the way he could make me laugh until I ached, before the familiar blinding pain follows and I must concentrate on nothing else except holding myself together until it passes. Or I may be lying safely in the bath at the end of the day and suddenly remember another bathtime, the night of Miles's birthday on the Sunday before he left for St. Anton, when I had heard the familiar ping of a text message received and read the thank-you he'd sent: Best cake ever, Ma, Will and I just polished off remains. Thanks for great birthday. Love you loads and see you when I get back xx. And so memory continues along its barbed, relentless course and I'm not safe after all. Now I remember the awful prescience of my reply: Had just been thinking how much I love you! It's been 29 wonderful years, and then his reply: And I love you very, very much. The following Sunday I would be on the plane to Munich; twenty-nine years and one week later his brilliant, funny, undomesticated, risk-taking, fearless, vital selfhood would be extinguished in one catastrophic blow to his brain. There is no escape. The bathwater is beginning to get cold. I must get out and get ready for bed.

GEORGE IS IN the bed opposite Miles and he is soon to be discharged. Like Patrick he, too, is homeless, but it has not been his choice. In one of his regular fights with fellow tramps he sustained a serious head injury, but is now recovered and walks about restlessly in his blue hospital pajamas. Garrulous and disinhibited, perhaps as a result of his injury, broken nose flattened to one side, not a full set of teeth, his presence is disconcerting with its hint of bewildered aggression.

He likes to come over to Miles's bedside when I'm there. Miles is a good man, he says. It's very sad, Miss. Please call me Lu, I ask him, but he refuses. Miss is easier, he says. He looks down at Miles and I can see George is genuinely sad, his tenderness like a secret gift he reserves for Miles and me, for his treatment of the nurses is abusive and his behavior towards the other patients dismissive and resentful.

One morning when I arrive on the ward he calls out excitedly before I can get to Miles's bed, Miss, Miss, Miles is talking!

I heard him talking last night! I was so happy for you. For a wild moment the whole world tilts and lifts and I am flying to Miles. He can speak! Nothing will matter any more now that he can speak— however slow his recovery might be, he will be back with us and can tell us what he wants, what he feels . . . What did he say in the night? Did he call for us? I can ask him! As I reach Miles's bedside the physiotherapist who is attending to him gives me a look that tells me everything. No, it's not true, it's just George's imagination and he's not quite right in the head.

The physiotherapist finishes her session and takes her leave. I want to be alone with Miles, away from everybody. I want peace, and silence, just the two of us. I'm tired. I'm so tired of negotiating people. But here is George, standing awkwardly in front of me. There are tears in his eyes. I'm so sorry I made that mistake, Miss. I was sure I heard him speak, but I think it must have been someone else. I'm really sorry. It's a dreadful world. He looks so forlorn, this big man with his crushed face, that what I feel for him could almost be love.

Two days later George absconds and is found by a nurse sitting in the sunshine on a bench in the square outside the hospital, drunk. He had got some beer—how, in his pajamas, nobody knows. The nurse brings him back up to the ward and he glowers like an insolent schoolboy at the ward sister as she admonishes him. You are not here for fun, George, the ward sister says sharply, and you know very well that you are not allowed to drink alcohol because it will prevent your recovery. I will have to tell the doctor that you have disobeyed his instructions. Now go to bed and sleep it off. George sulks for the rest of the day, does not cooperate with the nurses or therapists and growls at Hussein, the patient in the bed next to him, when he does his choking cough, George blocking his ears with his fingers like a child.

Two days later he absconds again but returns this time of his own accord. He walks past the nurses' station in an elaborate weaving diagonal. It could be funny but the nurse in charge, a stern, gray-haired Jamaican woman, comes out from behind the desk and reprimands him forcefully. George lifts his head up in a swinging movement that almost takes him off balance. Fuck off, he says, I don't have any black women tell me what to do. Right, my boy, she says. I'm reporting you to the ward sister. Well, you can all just fuck off the lot of you, he retorts.

After some time the ward sister arrives, together with the Jamaican nurse, and the curtain is drawn around his bed. I can hear George swearing and the ward sister calmly and firmly discussing with him what I imagine are administrative discharge procedures before the curtains are drawn back and the nurses leave. He is sitting hunched on the bed, crying. Despite his shameful and deeply offensive behavior, he cuts a pathetic figure. I go over to him. Are you all right, George? I ask. He looks up at me with his bloodshot eyes, fearful, confused, a feral creature that has finally been cornered. Miss, he says, what can I do? I have nothing. I have nowhere to go. I ask him if he has family he might go to. He shakes his head. No, he says, looking down at his hands, no, never. I never did.

How can this be, this pain of living? I get my handbag and, hoping he won't find this patronizing, I give him all I have in my purse, which is only a twenty-pound note and some coins. I'll miss you, George. A nurse arrives to escort him out and he leaves the ward.

THE TRUTH IS, we do believe Miles is trying to speak. When we are talking to him there are times when he will begin to respond by moving his mouth in what clearly looks like an effort to reply. On a few magical occasions we hear a whisper, his expression intense with the effort of it. Yes, yes, Miley, we urge him then, come on, you're doing it! You're doing it! We can hear you! Keep going! The whispering sounds continue and we listen intently, but they are indecipherable, he cannot frame the words. Eventually, exhausted, he closes his eyes and sinks back into himself, away from us.

The occupational therapist has advised us that we should only make one request of Miles during each visit. Give him time to respond, she says. The sheer difficulty for Miles of coordinating his movement or trying to speak will be exhausting, and too much at once would be overwhelming. It is difficult to hear this advice: Miles who, as his friend and colleague Jason described him, had the problem of being talented in so many directions it complicated his career choice.

WE ARE ALL beginning to notice a change in Miles's mood. A lot of the time now his eyes remain firmly closed when he is obviously awake and his jaw is set in a way I recognize, an indication of his deep frustration, if not anger. He doesn't seem to be making the same effort to respond when we try to engage with him, even when we know he is awake and listening. I think he's depressed, though that seems too facile a description of what he might be feeling. I mention this to the neuropsychologist and expect him to be skeptical of my oversensitivity, but he understands. He says it is entirely possible, but the problem is that treatment by antidepressants might mask any possible awareness by slowing his responses even further. He will monitor Miles, but as he sees him only once a week he suggests we keep a record of his mood. I am touched by this humane young man, probably the same age as Miles, who talks to Miles and treats him with such quiet respect. I ask him about my greatest dread, that if Miles does suffer real depression he might give up this gargantuan struggle altogether. Central to my dread is the danger that by making either too many demands of him or, worse still, the wrong demands, we may be the instruments of his withdrawal.

Has that ever happened? I ask. Yes, I have seen it happen, the neuropsychologist replies. It is a very real danger that overstimulation can cause a person to retreat, to give up the unequal struggle. We must never forget how difficult even the smallest physical action is for someone who has suffered a traumatic brain injury, how vulnerable the person is and how delicate the recovery process.

Miles's recovery is the thing I yearn for most in the world; how terrifying that I could unwittingly impede it.

WHEN I ARRIVE on the ward today there is a woman I have never seen before sitting in a chair at Miles's bedside, reading to him. He is lying facing her with his eyes closed and I can't tell if he is asleep or awake. The woman is middle-aged, graying hair pinned up in a wispy bun and wearing a long skirt, sandals, and trailing scarf; she's definitely not a member of staff. She doesn't notice me approaching and continues reading, leaning forward in her chair, and I can hear her enunciating the words clearly in an elaborate nursery-rhyme voice, as though reading to a very young child. I'm surprised by the proprietorial air with which she frowns on seeing me, closing her book with her finger in it still marking the place, a look of irritation as though I'm interrupting an important session with Miles. Hello, I say, I'm Miles's mother, Lu. I saw you were reading to Miles? She remains seated but now shuts the book, which I notice is *Charlie and the Chocolate Factory* by Roald Dahl. Gracious, I see you've chosen Roald Dahl. I wonder why you think that would appeal to Miles? The shock I feel is visceral; how *dare* she read that to him.

She stands up and faces me with an expression of resigned exasperation. I've been doing this for some years now, as a volunteer with my local drama society, which provides readers in hospitals. I always read well-known children's books in this ward because I think that is particularly relaxing for the sort of patients to be found here. She looks at me challengingly and I'm aware of a standoff existing between us, each pricklingly hostile like two teenage girls competing over the same boy. Maybe I should be showing gratitude that this woman has given her time to entertain Miles, but I am ice cold with fury that she should have been reading him a children's book, infantilizing him in such a cruel way. If he's awake, what conclusion could he draw from it? How demoralized must he feel? What does he think has happened to him? Thank you, but please don't come and read to Miles anymore, I tell her. He has a lot of family and friends and we will choose the writers we know he likes.

She turns to say goodbye to Miles but not to me and leaves. Oh god, Miles, was I really rude to her? How ridiculous that she was reading that book to you, especially when I know how you always disliked Roald Dahl. I want to howl with misery, with hurt anger and shame and the deep, cold dread that Miles has been patronized by a stranger. To see him through someone else's eyes as having been reduced to a child by his brain damage. Miles! Miles, of all people.

WHEN MILES HAS been at the ABIU almost eleven weeks I have a meeting with Dr. Stephenson and it is not unexpected when he tells me Miles will have to move on. By definition, the Acute Brain Injury Unit is for acute cases and patients are never expected to remain for more than eight to ten weeks at most. Miles is no longer acute and a place has become available for him at Putney. I know it is not where you wanted him to go, Dr. Stephenson says, but Miles is now at the stage where he needs long-term neuro-rehabilitation and Putney has some of the best available facilities for that. I hope Miles will respond well to being there. Please don't hesitate to get in touch with me if you have any concerns.

However kind he is, it feels like a death sentence: the Royal Hospital for Incurables. Though the name has changed, the meaning for me has not. But at least, I think, at least Miles was given a chance and he is in a very different place from where he was when he arrived at Queen Square. Then he was still in a coma; now he has had ten weeks of progressive therapy. He had the best treatment he could possibly have had at the time, and there are eight months left in the vital one-year prognosis deadline. We can still maintain hope for recovery, whatever it may be.

IV

It is the end of July, the hottest day so far in an already hot summer. The ambulance has been booked for early afternoon, which gives me time to pack up Miles's things. I empty his bedside locker, the books we tried and didn't succeed in reading to him, the bottle of essential rosemary oil that was said to be an agent for awakening, the tiny glass vial of holy water from Lourdes given by our beloved Irish cleaner and sometime nanny Dorrie, who loves Miles like a wayward son. He sleeps in his chair as I move around him, collecting everything together in his overnight bag, the old canvas one I remember him stuffing his things into so decisively whenever he packed. It doesn't take long to finish and then it is time for the final farewells. I have been doing this piecemeal over the last few days, catching, whenever they are on duty, the nurses and therapists who have made a special connection with Miles, to thank them with a gift and the hope that we may meet again, though we know we won't. The loss is ours; we must brace ourselves to be Miles's spokesmen afresh, to try to make people understand anew the person that was Miles before this terrible thing happened to him.

We will be setting off within the next half hour—to what? We may as well be stepping off the edge of the world. His time in the ABIU is over, and although every day we might have been inhabiting a nightmare, it had become, at least, a familiar one. I trusted the hospital and the neurologist in charge. I know nobody at Putney, I don't know anything about it except its enormous, grim façade. We will arrive, the two of us, like strangers to a doomed planet.

The ambulance arrives. I follow Miles on his stretcher up the ramp, together with Grace, the nurse who has been deputed to accompany him and do the handover. I've never been in the back of an ambulance before. A small square window at the top on one side lets in light and it is already stifling hot even before the doors are closed. Miles's stretcher is battened to the floor, Grace and I strap ourselves into our seats, the back doors are closed, and a few minutes later we set off. There is a strange sense of disembodiment being contained like this, feeling the motion and hearing the sounds of traffic and the world outside, but removed, invisible. The same as a prison van, I imagine. Miles is already sweating, as am I, the heat beating in through the metal sides. Grace is not sweating and looks ebony cool as she tells me how she likes this heat; she comes from Sierra Leone and always dreads the arrival of winter in England.

The journey takes an hour. I cannot imagine why the suspension in an ambulance is not considered more of a priority; Miles is thrown about by bumps and stops and around us things rattle and slide alarmingly. He is tense now, his eyes wide open, his body on full alert I can see. Grace is gentle with him and we talk a little about our lives in the intimacy of the moment. She reveals that she took up nursing when, aged sixteen, she lost her only brother in the war in Sierra Leone, and I am moved to tears by her story, ashamed at my self-absorption. Eventually we feel a long slow stop, followed by the bang of doors as the ambulance men disembark from the front. A heavy scrape of metal, the back doors are opened and we are let out into the glaring afternoon sun. We have arrived at Putney.

The ambulance driver and his assistant set off with Miles, directed by the uniformed porter at the entrance. Grace and I follow as Miles is wheeled down the long corridor that I and the children will come to know so intimately, a corridor that smothers the soul before you have even reached your destination, so long is it, the air so heavy with dread, the people one passes so heartbreakingly damaged. Occasionally I catch a glimpse of long green-lawned gardens, spacious outbuildings, and wide, leisurely paths; it could be the grounds of a grand country hotel except that the residents are all in wheelchairs. There are no guests here.

TAKING AN ELEVATOR up to the second floor we follow the porters down yet another bleak corridor before we reach our destination. A large square room appears to be the center of the ward. It is muggily hot, sunshine streaming in through three big windows along the far wall, none of which, I notice with surprise, is open more than a few inches. There is a nurses' station immediately on the right and beyond it I can see a semicircle of about twelve men and women of differing ages, all in wheelchairs, fanned out around an enormous television. Next to the television stands a blackboard with yesterday's date written on it in large white chalked letters and a picture of a smiley yellow sun. On the TV screen a picture flashes and jumps, accompanied by stalling gobbets of sound; whatever is showing is indecipherable. They must be having a problem with the reception and I wonder how the audience can tolerate it.

It is only then I realize that every one of the people sitting there is more seriously brain-damaged than anyone I have yet seen. With mounting dread I scan their faces. Some are blank, gazing out, calm in the way of something unanchored, floating free; others are contorted with tics and grimaces, as though engaged in a harrowing internal struggle. A young man is gazing at me, through me; he is magnificently handsome, tall and dark, as erect in his chair as a soldier, and half his skull is missing, a concave hollow of sunken skin. I don't know which circle of hell this is but I want to grab Miles's stretcher and wheel him away as fast as I can to somewhere we can be quiet and on our own, away from the horror of being witness to all this suffering. I don't want him to witness it and to realize he is a part of it. If I take him away he can never be part of it.

But a nurse is pointing out his room. It leads directly off the day room with a sliding door and it is so small that Grace and I must wait outside while the porters transfer Miles from his stretcher to the bed. When they wheel away the empty stretcher and Grace leaves with them I have the sense of Miles's tenuous lifeline to Queen Square being finally cut. He is adrift now; not a soul in this huge place knows him. Wide awake after the journey and the rolling and sliding from stretcher to bed, what is he thinking? He looks tense, his arms clenched. The young nurse who showed us the room left with Grace and nobody else seems to know we're here. I am tense too; I am adrift with Miles in a new place of such acute misery and loneliness I fear I might go under. How can Miles bear this loneliness? I will go home this evening, see Ron, the children, explain and be comforted. Miles will remain here, alone. And yet I don't know how to deal with this.

Eventually a nurse comes into the room. She is the ward sister, a crisp, elegant Filipina with a soft American accent. She introduces herself and when she begins to take Miles's obs, the sound of her voice explaining the procedure—Hello, Miles, I'm Erica. I'm going to take your blood pressure now—is calming for us both. She notes the details in a file that she leaves in a holder at the end of his bed and tells me that the ward doctor will be coming to see Miles shortly. She exudes a quiet, unhurried confidence and her cool demeanor is soothing in the oppressive heat of the room.

For the room is like a greenhouse. It faces west, and as it is now mid-afternoon the sun is pouring in through the one window that takes up most of the outside wall. When I try to open it I find it is locked to allow only a few inches' opening, the same distance as the windows in the day room. With disbelief I wonder whom the authorities fear is going to jump out of these windows. None of the patients is capable of it. Maybe someone once tried, a relative maddened by the claustrophobia of the place; whatever the reason, it makes it feel even more like a prison. It is not yet the end of July, and August is forecast to be even hotter than it is now. The room will be unbearable.

There is a basin in the corner and I run the water for some time before it feels cold. We will have to bring ice packs in when we visit, I think, but for now I wet some paper towels to cool Miles down. He closes his eyes as I place the folded wet towels on his forehead and I talk to him, telling him again where we are and describing his new room to him. I tell him that a doctor is coming to see him, that this is a cutting-edge rehab hospital, repeating myself. I hope he believes it; I want to believe it. But as I look up through his open door into the day room beyond I could be witnessing a conference of the damned.

Some long time later the doctor arrives. Before Miles left Queen Square Dr. Stephenson had suggested I flag up right from the beginning that we would like to provide extra therapy for Miles if it is possible. After we've made our introductions I mention this.

What do you mean? asks the doctor. Well, treatments like acupuncture, for example, I answer. All the patients' relatives feel the same, he says. Everybody wants the best for their own relative. He hasn't answered the question and I feel strangely demeaned, as though I've stepped out of line. I don't yet know the rules here.

As SOON AS he is able to, I want Miles to come home and live with us. I'm apprehensive about mentioning this to Ron, for I'm fully aware that until Miles has recovered sufficiently it will dramatically change our way of life. Ron, it turns out, raises the subject before I do. We should think about where Miles will go once he has been stabilized at Putney, he says. We could consider altering the house to accommodate him—it wouldn't be impossible. Relieved and grateful for his generosity, I begin to make plans. A friend who is an architect comes around and by the end of his visit it all seems straightforward. Miles would live on the ground floor, the drawing room made over into his bedroom and the small sitting room next door converted into a wet room where he could be gurney-showered. It is directly under our bathroom upstairs, so the plumbing could easily be achieved. We would make the kitchen our family room and convert the basement to provide accommodation for carers.

I'm acutely aware of how privileged I am, both that Ron is prepared to accept such disruption and that we have the space and can afford to make the changes. I was privileged to be able to stay in Innsbruck for six weeks; now that I'm back I can afford to dedicate my days to Miles. Ron has cushioned me from the practical burdens that so many people in my position have to endure. The knowledge that Miles will be able to come home relieves me of a major anxiety; I have a sense of having rolled away an enormous boulder blocking the path ahead.

* * *

EVERY DAY AT Queen Square Miles spent some hours seated in a wheelchair, as he did in the last weeks at Innsbruck. I have learned that it is a crucial aspect of his rehabilitation, helping to alleviate spasticity and the risk of bedsores as well as keeping his chest clear by being upright. It is easier to cough sitting up and luckily Miles has a strong cough reflex, but chest infections are a constant danger for unconscious and bedbound patients. He was also given splints to wear on his legs and arms to combat spasticity, to prevent muscle contraction and ensuing joint deformity. Now I discover that at Putney he will not be placed in a chair for the first three weeks, during what is known as every new patient's "assessment period"; nor will he wear the necessary splints, which apparently here take two to three weeks to be provided. One of the basic tenets of neuro-rehabilitation is that it is important to be proactive from the beginning rather than have to deal with secondary changes later on. I don't know who to turn to, and call the Queen Square head injury nurse for advice. She is as shocked as I am, says that if he remains in bed that length of time all their hard work will be undone. Miles's admission notes from Queen Square gave details of his daily therapy. I don't understand why they haven't been acted on and take the matter up with the physiotherapist. I understand it is difficult for her, because she is constrained by the hospital regulations. In the end I tell her that if necessary I will look into getting a wheelchair myself for Miles. He cannot be left in bed for three weeks; apart from anything else, it will be hugely demoralizing for him.

It is the second day and I realize that I am probably marked now as a difficult relative. A young speech therapist comes to examine Miles, and hearing the end of my conversation with the physio she is conciliatory. I clearly need soothing. It's a beautiful day, she says, why don't we go down and have a cup of tea in the garden and I'll show you the grounds? Sitting on a bench in the sunshine she explains the standard arrival procedure for new patients. You mustn't be concerned about it, she says. All the patients plateau for the first few weeks after arrival, sometimes for months, and they can regress. But then they will start to go forward again. She tells me this is a necessary part of the very thorough assessment procedure they have, but I have not been soothed. It seems to me frighteningly complacent.

Eventually Miles is "fast tracked." He gets a chair in twelve days and splints in ten. In the meantime his spasticity has increased and he has developed a chest infection from being immobile, which must be treated with antibiotics. His mood is bleak and we fear he is retreating.

MILES IS BEING put to bed and I am waiting, as one of us waits every evening, to make sure that he has been comfortably positioned for the night. We sit on the sofa of the day room while two carers wheel the portable hoist into his room and close the door behind them. It takes about thirty minutes and if Miles is lucky the process of hoisting him out of his chair to swing him onto the bed, remove his leg and arm splints and then his trousers, change his sanitary pad, empty the urine bag, wash him, and clean his teeth before positioning him for the night will all be carefully and gently done. Otherwise we must endure the sound of Miles's groans or more often the long drawn-out roar that has become his signature sound. That's Miles, people on the ward will say, hearing it from afar. He's certainly got a good pair of lungs, the father of a patient in the next ward said to me, no doubt trying to cheer me up. It is a sound that reverberates through me. I hear, I feel, his anger, his humiliation; I want to roar with him. And I am ashamed of myself, because I am embarrassed by the noise, by the exhibition he is making of himself; I am ashamed on his behalf and also, sickeningly, on my own.

Tonight the groans and roars are continuous and I'm concerned it may be more than furious humiliation. I'm about to go into the room to find out when the door opens and the carers, Bula and Sam, take their leave, saying good night, their job done. As I enter his room Miles is lying on his side facing me, his face flushed deep red and sweating, his eyes too wide. God, darling, what on earth has happened? I test his pulse rate with the portable finger clip and it reads 120. Is something hurting you? His eyes widen even further and I notice his right arm is bent at a peculiar angle underneath him. Pulling back the sheet to adjust it I am astounded to see that his hips and buttocks have been positioned flat on the bed with his legs stretched out straight. His torso is twisted at the waist, the upper half of his body on its side, his shoulders at right angles to the bed, while the lower half is flat and parallel to it. Oh Jesus, Miles, no wonder you're uncomfortable! How could they have done this? I'm so, so sorry you have to endure this. I try to turn his hips but he's too heavy. I can't move you on my own, Miles, I'm going to call those two idiots back to do their job properly.

I find the men and ask them to come back to Miles's room immediately. Being a carer is a thankless job and underpaid, but right now all I am concerned about is that they have done their work carelessly and the consequences were traumatic for Miles. One look at Miles without the sheet covering his lower half and both men understand. I ask them to read the physiotherapist's guide on positioning Miles and watch as they reposition him. When they have finished he is lying at ease at last, the tension gone from his face. Thanking them, I ask them to stand in front of me for a moment before they go. They look understandably sheepish but I am adamant. Maybe if they can understand Miles's discomfort they will think about it more closely when positioning him, and other patients, in future.

So I ask them to stand facing me, and then to twist their right shoulder forward and to the left as far as it will go without moving their hips. I do the same. It is extraordinarily uncomfortable and none of us does it longer than a few seconds. The carers apologize, saying they didn't realize how uncomfortable it would be. Then Sam says, Our problem is that normal human beings can tell us when what we're doing is not right. The room is very small and the three of us are standing right next to Miles's bed; he has heard and I watch his eyes slowly closing. Okay, you can go now, I tell the men.

Miles, oh god Miles, Sam is not educated, he is a kind man but he has the IQ of a bear. He doesn't know the meaning of what he's saying. But Miles knows what he meant and so do I. There is nothing I can do to retrieve the situation; the words hang in the air. I feel him retreating far within himself and all I can do is lean over the bed and put my arms around him, staying like this until I know he is no longer there.

Before I leave I find Sam and tell him I would like a private word with him. We go into an empty side room and I ask him if he is aware of what he just said to me in front of Miles. He has no idea and looks concerned. You said: The problem is that *normal human beings* can tell you when what you're doing isn't right. As I emphasize the words, Sam realizes, looks appalled. Oh, that's awful, I didn't mean to say that, I'm so sorry. I respect Miles very highly. There are tears in his eyes. I am so sorry for him, he says.

Of course he didn't mean to inflict pain. I'm tired and I want to go home now. Thank you, Sam. You understand. I take his hand

and we remain for a moment facing each other, sharing the terrible pity I dread for Miles. I'll see you tomorrow. Good night.

RON IS ABROAD on business and, lying alone in bed that night, unable to sleep, I am thinking about Miles lying those few miles away from me across London. How can he sleep, how can he bear it, even when he is properly positioned? Stuck in one position for a minimum of four hours until the carers come and turn him over? And then to lie on his other side for the next four hours?

I am going to do an experiment, to find out what it feels like.

First I need to get up and take some extra pillows out of the linen cupboard. Then I get back into bed and turn onto my side and try to remember the position that has been devised to help his spasticity, the stiffening left leg and left arm in particular. He will have been placed on his side because he cannot be left on his back for fear of him choking. I turn onto my left side, left leg very slightly bent and right knee bent over it, supported by a pillow. My hips are more or less in a straight line, at right angles to the bed. Left arm bent out slightly away from my chest, right arm stretched a little further and the elbow resting on a pillow. Two more pillows under my head, my neck aligned with my spine. I think that's it. I know there is also a large plastic oblong wedge placed between Miles's back and the raised metal side of his bed to stop him rolling backwards, but I can't set that up. Now I'll time myself and see how long I can last.

Four minutes pass and I have to stop. It is impossible. What began as a slow-growing claustrophobia, an internal stifling, inch-by-inch spread outwards into my limbs—arms first, then my back and legs, my feet and ankles, particularly the ankles, then my neck. A deep physical agitation which I could feel building up to a crescendo of what I can only describe as *psychic* pain. And Miles must endure the physical pain too, his muscles and joints already pain-fully stiffened, slowly atrophying.

MILES HAS BEEN at Putney now for three months and my life has evolved into a routine. Visiting hours are from twelve noon until eight in the evening. The journey by car takes an hour on a good day, so I leave Greenwich at eleven, driving the circuitous route that avoids congestion charging. Through the Old Kent Road, Elephant and Castle, down to Lambeth Palace and then along the river, past New Covent Garden, Battersea, and the glinting ranks of glass and concrete apartment blocks that have begun to fringe the Thames. I love this city, as did Miles; we often talked of it, trying to understand its essence, the vibrancy and recklessness, Miles said, and yet its calm containment of all our hurtling lives.

Turning away from the river now to enter Putney, driving up the final hill and the hospital looms into sight, its solid façade upholding the ordinariness of this respectable suburb. The irra-tional anger I feel for the building, for that sign, Royal Hospital for Neuro-Disability, belying the shattered lives it fronts. Entering through the porter's lodge, driving past the elegantly manicured parking area reserved for hospital management, the road winds around the side of the building past Miles's ward to the visitors' car park at the back. I dread the moment of looking up and knowing that he is *there*, behind that window, contained and separated in every conceivable way from me, from us, from his life as he should be living it, thinking it. Longing to see him, dreading the confron-tation with his reality.

But at least I am expecting to see him now, unlike the eve-ning Ron and I were in a cab being driven back with friends from a night out in West London. It had been a good evening, theater and dinner afterwards, a happy distraction with old friends. Ron or

Michael had said something funny and we were all laughing when I looked out of the cab window and saw the great stone building lowering from the side of the road. Miles was there, yards away from us. The shock, like being unexpectedly stabbed; our terrible echoing laughter. Lights were on in the day room. Was he awake, lying in the same position he'd been put in hours before, in pain, unable to move or call anyone? Ron reached over to hold my hand as I cringed back into the darkness.

WHEN HE CAN, Ron comes from his office to visit Miles at lunch-time, a treat for me as well. Most days I spend the afternoon with Miles in his room or, when the weather is fine, take him out into the garden, where I try to find somewhere shady and isolated. The gardens are the luxury of Putney and it is possible to be on your own. I have come to recognize the relatives who feel as I do, who glare at anyone who dares to share the same bench or park a wheelchair too close. There are the others who gather together, their charges ranged in a cluster of wheelchairs beside them as they exchange banter like old pub friends. It is all a matter of survival.

In the evenings the children or friends arrive after work, for everyone involved a valiant effort, given the laborious journey required to take the train from central London and the long walk from station to hospital. We chat together for a while with Miles and then I leave. Recrossing the city it is rush hour now and I long for the sight of a red light ahead, knowing I will have those few blissful moments before it turns green to close my eyes and imagine sleep before I have to set off again.

I drive to Putney and drive back in the comfort of my car with music I've chosen to listen to and I know at the end of each day I will return to a house I love and a man I love. Ron will be there and as I shut the front door I can let go of the thing that has held me together, can unravel whatever it is and know I am safe here. Ron will pour us each a glass of wine and together with him the peace of the house will absorb, for that moment, the pain. I imagine another mother who might return from the hospital after a long, crammed tube ride to her home, perhaps in one of the bleak tower blocks I pass on my journey, its dimly lit stairwell and graffitied elevator offering no respite and a partner waiting for her who demands and does not understand, maybe a partner whom she has disliked for some long time even before this devastating thing happened in her life. How does she survive? Or the families that have lost the bread-winner to brain injury, where there are young children who must come to terms with a mother or father in such a condition. How do they manage?

DURING HIS TIME here Miles is exposed to various different approaches to occupational therapy. There is music therapy, massage therapy, there are audiobooks that can be started or turned off by a nudge of his thumb, sensory sessions with textures, smells, colors, lighting. Large printed instruction cards are held up in front of him: BLINK, STICK OUT YOUR TONGUE, CLOSE YOUR EYES. There are visits to the computer therapy room on the ground floor, where a selection of advanced computer hardware and software is available for use by the severely disabled, with specially adapted keyboards and switches as well as eye-gaze systems, whereby the patient's eyes can direct the cursor across the screen. All the therapies attempt in some way to stimulate the senses, reawaken memories, goad interest; the phrase used is "to evoke potential," which means to find something, anything, that will reignite and fire up the dormant consciousness. Above all, the goal is to try to find some way in which Miles can communicate.

We are amazed and thrilled when on a number of occasions Miles responds positively. He blinks on command to the instruction cards held up in front of him or he puts out his tongue, and although his responses are not consistent it does mean that he has retained some kind of vision. His most consistent response is a slow blink to indicate that he is listening and suggesting assent to a question, though there are also times when he is awake and attending to the therapist and does not blink to respond. It all confirms what we have known from the beginning, that he is undoubtedly aware some of the time. What it also reveals is that even when aware and attentive, he is unable to initiate; he can only follow a command. To know Miles is to know his particular proactive nature, and this is one of the most distressing diagnoses to accept.

He begins each new therapy with clear interest, his eyes wide, the look on his face the one we now know means he is listening intently. He makes an obvious effort to do what is required of him, often involving huge physical effort as he is made to work against his spasticity. At the beginning there is a strong sense of his own optimism, that he, too, is hoping this will be the key, and as we cheer him on we feel the familiar mix of hope and pride rising: this is *Miles*, he will do it, he always has done. Excitement tainted by a sadness too painful to acknowledge as we watch him quivering with the physical effort to follow the simplest demand. Yet as the sessions are repeated in the damning quest for the therapists' Holy Grail of consistency, so Miles's interest wanes and his responses drop off. He cannot keep it up, he is defeated. I have seen him sometimes, awake and alert with me before a session, immediately close his eyes as the occupational therapist begins to speak. Nothing more happens. Eventually she puts the cards away, turns off the audiobook, shuts down the computer. We'll try again tomorrow, Miles, she says. You've been doing so well, but I think perhaps you're too tired today. When she leaves the room I want to shake him despite his misery, You've got to keep going, Miles, no matter how boring and repetitive it is and no matter that you sometimes can't do it. You've *got* to keep trying. You have to *show* them you're there. It's not enough that we know. We love you so much, we adore you, you know that, don't you? I am ashamed at my cruelty, constantly goading him on like this. I don't want to accept that he can't do it; if I do that there can be no more hope for him, and hope is our lifeline. The therapist is guarded at the end of the session. I'm afraid it is a symptom of the minimally conscious state, she says to me, the inability to respond consistently. We know Miles is aware some of the time. Perhaps a different approach will be more successful with him; I'll keep working on it.

MILES IS ASLEEP in his wheelchair and Marina and I are sitting in his room with the door closed, enjoying our shared closeness to him in this rare interlude of peace and privacy. It's a Saturday, and since the therapists don't work on weekends there will be no interruption; we can relax together until it is time for him to be put to bed in a couple of hours. Marina has come up from Oxford and will return this evening, so it's a luxury to have some time with her on my own and to catch up on her news. She makes this journey to see Miles a couple of times a week and, knowing the pressure of work she's under, I am concerned about her health—she contracted glandular fever last year and her immune system is not robust. I am concerned, too, about her dealing with Miles's situation on her own, for I fear that, away from home and the support of the immediate family, she internalizes her deep distress, despite the number of friends she has. It is too private a thing to share, too painful, too difficult to explain. Her friends are young, they're students living their own lives at full tilt; the ordeal she is undergoing is not yet within their experience and it is easier for her not to burden them. So she keeps it to herself and leads a double life.

She is sitting now with her chair pulled up close to Miles so that she can rest her head on his shoulder. Even though her eyes are closed it doesn't look comfortable; none of us can find a way of making physical contact with him that feels relaxed or natural. I reach over to take her hand and as she looks up at me I am shocked to see the utterly bleak, deadened expression in her eyes.

Here I am, she says, hugging my brother, mourning my brother.

It strikes me then that she has articulated the essence of our situation—of losing Miles and yet not losing him, of having to come to terms with the grief of his loss while at the same time trying to comprehend and negotiate his continued existence.

I'M WITH SHEILA, the senior speech therapist, in Miles's room. She has just had a long session with him and she tells me she is pleased with his progress. He is exhibiting the bite reflex less and less often, she says. It is a good sign.

If only I had known. Sheila has shown us how to do orofacial therapy with Miles, choosing a calm moment to stroke his cheek and then open his mouth very gently to run a surgically gloved finger along the gums. The aim is to give him the added sensory experience, and to accustom him to it so that he cooperates more easily with his daily oral hygiene routine. It is not an easy thing getting a patient with TBI to open their mouth.

I cried out loud when Miles bit my finger. Pain, and shock, and fury; it felt vicious and intentional. I left him and stood at the window of his room with my back to him and wept. Fury followed by the misery of guilt. Such an invasion of his privacy; how infuriating must it be to have me prodding and poking about in his mouth, how dare I now feel anger at his response. I'm trying in vain to rationalize the deep hurt I feel, what felt like his furious rejection of me. It was frightening, the force of it and the pain. The dent in my finger lasted for days.

Now I think back to the time in Innsbruck, perhaps two weeks in from Miles's accident, when his friends Matt and Ollie had come out from London to see him. During their visit to the hospital a nurse told them how Miles clearly hated having his teeth cleaned and would bite the brush so hard she wasn't able to continue. He would clamp his teeth on it and not let go and she worried he might snap the brush. Matt and Ollie thought it was a perfect example of his force of character and general impatience with things that got in his way, and we all agreed and laughed with pleasure at the idea of it. How typical, we said, just the sort of thing he would do when he's irritated. We loved him even more for that show of obstinacy and irascibility, but we also thought it was exciting news, that it showed how close he was to the surface and very soon we would be able to tease him about it.

And so I discover the truth about Miles's apparent show of irritation and independence. I learn about the notorious bite reflex, so feared by speech therapists, that appears in adults with severe neurological impairment. It occurs in association with what is described as "marked sensory disturbance"—what does that mean exactly? How will I ever know? But far from showing he was close to coming out of his coma it was an indication of the severity of brain damage Miles had sustained. He couldn't help it—it is an involuntary response, and so powerful in some cases, I read, that the power of the bite is said to be equal to 90 kilograms of pressure.

The good thing is that his bite reflex is diminishing. His swallow has improved too, although he still cannot manage liquids, let alone solids, safely without choking. But he still has a trachie, the hated plastic protuberance that has come to embody

TBI for me, its ugly, demeaning marker. I want it removed; that was the aim of the speech therapists at Queen Square, but here at Putney their approach is more conservative. I do not think it is ambitious enough and say so. There are arguments. Your mother is very confrontational, the junior speech therapist says to Marina. We all agree with her, says Marina furiously and returns home to tell me.

Apart from the discomfort for Miles, if there is any chance he is going to speak again a trachie could inhibit his initiating speech. Erica, the lovely sister in charge of this ward, thinks Miles is ready to have his trachie removed too, and she takes the responsibility upon herself, asking the ward doctor's permission. She removes it, despite the speech therapist's advice, a brave thing to do but entirely in keeping with the sureness and compassion of her nursing skill. She is a beacon in this ward, her calm confidence and her beauty. Miles visibly relaxes in her presence, turns towards her when he hears her voice. I could love her for her ambition for Miles.

I AM CONCERNED about the quantity of drugs Miles is prescribed. His daily drug list reads like a junkie's dream cocktail—I am told by a friend who visits Miles that a number of the drugs he is prescribed demand huge prices on the experimental black market. Baclofen, dantrolene, tizanidine, gabapentin, atenolol, modafinil—how can his weakened body tolerate such a bombardment? Baclofen, dantrolene, and tizanidine are given to combat spasticity, gabapentin provides neurological pain relief, atenolol is a beta blocker, and modafinil a stimulant. When I look them up the individual known side effects can include nausea, dizziness, double vision, headaches, numbness, tingling in the limbs, cold hands and feet, liver damage, depression, even, should he be capable of them, suicidal thoughts. Apart from the stimulant modafinil they all cause increased drowsiness. Surely any moments of awareness Miles has must be seriously compromised?

I make an appointment to see Dr. Jackson, the ward doctor. Unlike the doctors at Innsbruck and Queen Square, he appears to keep himself intentionally aloof from relatives. When I enter his office he looks up from his desk with undisguised irritation. How can I help you? he asks, screwing the lid carefully back on to his fountain pen. After I have told him of my concern he shifts in his chair and sighs resignedly. In my opinion, he says, it really is not a good thing for relatives to try to inform themselves about medical matters. It's much better all around if they just leave it for the doctors to get on with. I can feel my anger rising. Dr. Jackson, that is the most patronizing thing anyone has said to me. If I don't understand something I will always try to find out about it. In this case we are talking about my son's life and as he is unable to speak for himself, I am his spokesman. Surely you understand it is my duty, my responsibility, to try to understand his situation? I'm not telling you how to treat him, I am just telling you that, given the crucial need to encourage his awareness, I am concerned about the quantity of drugs he is being prescribed.

I do understand how irritating it must be for doctors when relatives question their expertise, but there is too much at stake for me here. Dr. Jackson is clearly not used to being questioned and his surprise at such impertinence is plain. Miles's situation is complex, he says coldly. His needs are complex. That is what I am treating. But suddenly the coldness subsides. You know . . . He stops for a moment, then he continues: I have two daughters, the oldest one just a few years younger than Miles. They are also very gifted academically. He goes on to tell me about these daughters, how hardworking and grounded they are compared with so many of the youth today, how proud he is of them. He doesn't say it, but I think he is telling me he understands, he is a parent too. How difficult must his job be, every day to be treating such damaged people and having to confront their desperate and confused relatives; perhaps keeping aloof is the only way he can maintain his equilibrium.

A few days later Erica tells me that a decision has been taken to try to reduce Miles's medication. It will be a slow process, one drug being reduced at a time so the effect can be monitored. Gradually Miles comes off tizanidine, dantrolene, atenolol; there are no adverse effects and his spasticity does not change. As soon as they begin reducing baclofen it deteriorates and similarly with the reduction of gabapentin; Miles will always require both these drugs. But at least they have been proved to be necessary and I am grateful to Dr. Jackson.

MILES AND DRUGS: how ironic that I am more concerned about his drug intake now than I was when he was experimenting with them himself. At fifteen he was a full-blooded teenager, roiling with hormones, his hobbies no longer simple boyish ones but skateboarding in derelict urban places, going to raves, breaking whatever rules he found it fun to break and, crucially, those he thought constrained without necessity. Like so many adolescent boys before and after him, he read *The Doors of Perception*, *On the Road*, *The Naked Lunch*, Ferlinghetti, Ginsberg.

A Saturday night at his boarding school, long after all the boys should have been signed back into their houses. Miles and Rick are still out in the town, exuberant with whatever it is they managed to get hold of, regaling each other with the amazing insights they are now privy to. Suddenly Miles stops in his tracks. Hey, Rick, come and look at this, he calls to his friend, you've got to come and look at this. It's awesome. There's a bush here that looks exactly like Miss Nash. He leans forward with great deliberation to inspect the bush and then starts to prod it tentatively. Whoa, Rick, you've got to come, he says as he continues prodding, this is definitely weird. Rick joins him and now both boys are peering in amazement and delight at the strange apparition they see before them. They reach out to touch the bush, and then, very clearly and very slowly, it begins to speak back to them.

It *is* Miss Nash, it says. They have been standing in the middle of the street at 3 a.m. prodding their French teacher in the face. She escorts them back to their boardinghouse where, he tells me later as an adult, he spent three of the most nightmarish hours of his life so far left to sober up in the neon-lit washroom.

ONE DAY GEMMA appears at the doorway to Miles's room. Her own room is just along the corridor and the door is always closed, a large unmissable sign on it that says in thick black print: THIS IS GEMMA'S ROOM. DO NOT ENTER WITHOUT GEMMA'S PERMISSION. I have seen her sometimes in the distance, being pushed along in her chair by a carer, and she looks as regal as a princess enduring a royal visit. One of the nurses tells me that calm and sweet as she looks she is a demanding patient, that she dismissed Dr. Jackson, her appointed doctor, because she does not like him and requested another whom she preferred. What a girl, I think.

She has come today to introduce herself to Miles. She asked the carer, Donna, a motherly Filipina, to bring her; Donna has left her own children behind in the Philippines to support them from afar and treats all the young patients as her surrogate family. I've come to visit Miles, says Gemma to me simply, in a voice so quiet it's almost a whisper. I've seen him a few times since he arrived and I wanted to say hello. Donna has placed the chair in the doorway so that she is facing Miles, who is seated in his chair by the bed and looking the other way. Hello, Miles, she says, I'm Gemma. He doesn't respond. She is a formidable girl, sitting there, her manner at once imperious and sweet, a combination, I think as I look at her, of the lack of movement, the lack of anything extraneous about her except the words she is uttering, and the shock of her extraordinary beauty.

For close up she is beautiful. Partly because of her luminous eyes and perfect creamy skin, partly because her moon-pale body is strangely motionless as she looks back at you. She sits so erect in her chair, her arms on the arm rests, nails perfectly manicured with the lightest sheen of pearlized pink. Everything about her is carefully executed: the understated makeup, just the lightest touch of eye shadow and lipstick; her dark hair cut to frame her pale face; the perfectly coordinated blouse and long skirt; and her earrings, dangly and sparkling, even in the daytime.

Surprisingly for someone so beautiful she has the sweetest smile. There is a transparency about it, as though you can see through to something quiveringly alive, and you think perhaps that is why she seems as fragile as a butterfly trapped under glass. But her smile is the only point of expression in her face, and only when you realize that do you take in that she is breathing by means of a corrugated white plastic tube that leads from the tracheostomy in her throat and winds down behind her into a box at the back of her chair. The box is her portable ventilator and she can only speak on the out breath; talking to her is a slow and difficult process for both of you.

Three years ago, aged twenty and at home one evening with her boyfriend, she collapsed with no warning and was rushed to hospital. When she came around she was paralyzed from the neck down and on a ventilator. It was discovered that, as the result of a freak condition, part of her spinal cord had from childhood not been growing in tandem with the rest of her body and had finally snapped. There was nothing the doctors or medical technology could do; her paralysis would be permanent. After spending the first two months in her local hospital she was moved to Putney and has been here ever since. Her boyfriend broke off the relationship; he was young and could not bring himself to see her after that traumatic evening.

Following her first visit she comes to see Miles regularly and unannounced, despite her fierce approach to her own privacy. She brings him gifts, CDs of her favorite music, DVDs of films she thinks he might like, books to be read to him. She asks me if she can have a photograph of him to put up in her room and chooses the one in which, she says, he looks like a film star. Donna tells me Gemma has fallen in love with Miles.

The children and I find it difficult; we want to concentrate on Miles when we are with him and instead we must talk to Gemma, in itself an arduous process as she waits for the breath to speak, her voice so faint we must strain to hear. There is the added poignancy of her unrequited feelings for Miles, for he always looks uncomfortable when she is there, as though this is an intrusion for him, too.

She never has visitors. I assume her family must live a long way from London but she doesn't discuss them or her home life, except to tell me she is one of five siblings. Later I discover they live in South London not far from me. Donna says they don't like coming to Putney, because they find the people there frightening. Instead Gemma invites Marina to accompany her shopping and on outings to the cinema or a Persian restaurant with Omar, the Kurdish paraplegic ex-soldier who occupies the room next to Gemma. Marina goes with her, setting off from the hospital in an ambulance, Gemma in her wheelchair, a carer to attend to her, Marina trying to shield her from prurient attention from the public—it is demanding and Marina is exhausted when she comes home. I would like to protect her from this added strain, but then she says, How can I refuse her when she asks me? It would be too cruel.

THIS MORNING DR. Jackson informs me that Miles has been selected to take part in a research project being done by the Wolfson Brain Imaging Centre, part of Cambridge University. Neuroscientists under the auspices of something called the Impaired Consciousness Study Group are researching "possible covert brain activation" in low-awareness states. He would like my permission for Miles to travel up to Cambridge and spend five days at Addenbrooke's Hospital, where the research will take place. This is thrilling news. It is the same team of neuroscientists who are responsible for the extraordinary story that's been in the news lately. I have read about it—a young woman thought to be in a permanent vegetative state who, when asked to imagine playing tennis or moving around her home, was observed under fMRI, functional magnetic resonance imaging, to activate the areas of her brain indistinguishable from healthy volunteers. How incredible that Miles is to be seen by the same neuroscientists who did this. Then the familiar twist of apprehension—will we or won't we be given the definitive news we want to hear?

Miles is awake and I tell him the story about the young woman, that he has the chance to be seen by the same research team in Cambridge. He is alert as I start talking and then as I continue there is the recognizable shift in his expression, a quiet, focused intensity, as though he were in a noisy room and straining to hear. Miles, I can see you understand me, I tell him. I hope you never doubt this, even when sometimes I don't understand you and I get you wrong. This is going to be an amazing opportunity for you, to give the doctors proof of your awareness so we can be certain you get the right treatment while you're recovering. Because you *are* recovering, my darling. I hope he doesn't hear any change in register; I want so much to believe it myself. Week by week we all see the changes, I tell him, even though it might not feel like that to you. And going to Cambridge will be interesting for you, a change from the routine, the monotony, I know, of life here. Will and I are going to come too—he's taking a week off work to be with you because it is so important. I think Will may also be concerned about me being on my own, but whatever his reason I am relieved he is coming.

I have been worried for some time that our pep talks are unconvincing. From an early age Miles's clear, fierce intelligence compelled the truth from people; he saw through any dissembling—his infallible, built-in bullshit detector, a friend described it. I think he believes me today; perhaps he is persuaded this research can liberate him. It is always clear when he is unconvinced—I think of the computer program he works on with the occupational therapist, a program that is by necessity basic to the point of humiliation, that would be fun for a three-year-old. As the therapist and I urge him on, trying to keep him motivated, I can feel him withdrawing, as though resolutely not cooperating when the carefully enunciated computer voice tells him to find the cat from a picture of cats and dogs. The visible shift of tension that crosses his face suggests defiance if not anger. The physical effort he has to make just to press the switch is herculean and the lack of consistent success must be unbearably disheartening. He was always impatient with failure. But today he seems convinced by my pep talk. The responsibility is fearful. What if Cambridge is a failure? Could my encouragement be another act of unwitting cruelty? But what else can we do, except continue to try to give him hope, to keep him motivated? For his sake—and ours.

Before leaving for Cambridge, Will and I meet the neuroscientist who will be doing the research with Miles. A slight young man with pale, thinning hair and a boyishly enthusiastic manner, he is not what I imagined for an eminent neuroscientist. I warm to him immediately as he introduces himself to Will and me and then turns to Miles. I'm Martin, he says, and I'm hugely looking forward to working with you. He goes on to explain where and when this will take place, speaking to Miles as though he were meeting a new and respected colleague who is about to join him on an important project. Miles has gone quite still, listening and looking up from his wheelchair at this young man with a yearning intensity that I find agonizing to see. It is as though I have glimpsed the scene unwittingly through a half-open door. And then an image superimposes itself, Miles as he was, standing there engaged in this conversation, strong and upright, his dark looks in vivid contrast to the paleness of Martin Coleman and both participating in the rapport of shared intellectual vigor.

Dr. Coleman has asked us to bring a collection of family photographs for him to show Miles under fMRI. I rummage through the old copper trunk that houses our mess of photographs, wishing I had been more organized about their storage. Picture after picture enshrining the family, I realize, and the unit of four children intact, in gleaming health, no trace of a shadow. Miles aged six, proudly astride his uncle's motorbike, Will as a grinning eight-year-old Batman, three-year-old Claudia having a tantrum on a ski slope, her expression the one we all found so adorably funny, Marina aged seven on the beach in Cornwall, a gleaming shrimp of a thing. Sitting there on the carpet in the playroom, surrounded by the remnants of a life lived once upon a time without any tremor of foreboding, I think: I had that. At least I had that. And then the ripple of pain begins and as I go under, I can barely breathe.

In Cambridge, Will and I spend each day at the hospital, leaving Miles in the late afternoon to return to our hotel. We sit for a while on the cool terrace overlooking the river, sunlight slanting across the green Backs of the university as we talk through the events of the day. We are both wrung out; seeing Miles in this new environment has been freshly painful. In a way, we realize, we've been lulled by the routine of Putney and must now, with so much at stake this week, confront our hopes and fears with a new intensity.

Each day Miles undergoes a different form of testing with Dr. Coleman. He responds to commands both verbal and written in four out of five trials. We are amazed to see his intense efforts to cooperate and he is clearly exhausted by the end of each day. When the fMRI is done it is confirmed that he does not retain a full field of vision, the damaged right occipital lobe remaining blacked out, though the left side lights up to photographs of the family and famous faces. But during the seminal test he does not succeed in performing the crucial mental imagery tasks. His brain does not light up when asked to imagine playing tennis or moving around the rooms of his home.

Will and I hear the news with bleak resignation. Dr. Coleman stresses that a negative result cannot be interpreted to say Miles is unable to perform these tasks, since false negatives occur in healthy volunteers; he also notes that problems with Miles's eyesight and spasticity could be masking his ability to respond, as well as his inability to initiate actions. I fear that he is trying to be kind with these caveats. Getting to know him this week I have a sense of an almost spiritual mission to achieve, through his research, a world-wide alleviation of the suffering and hopelessness in low-awareness states and this extends to his concern for the relatives. At the end of the week I can see he is sincere when he tells me how much he has enjoyed working with and getting to know Miles. He has worked incredibly hard, he says, and I would like to review his situation in six months' time. I very much hope things will continue to improve for him.

It is true—not since Miles came out of his coma have I seen him making such a consistent effort to engage. When Will and I sit in with him during the computer work with Dr. Coleman we both recognize his clear interest in what he is being asked to do and can see his determined attempts to succeed. How can I tell him he failed the central challenge, the fMRI test? I cannot, I dare not, undermine his hope in any way. For the first time in my life I must lie outright to Miles, to whom one could only ever tell the truth.

RON IS VISITING Miles over lunch today and I take the opportunity to meet up with a friend at a restaurant near the hospital. We've known each other since our early twenties and have shared most of the events of the ensuing decades with sympathy and brio, the kind of intimate friendship that leaves one nourished through laughter. Through the painful years of my divorce, with her I could laugh.

She loves Miles, has known him from the bump in my tummy to the last time when I saw her helplessly flirting with the handsome young man who was teasing her so fondly. When we meet for lunch she asks me immediately, How is he? I wish she hadn't. There is no change, I tell her. I'm going to see him later. Let's talk of other things now.

The truth is, I don't ever want to be asked how he is, even by close friends. It is a question I dread. I understand why people ask it, but what answer can I give? Nothing has changed and there is nothing to say; the particular pain lies in having to confront that out loud. If I'm enjoying the relief for the moment of not thinking about Miles's situation, I don't want, without warning, to be suddenly made to. I talk about this with another friend of mine, Jennifer, who was at lunch that fateful Sunday in March. She is now undergoing chemotherapy for breast cancer and she understands. Someone I don't know terribly well came up to me at a party the other night, she tells me, and I could see the expression on this woman's face suddenly changing into that sort of do-goodery voyeurism I dread. How *are* you? the woman then asked me, her head tilted dolefully to one side, and I couldn't help it, Jennifer says, I just replied—Do you know, I was feeling absolutely wonderful until you reminded me. I love Jennifer. It is not only because she's a psychiatrist or that she now has cancer that she understands, for from the beginning, from her early phone calls to me in Innsbruck, she knew. Grief is private, only to be shared by choice. Intrusion, even when well meaning, exacerbates the pain, ratcheting it up out of nowhere like suddenly knocking an already broken limb.

I am still a figure of dread, the mother whose son is in a coma, but I am more approachable now. My maimed state has become familiar. Though I know it is understandable for people to ask how Miles is, my defenses remain fragile, easily breached, and there are other recurring and more invasive questions than "How is he?" As a family we are learning to see these questions coming and to fend them off, inevitably asked by people we know less well. Are Miles's eyes open? they ask. When you're with him does he know you're there? Can he speak? Can he hear you? Can he eat normally? Does he know where he is? Does he look the same? Taken by surprise, we begin by answering them, but one question seems to lead insatiably to the next until our painful, unwilling sharing of Miles's predicament turns to bitter resentment. The niceties of behavior have, it seems, to be observed; somehow it feels incumbent on us to be polite and appreciative in the face of people's concern. But this does not feel like concern, it feels like curiosity bordering on voyeurism. Thank you for asking, I have now learned to say, but if you don't mind I would rather not talk about it. What I want to say is, Why are you asking such a question? What is your real interest in the answer? His predicament is private; your curiosity makes this feel like a freak show.

I don't like this sullen protective anger as I try to deflect the conversation. Interacting with people used to be uncomplicated. I think of Jacqueline, who lost her twenty-four-year-old son in a car crash, telling me that she could no longer speak to two of her former close friends because they said the wrong thing after his death. I remember thinking at the time what a pity it was that she was so implacable, that her friends would never have meant to be upsetting. Now I understand, though I wish it wasn't so.

But the friends who do understand have been the crucial backbone of support from the moment of Miles's accident. Extraordinary, undemanding thoughtfulness: bringing home-cooked meals, pot roasts and fresh loaves; gifts of massages, facials, spa treatments, books; cards dropping through the letter box with random news that delights; invitations to the theater, art exhibitions, meals; or just regular phone calls to chat about things other than Miles. The friends on whom I know I can call in moments of despair, who will listen without instructing or intruding. And the young friends of Miles who continue to visit him despite the difficulty are a constant deep source of comfort for us all.

I think now of the parents of a girl on Miles's ward, Hamad and Yasmin, who want no outside distraction in the long vigil as they wait for their daughter Mia to wake out of her coma. They do not accept the doctors' diagnosis of persistent vegetative state, despite Mia having lost a large part of her brain in a car accident and her showing no response of any kind in the four years since her accident. Old friendships abandoned, they have made a new social life within the hospital, joining the groups of relatives who find comfort in sharing the lives and stories of their damaged children. All the people who make up this group are parents and all are hoping for a miracle.

Many are people of faith. Hamad and Yasmin are Muslim; five times a day they leave Mia and go somewhere private in the hospital to wash and pray. During Ramadan they fast until sunset. Each night they have supper in the canteen, for they will arrive home too late to eat. Leaving home every morning at ten they drive the two-hour journey to Putney to arrive in time for the opening of visiting hours at noon. They leave at the end and drive the two hours back, arriving home at ten. She will wake, they say, and we must be here for her when she does. Our life before this thing happened is of no importance.

Not only are their old friends now irrelevant, but their two younger children are lost to them too. Both are teenagers still at school and I think the loss of their older sister must be complicated by resentment, for they never come to visit her. My young son is more interested in parties and girls, Hamad says. He has even told me that he finds Mia disgusting to look at now. I will continue to provide a home for him and my other daughter, but that is all; they have abandoned Mia in her hour of need.

Hamad is a warm, sympathetic man but on this he is unrelenting. Yasmin remains quiet as he speaks, her beautiful face framed by the rich blue of her headscarf like a living Pietà. How can she bear this triple loss, estranged from her younger children as a result of the tragedy that has taken away her first child? Alone, sustained only by her faith and the shared obsession with Hamad, she waits for the miracle of Mia's awakening.

It's raining, a bleak gray summer's day. Miles is awake and Claudia and I are chatting in his room, including him in the way we have become accustomed. It's easier to talk to him when there are two or more of us and the conversation is no longer one-sided. It's raining today, Miles, I tell him. I remember us once discussing how strange that rain can make us feel restless, gloomy, cut off from something more exciting, but when we're in bed the sound of it is so soothing and pleasurable. Do you remember, says Claudia, how we used to love swimming in the rain in France? You were the first to suggest it, Miles, and we all joined you and had the coolest time ever. The usual fleeting frisson of apprehension that maybe he doesn't want to be reminded, but his expression doesn't change from a look of calm interest. It occurs to me then that he hasn't felt the rain in over a year. Why don't we take him out in it now, I say to Claudia, we can let him have that sensory experience. It's warm enough, it can't do him any harm and he's due for bed in an hour so if his clothes get wet they can be changed straightaway.

We set off out of the ward, wheeling him to the huge elevator that takes us down to the ground floor. It feels like an adventure and as we push open the doors that lead from the visitors' room into the garden the questioning looks we get from staff and visitors make it feel even more so, as though we're breaking school rules. The garden is quite empty, a clean sea of green lawn between the gleaming pathways and dripping wooden benches. What heaven, says Claudia, let's run. So we do, propelling Miles what feels like dangerously fast along the slippery tarmac paths. I remember doing this with the children in their pushchairs, their shrieks of delight. The rain is as fine as sea spray on our faces and Miles closes his eyes in what I hope is pleasure as we run, enjoying the movement and this once familiar, elementary thing that now seems to me so poignant. What else have I not thought of, of all the ordinary things he loved that are removed from him now?

* * *

THE SHOCK OF disgust. The day I come home and I'm shouting at Ron: I can't stand it anymore, Ron. Do you realize what I've been doing all afternoon? Miles has had a bad day; *I've* had a bad day. All I've done is watch Miles sitting in his chair like a hopeless idiot—I contort my face grotesquely to imitate Miles when he is distressed—and he *would not* relax his legs down from the ridiculous horizontal thing he does with them when his spasticity is bad, he *would not* unclench his arms. He dribbled and coughed and then he choked while I suctioned him—great gobbets of phlegm came up. His brain is scrambled, I can't stand it, his life is *finished*, done for, over, kaput. The whole thing is just *preposterous*, Ron, do you hear me, I can't bear it anymore. How on earth can I help him when he's like this? I am in the swing of it now, shouting and gesticulating, and Ron is letting me do this. It is painful for him because he loves me and he loves Miles, but he has lost part of me to Miles—part of me has been damaged with Miles. We can't return to the simple, pure happiness we had together before this thing happened.

SOME WEEKS LATER Ron wakes at night with a stabbing pain in his stomach and severe nausea. It has receded by the morning but it was so sudden and so violent I ask him please to see the doctor that day. He does, and is immediately referred for tests.

I have come to meet him in the clinic after the test and we wait together for the doctor in the small, curtained-off cubicle where he has been resting as the sedation wears off. I've driven straight from Putney, so I tell him how Miles was this morning and then we chat about other things, keeping at bay the fear that hovers unspoken. The doctor finally arrives, straight from the operating theater and still in his blue cotton scrubs. A kind man, he can't soften the blow. He has found two large tumors. I honestly don't know how you have remained functioning normally, he says. You must have quite remarkable strength. He stays with us for some time and I gather that he knows about Miles. Ron must have told him; I don't ask why but knowing Ron I fear that he knew something was wrong but postponed finding out, not wanting to burden me further.

It is the end of November and when we leave the clinic the afternoon has darkened already, shrouded in gray drizzle. As we drive home the windshield wipers scrape relentlessly through the mist of our incomprehension. Hope comes to the rescue, that primordial survival mechanism—how else could we face this? If the tumors are removed and the cancer hasn't spread, then that will be the end of it. Ron hasn't lost weight, that's definitely a good sign. There is no history of cancer in his family. We know lots of people who have survived cancer and are still going strong.

We've exhausted the subject by the time we get home. Belinda and Amelia, Ron's daughters, are waiting for us. Now in their late thirties, they are of a different generation from my children, but the merging of our families has been a happy one and Miles's accident has cast a shadow over their lives too. Now Ron must tell them that he has cancer. They lost their mother to cancer ten years ago and I know what dread this news will hold for them. By the time we have supper together the subject has been exhausted once again, the shock absorbed. The girls' relationship with Ron is a close one and both live nearby; there will be a lot of us on hand to support him through whatever lies ahead. We don't talk about cancer over the meal and instead enjoy a bottle of the wine we normally save for special occasions, though our conversation is tinged with strange urgency.

I wake in the night and realize that light is coming from under the closed office door, the room next to our bedroom which is usually left open. I get up and Ron is sitting at the desk in his dressing gown, writing. It's all right, he says, please go back to sleep. I just need this time to work things out. I go back to bed. I understand; Ron has a habit of facing any problem, work or personal or of someone else who has asked for help, by writing it out to reach the decision that he will stand by.

Before he leaves for work the next morning he brings me my morning cup of tea and sits down on the bed. I have made up my mind, he says. We are going to put this on the back burner. I want life to continue as normal—you've got enough to deal with and it must not intrude on our total commitment to Miles. Oh, Ron, how can you say that? I take his hand as we share the crushing weight of this new, pernicious thing that has entered our lives with such callous timing. I can't possibly put it on the back burner, I tell him. Of course I can face both things together. And we will emphatically face this together.

What I can't acknowledge is the truth, that loving Ron with the intensity I do, it's not the same as a mother's love. I don't want to be put to this test. I must not let Ron feel he is taking second place, on the back burner.

Two days later Ron undergoes surgery to remove the tumors. I am with him when the surgeon tells us the pathologist's results. He has stage IV cancer that has metastasized to his liver.

The surgeon inspires confidence, he is serious and concerned and he is not unoptimistic. Ron will have chemotherapy to shrink the small tumors in the liver and then surgery to remove them. He could remain clear of cancer after that for some long time.

This cannot happen to Ron. We cannot let this thing happen to Ron. How does the mind respond to calamity? But this time we understand—I think we do—what the calamity is. It is cancer and it can be targeted. Ron can survive this. He must survive this. He is talking calmly to the surgeon who sits across from us at the end of the hospital bed and they are discussing logistics, when the chemotherapy should begin, how long it will take. The surgeon says that time should be allowed for Ron to recover his strength from the operation, which was major surgery; chemo will begin after that.

When he has left the room Ron takes my hand. I'm so sorry, he says. Such an extraordinary man, even now not thinking of himself. He could never, ever be a burden to me. He has only ever, will only ever, nourish and uphold me.

RON'S DIAGNOSIS MEANS we must put on hold our plans to have Miles living at home. We cannot have the disruption of builders doing major work in the house while he is recovering from his operation nor while he is undergoing chemotherapy. It is an added bitter blow, but I remind myself it is only a deferral. Once Ron is better we will reimplement the plans.

THE FIRST CHRISTMAS. Belinda and Amelia come for our traditional celebratory breakfast; so far everything is as normal as it can be, except Miles is not here. Later the children and I drive to Putney through the empty streets of London, the river placidly aloof alongside us in the wintery sun. We arrive and Will carries in the cooler filled with champagne and glasses, plates of smoked salmon sandwiches, Christmas cake, the girls and I laden with carrier bags of presents. We take Miles down to the empty ballroom, the girls playing a duet on the grand piano while he faces them, rigid-jawed, in his chair. Nothing we can say lightens his mood. Shiny multicolored strips of Christmas foil hanging from door frames, tinsel and sprigs of holly over the dull watercolors and we sit on gray plastic chairs around the piano to eat our picnic lunch. At last Miles drops off to sleep so we talk among ourselves and then we're laughing wildly because actually the bizarre dreadfulness of the moment is hilariously funny and laughing is a huge, delicious relief. Taking Miles back upstairs we give out the presents for carers and nurses, key rings and pens for the men, boxed, scented soap and scarves for the women. How fond we feel of each other, how affectionate they are with Miles. But under our show of gaiety lurks the truth. Remember this time last year, Miles's fling with the Icelandic girl, a friend of Tom's he met on Christmas Eve who fell for him and happily accompanied him home for the night, his waking Ron and me as he crept down the stairs with her at six a.m. so she could go back to Tom's parents' house without their noticing. His rueful hangover, sleeping on the sitting room sofa while we went out to friends' for lunchtime drinks, regaling us in the evening when he recovered. His delight in the evening meal being spent on our own, just the six of us, his ideal Christmas, he said. Handing out presents from under the tree beforehand, his own for us all elaborately wrapped and generous. The gusto with which he enjoyed every part of the ceremonial meal, his skepticism when Claudia offered to cook it instead of me and then the shower of compliments that she had done it all to perfection. The decimated goose and Stilton, his favorites. All of us sitting around the fire afterwards enjoying the end of the port. What could be better than this? he asks. Great food, a good fire, and family.

We sit in the day room while Miles is put to bed and then we drive home, in time to bathe and change and gather around the tree, presents and more champagne, a festive dinner tonight for five. Miles's absence is a tangible thing, his presence at Christmas always so intrinsic to everything about it, but there is something else tonight that flits like a moving shadow between us. It is the specter of Ron's cancer. His treatment starts in the New Year.

* * *

Ron has been having chemotherapy for months now and somehow it has merged quietly into the new pattern of our lives. It helps that so far the side effects have not been troubling, though he is beginning to lose his hair. Thick and curly and once fair, it turned to white before I met him and I love it. We go to Lock & Co. and choose him a hat, a dark navy fedora. You look ridiculously handsome, I tell him, it's really a tragedy you haven't always worn a hat. His treatment is making us optimistic and whatever other side effects there are, he doesn't complain about them. Life continues as normal; he has succeeded in putting his illness on the back burner.

There is a large indoor pool at Putney, one of the many amenities for the patients, and the physiotherapist Sarah tells me she has decided to take Miles swimming. The theory is that the weightlessness of the body in the warm water helps spasticity, aiding the patients to relax their muscles. By regularly experiencing this relaxation they may regain some movement, while the pleasurable new sensory experience might help encourage further wakefulness.

For the hour's drive to Putney I try to keep hope submerged but it doesn't work, I can't suppress it and I have sudden little bursts of sweetness—maybe this will really be pleasurable for him, maybe it will be the catalyst for his recovery. For some people it has had amazing results. Nervousness as I enter the building, a modern wing just beyond the car park, the air getting warmer and thicker as I near the pool, saturated with chlorine, much worse even than the indoor pool in Lewisham where I used to take the children for swimming lessons. Of course, almost all the people who swim here are incontinent. Taking off my shoes to step through the antiseptic footbath and onto the pool side is like entering a sauna, the air suffocatingly clammy.

The session is about to begin. Sarah is in the pool and Miles—he is suspended above the water, swaying slightly in his sling as the hoist is maneuvered by Harriet, Sarah's assistant, who is strong and stout-legged in her swimming costume. Miles could be a wounded animal being airlifted for treatment like one sees in nature programs; his eyes are black with fear. I realize that I have never, in my life, seen him look fearful. Sarah is soothing him, talking to him as one would to a child: Miles, it's okay, I'm here to receive you, you can't come to any harm, Harriet and I will hold you in the water, you're going to be fine. His legs are rigid, stretched out straight from the sling so that it looks precarious, as though he might slip out. His arms are clenched up to his sides, fists together under his chin, his broad shoulders now contracted and narrow. He is wearing a nappy under his shorts. He looks small in the air above the empty expanse of water, his once powerful body shrunk to this.

In the water he is no better. Sarah and Harriet are supporting him, Sarah behind him, holding him under the arms, Harriet supporting his legs. But Miles is more rigid than ever; this is a disaster. He doesn't feel safe, and how can he, when he has no control over his movements? The thing he has always sought to avoid, feeling safe. It is a grotesque parody of his life.

WHERE DID IT come from, Miles's need to push every experience to its furthest limits? He agreed with the saying, he told me once, that the greatest hazard in life is to risk nothing. From the beginning he sought out danger and it was as simple as that. He needed it in the way that a mountaineer continues to seek out an ever more challenging rock face, and though the usual explanation is that it's for the adrenaline rush, I felt it lay deeper than that. It seemed more a need to confront and combat any personal fear; the thrill was in the personal, private victory.

Like the time he went cage diving with sharks. As every other person who saw the film *Jaws* did, he had a consuming fear of sharks and so one of his greatest thrills was to arrange, as soon as he knew we were going on a family holiday to South Africa, to go cage diving. I have the video of it: he and another young man in their black wetsuits like seals in the sea in a steel cage attached to a small boat, and the lazy eyes of the great white sharks circling them a hand's width away, occasionally thumping the cage violently as they appear to try to reach the men. He described the experience as the most exciting of his life so far, even the buildup to it. Setting off at four in the morning to travel up the Eastern Cape coast through the dawn to Gansbaai, from where the small fishing boat departed, the scenery wild and the dawn ethereally beautiful, and he felt a sense of uncontaminated connection with nature, and with himself.

The anticipation of confronting pure fear emptied his mind of all its clutter. It felt cleansing, he said.

THERE IS AN article in the newspaper about a woman who is paralyzed following a riding accident. The story is very moving—the young woman was a gifted competitive rider and her world has ended. But, I think, and she can never think this, the wonderful thing is that she is not brain-damaged and she can speak. We are party now to the weird hierarchy of injury, where before Miles's accident her plight would have seemed inconceivably dreadful; now we are envious of it. She is so much higher up the ladder, and Miles is right at the very bottom.

She can speak, and she says no one will believe that one of the worst things about her injury is that when she has an itch she cannot relieve it. She cannot scratch her nose when she wants to. I register a small shock of horror. Why didn't I think of it before?

It's been more than a year since Miles's accident. He and I share the same ridiculous affliction of having a sensitized nose which regularly, for no explicable reason, becomes agonizingly itchy. This means that at random moments we are assaulted by an overwhelming need to scratch our nose, and by scratch I mean really scratch hard, preferably with something like a wad of rough kitchen paper, and then to rub it as viciously as possible backwards and forwards, up and down, until the itch has been quelled into submission. If the situation doesn't allow such comical movements we must make do with a quick surreptitious push of the nose side to side or a hard pinch, but the itch will not have been satisfied and we must continue to suffer.

For some time I have been puzzled by a look that has come over Miles's face at odd times since he came out of his coma, a look I haven't been able to interpret. All of a sudden he begins to frown, his eyes shut tight and his whole face tenses, like the quivering moment just before a sneeze. But there is no sneeze and he remains frozen in this grimace until eventually, as though with Zen-like effort of will, his expression begins to subside into its former stoic blankness. When it has happened I've not been sure if he is in physical pain or whether he is suddenly experiencing emotional distress of some kind, perhaps a memory he cannot bear to go back to and is trying to shut out of his mind. Now I'm sure I know what it is. I do an experiment in front of the mirror and there is no doubt—my grimace exactly replicates what I would do if my nose was itchy and I couldn't scratch it.

When I am with Miles the next day I read the newspaper article to him. I can't bear to think, I tell him, that you must have felt the same. He is alert this morning and I can feel him listening to me, though his expression is a little tense. Miles, I thought I might just give your nose a bit of a scratch anyway and see if you like it—I know myself it's never unwelcome. Going to the paper towel dispenser above the basin in his room I tear off four sheets and scrunch them up into a ball. Okay, I've got some paper towel and I'll give it a go and see how you feel. As soon as I begin he closes his eyes in the way he does when Marina gives him a head massage, his face and limbs softening back into the chair. When I stop his response is unambiguous. Slowly and deeply he inhales, and then he exhales in a long, drawn-out sigh of undeniable relief, his face and body now completely relaxed. It is a sweet sensation, giving him this pleasure.

As A SMALL boy Miles was prone to ear infections and the doctor would prescribe a particularly vicious-tasting bright orange antibiotic. He made a great fuss on first tasting it, said it was disgusting and it would make him vomit. But I insisted fiercely and the matter was closed. Having been overruled he accepted my authority and then stoically and meekly took the medicine three times a day as he was meant to. Some years later he confessed he had poured the medicine down the sink when I wasn't in the kitchen and refilled the bottle with orange juice. How we laughed then and how happy it makes me now to think of it, another scrap to add to my album of memories.

SUMMER HAS COME around again. It is a beautiful sunny afternoon and the luxury of the gardens at Putney is being appreciated to the full by residents and visitors alike. Marina and I are sitting on a bench in the rose garden with Miles next to us. He is asleep and we have positioned ourselves behind him in such a way that we can't be seen staring at two people occupying the bench nearby. It is Jack and his father, and Jack has just begun to speak. We are feasting on him, on the stiff, halting movement of his mouth and the intensity of his expression, and we're also feasting on the look of rapturous happiness on his father's face. Our voyeurism, our envy, is a wretched thing, but we can't stop ourselves.

Jack came into the ward some months after Miles. Skateboarding on a London pavement, he was struck by a truck that had mounted the curb and it threw him into the path of an oncoming car. There is a look about him of Miles, perhaps his longish face and dark hair, or perhaps just his youth and because Miles also liked skateboarding when he was younger; Jack probably snowboards too and I imagine they would have things to talk about. At first, on arrival, he appeared to be in a persistent vegetative state, his face completely blank, unmoving, his eyes black and unlit. His mother accompanied him with the angry, haunted look I understood. But gradually his eyes began to lighten until their expressiveness became a shocking thing to witness—you could literally *see* that he was trapped inside. We can't get that from Miles because of his damaged sight, a major pathway to the brain lost; it is somehow an insultingly unfair cruelty in the circumstances.

Some time passed after Jack's eyes regained expression before he began to speak. I imagine the moment when his parents heard him say the first words. I indulge myself, imagine the pure, heart-leaping joy of watching Miles emerging from his tomb of speechlessness.

Jack has succeeded where Miles has failed. I am ashamed to admit my envy, and my shame: envy of Jack's family, shame that Miles hasn't made it, like Jack has. But it is more complex than that. Even the fact that this has happened to Miles at all is somehow a failure—we have all failed. We have failed to help him, to find a cure for him, and he has failed to achieve the future he deserved. Our love can be no consolation. As Marina and I sit together in the mild sunshine with Miles asleep next to us, we talk about it, understanding each other. Who else could, who had not experienced the same thing? How can one explain the disgrace, in these circumstances, of feeling competitive, ashamed, envious?

Sarah, the young Australian physio treating Miles, understands, in a way. When I arrive one morning she asks me if I know a friend of Miles's called Angus. I can't think of anyone. No, I reply. Why? He came to visit Miles yesterday, she says, and he was strange, unlike the other friends that come. She clearly feels reticent about telling me more in front of Miles. So we go outside his room and she tells me that Angus was agitated, nervous meeting her, then gushingly emotional as he saw Miles, knelt down in front of his chair and tried to hold Miles's hands. I thought he might be stoned, she says, he was so weird and jittery, but arrogant, too. He told Miles how upset he was seeing him like this. He remembered Miles at school, his success, the promise his future had held, and he prayed for him. Miles tensed up terribly, she continues, he didn't like it and was obviously distressed so I had to ask Angus to leave. I hope you don't mind? The thing is, she said, I got this awful feeling—he had come to see how the mighty have fallen.

I am very grateful to Sarah for protecting Miles. Looking in the visitors' book we keep in his room, I see that Angus has left a message and now I remember him: he was at school with Miles. They weren't particularly close friends and have not seen each other since. He was exceptionally gifted at sport, the school's star sportsman, but they competed academically.

As a family, we made the decision at the beginning that we would allow only very close friends and colleagues to visit Miles. We all felt that in the same situation that is what we would want and, more important, knowing Miles, what he would want. Being with him is an intimate experience. He is vulnerable; so much of his condition makes humiliation possible. He coughs, he chokes, he has to be suctioned, his Conveen can leak and soak his trousers, he can't control his movements. If he is in pain his distress is piti-able. Who would want, then, to be exposed to someone one doesn't know well?

Angus has left his number in the visitors' book and I call him. I don't want to assume a negative motive for his visit—indeed I have no reason to—but I don't want him to go again. I tell him about the family's decision, that we would like people to contact us before visiting Miles, that his situation is very painful for him and that for the time being, until he is better and can tell us who he would like to see, we wish only his close friends to visit. I understand Angus and he have not been in touch for some years. I thank him for his concern for Miles but hope he will understand if I ask him not to visit him again until I can ask Miles's permission. He does under-stand. Thank you for being so gracious, he says. I appreciate your kindness.

I am thrown by that word, *gracious*; have I been unfair? But what can I do except rely on my instincts?

ONE OF THE hardest things for us about Miles's situation is the indignity his life has been reduced to. Certainly the indignity of being doubly incontinent cannot be adequately imagined. Miles wears a nappy, a mocking replica of the miniature ones babies wear. The nappy is to collect feces; when it is soiled he must be washed and changed by the carers. For urine a rubber Conveen is placed over his penis, as a condom might be, but in this case it is the upper end of a long tube that leads out of one side of the nappy to a bag attached to his leg with Velcro straps. The urine bag must be carefully monitored and I have seen another patient in a dreadful state after his bag filled and there was nowhere for the urine to go.

Quite frequently the Conveen slips off, discovered only when Miles's trousers and chair have become soaking wet. The cover of the wheelchair seat is dark gray and if his trousers are dark too, it's not immediately apparent. But we have learned to recognize the look on his face or the movements he makes to indicate discomfort, the latter usually by an involuntary raising of his leg as it causes his spasticity to increase. It is a nuisance for the carers—they have to take him back to his room, hoist him out of the chair and onto the bed, change his clothes and wash him before dressing and rehoisting him back into the chair.

I think about the time when Miles was at primary school and there was a little boy called Ted who suffered from a rare degenerative disease. He was small and delicate, his movements severely uncoordinated and his speech slurred so that it was difficult to understand him. The class was small and the teacher a beautiful fey young woman whom the children loved, wrapping themselves in her long skirts whenever they needed comfort; she understood and delighted in their differences, allowing no pressure to intervene in the business of being a small child.

One day when I collected Miles after school he was quiet and remained preoccupied as we walked home. Usually the walk was a tumble of stories from the day in between climbing walls and leapfrogging over bollards or racing with the other children, but today he walked silently, holding my hand. When we got home and I closed the front door he burst into tears: Ted weed in his chair and it went all over the floor and everyone laughed. It was horrible for Ted, it wasn't fair, Mama, he couldn't help it. Will the doctor make him better?

Ted died a year later. I didn't know his mother well and was surprised when, seeing her in the street and wondering what I could possibly say to her, she came across to me. You're Miles's mother, aren't you? she asked. I said I was, and how sad I was to hear about Ted. I felt awkward; I remember thinking, and then saying to her, that I couldn't imagine anything worse than losing a child. She waited for me to finish and then she said, I've wanted to speak to you because I wanted to tell you how kind Miles was to Ted. He told me that Miles always protected him when he was teased by the other children. I'm very grateful to him for that.

SATURDAY EARLY EVENING and Ron and I are driving home after spending a long afternoon with Miles. He was awake and alert for most of the time, so it should have been a good visit, but I am in tears and Ron is struggling to console me. Something has suddenly given way; I can't help myself though I know how he hates it when I'm unhappy. It is my greatest aim, he said, just after we met, that you will never be unhappy again. I remember thinking that I understood for the first time how it felt to be truly cherished.

What is it, exactly, lovey? he says. He is driving and keeps looking at me concernedly and I would prefer him to keep his eyes on the road. Miles looked well today, he says, and I thought he was very much present and with us, didn't you? He seemed more relaxed than usual too. I don't reply and he continues. You were wonderful with him today . . . It's no use, he gives up now and we drive on in silence. My eyes are closed, I don't want to hear any more, I am consumed by this fresh wave of pain that has welled up and threatens to suffocate me and all I can do is concentrate on trying to find my breath to keep myself from drowning in shame.

Shame, and guilt. Ron has cancer, he is undergoing chemotherapy and he has spent his Saturday afternoon at Putney. And I'm feeling guilty because I took the easy option with Miles. I didn't have the strength to keep up with the burden of a one-sided conversation, the effort of finding something new to say, of trying to imagine what he *really* wanted to hear. The trouble is, I just don't know what he really wants to hear from me. All I can think of now that I've left him is the sound of my facile glib chatter and the relief I felt when for a while he closed his eyes and I no longer had to speak.

When we get home Ron takes me in his arms. Would you like to go out for dinner? he asks. Would that help take your mind off things? I feel deadened and it's Saturday evening; I must pull myself together. No, darling Ron, let's stay in and I'll cook something easy. I love you. How could I manage without you? Let's just celebrate being here together.

I must not think about Miles lying alone in bed in that room.

TWELVE MONTHS HAVE passed since Miles's accident, the vaunted one-year marker of recovery. We have traveled a long way since the idea consoled us, when a year seemed a lot of time for improvements to happen. Now it seems too short. Miles has been officially diagnosed as MCS, in a minimally conscious state, as opposed to PVS, persistent vegetative state. PVS, that terrible rubric that demeans a person already demeaned through the tragedy of irreversible brain damage, somebody whose conscious life has been extinguished but whose body remains alive. How needlessly painful and insulting that word *vegetative* is. Coined in 1972 by the Scottish surgeon Bryan Jennett and the American neurologist Fred Plum in an article in *The Lancet*, its use is now firmly entrenched but bitterly resented by any relative of someone actually in that state.

Miles is definitely aware but his awareness inconsistent. The irony, that now we know MCS to be infinitely more devastating a sentence than to be PVS. He is able to suffer excruciating pain, humiliation, anger, misery, frustration, loneliness, boredom—all the same sensations and emotions as before, but imprisoned in a twilight world of incommunicable solitude. And what does this mean, in terms of the one-year marker for his prognosis?

For us it means that one moment he is with us intensely, responding to what is being said with his, by now, familiar movements and expressions, and the next he may be out cold, as it were, he might as well not be present even though he's awake. He crosses over into consciousness; he retreats. He slips back and forth. There is a constant sense of the permeability of consciousness, of Miles's existence in a place of fog and swirling mists that now and then will lift to reveal patches of pure blue sky. And there is the unbearable thought that at those moments he understands and is aware of what he no longer is.

We cannot accept that this is all the future holds for him. Doctors no longer refer to his long-term prognosis; I understand what I suspect is their reasoning, that if we can't accept it, there is no point. For, emphatically, I will continue to fight for Miles's future prospects. I will do everything in my power never to allow him to be sidelined into an acceptance of stasis.

The diagnosis of MCS means that we are in this for the long haul. We need to find a care home that is closer to where we live. I am shocked to discover that the primary care trust (PCT) has designated Miles as needing minimum funding for future treatment such as physiotherapy, occupational therapy, etc. A battle ensues— in effect this would mean giving up on his rehabilitation, and I am determined that Miles should continue to have ambitious treatment. He is a young man who, some of the time, is vividly aware; it is inconceivable that he should be allowed to atrophy physically and mentally, stuck away somewhere out of sight and out of mind. The severe and painful deformity that occurs in TBI patients denied regular physiotherapy is well established.

Rosemary, the redoubtable Putney social worker, is supportive and arranges a meeting for me with the appropriate person at the PCT. Going to the meeting I feel like a barrister defending against the possibility of a life sentence. I have done my research and planned my argument but, above all, I know I must not let myself become emotional. The result today will be pivotal to Miles's future; the matter is deadly serious. Each of the PCT's patients in Miles's position represents a tragedy, so I cannot plead for him by using my grief, much as I want to weep with despair at what the meeting really represents. For, in truth, what I am asking for is that my brain-damaged son should be allowed a future with some hope, rather than a future with no hope at all. It is as simple as that. At the end of the meeting it is impossible not to cry with relief when Miles is given the go-ahead for continuing rehabilitation.

The children and I have been visiting possible care homes. They are so bleak and dispiriting, the people in them so wretched, the atmosphere so inured to suffering, that despair begins to take hold of us all. And then Will and I visit Gael Lodge, a care home in South London twenty minutes' drive from us, and as we walk through the doors we know we have found the right place. We see an extraordinary thing, a residential care home where, despite the severely damaged men and women whose home it is, the atmosphere is not unhappy. It is clean and bright and homely. Most important, it is immediately clear that the residents are being treated with respect; in fact they are being treated as *people*.

V

The date is set for Miles's move. The manager of Gael Lodge, Rachel, a former palliative care nurse, has been in touch with me to discuss Miles's requirements. She is surprising and formidable. Extrovert, dyed blond hair, a vibrant dress sense and exuberant jewelry, she is the type of whirlwind character who carries everyone along with her, sweeping away their problems in her wake. Underneath the colorful exterior I sense a serious, steady core and know that at last we have found a safe haven for Miles.

Rachel invites me to visit Gael Lodge before Miles arrives, to see his room and talk about his needs. The room is in the small high-dependency ward and it is being freshly painted, as is the custom before a new arrival. I'm able to make a decision on the available furniture and can choose a chest of drawers rather than the tall wardrobe at present dominating the room. I'm introduced to Jana, the ward sister, a motherly, softly spoken woman whom I warm to.

On the day of Miles's move I get there early. He arrives by ambulance, seated in the wheelchair that now belongs to him. It is one of the advantages of Putney that it has the expertise and facilities to customize the wheelchairs, in Miles's case overseen by a remarkable inventor and engineer, Dr. Steve Cousins, head of Biomedical Engineering Services at the hospital. Talking to him helped me understand the importance of accommodating the complex seating and postural needs of TBI patients, and I realize what a luxury it is to have this chair for Miles, perfectly customized for his particular disabilities. Despite the many disagreements and upsets during his time at Putney, I am aware that there were a lot of people who committed time and skill and great effort to his rehabilitation.

Today, in spite of the long journey from Putney, he appears relaxed and clearly alert. There is no doubt he is aware that he is somewhere new, and he is curious. As I look at him waiting expectantly in his chair while introductions are made, I realize that what I am seeing on his face is a new expression, it is one of *hope*, and suddenly I am filled with a misery so acute I feel faint. The innocence in his look, the innocence of his hope—I have betrayed him. With deep dread I think of the conversations I have had with him, telling him about Gael Lodge, how excellent it is, how here he will begin to recover. I have wanted to protect him from despair, from the knowledge that he will now live forever in a care home. Am I protecting only myself? How will he deal with the inevitable truth? How can I have let him down like this?

UNLIKE PUTNEY, GAEL Lodge is a care home and as such it lacks hospital facilities. There are a number of occasions when Miles is required to attend hospital for outpatient appointments, such as having his PEG changed, his wheelchair adjusted, or for specialized

Botox injections to help his spasticity. The normal method for transporting him to and from the hospital is by ambulance, but their timing is unreliable and particularly so on the return journey, by which stage he is usually rigid with distress and exhaustion yet can be left to wait with his carer for hours before being brought home. I have decided to look into buying a customized van that will accommodate him in his wheelchair and do the journeys myself, and I am able to do so because of the generous financial help Miles has received from his company. Having our own van will also mean we can bring him home for the day at weekends, which we all hope will be enjoyable for him as well as giving the children respite from the arduous public transport journey they must make to visit Miles at Gael Lodge.

Now that I have the van, accompanying Miles to the hospital becomes a mission I dread. First I must collect him at least an hour before the appointment, finding somewhere to park with enough space behind it to allow for the metal ramp to be let down and have Miles in his wheelchair positioned at the end of it. This is a delicate process since his left leg now protrudes at a right angle from his chair, the muscles rigid from spasticity and the knee joint permanently locked, and to bump his leg accidentally will cause him severe pain. Once he is properly positioned, two giant metal hooks at the end of a long mesh cable must be fixed either side of his chair, which is then winched up the ramp by means of a hand-held electronic control. The ramp is steep and Miles tilted at an alarming angle and the tension as he is slowly pulled up into the van is shared by us both: mine the fear that the cable might break or come loose and the chair hurtle back down; his alarm, always evident at this stage, compounded, I imagine, by the sensation of perilous tilt and movement as well as the high whining noise of the controls. When finally in the van his chair must be firmly secured with more hooks and straps, the ramp folded back up, and a final check made that I have all the necessary equipment—suction machine, sterilized water, required drugs, syringe, etc.—before we set off. A Gael Lodge carer will accompany me, sitting in the back with Miles.

Arriving at the hospital the ramp procedure must be done again, even more alarming in reverse as Miles's chair descends backwards down the steep ramp. But it is entering the hospital I fear most of all. The sudden glare of exposure, people staring at him, lingering to see in close-up this young man suspended outside their world, his head and body strapped into a chair, his distorted limbs rigid with tension. Miles dreads it too. His eyes are blank and unseeing, but somewhere inside he is all too clearly sensing the attention. Humiliated and proud, his jaw begins to tighten and I see his mouth turning down on one side in the way I know means furious misery. And I am filled with furious bile—I hate all these gross people with their pig-eyed billowing faces, the shriveled old people with their smoked gray skin and corncrake voices, all filling our space, intruding into our painful private world, staring. Every one of them unabashedly staring. Fuck the lot of them, I whisper in Miles's ear, you are magnificent. These people can go to hell.

What is this? Is it inverse self-pity on my part? Or misplaced pride? Or just plain viciousness? For I am mean-eyed too, as I continue pushing Miles through the crowded foyer, I am shriveled and sallow. These people around me are not here for choice or amusement, it is a hospital and I know nothing of their stories. But I could, I feel like I really could, without a tremor of guilt, kill anybody who intrudes into Miles's pain.

I HAVE BEEN watching the Gael Lodge doctor on his rounds, Dr. Jensen, or Matthew as he is known. A tall, dark-haired man, there is something about him that makes me think of Miles; he is probably not much older and I can imagine them as friends. His manner with his patients is at once contained but assertive, businesslike but kind. There are a lot of patients demanding his attention, even those who haven't been referred for this visit, and I watch him listen attentively or engage in their banter, his warmth and humor with such damaged people an uplifting thing to witness. It takes a particular type of person to relate to them in this way, seeing through to the inner need of each without their being able to articulate it.

Although he knows Miles, we have not yet formally met. Today he comes over to where I'm sitting in the day room next to Miles, who is asleep now, and introduces himself. He asks how Miles is doing and we chat for a while. I have seen you with him, he says, and I've observed his times of obvious awareness. When he is awake and alert he is very actively present. He understands his situation, doesn't he? There is a clear sense of determination about him. It must be deeply frustrating for him and very painful for you.

I am flooded with relief—here is a doctor thinking about the situation from Miles's point of view. Dr. Stizer in Innsbruck, Dr. Stephenson at Queen Square—it is a rare thing. I can let down some of my guard, I need not be on continual high alert, a vigilante day and night protecting Miles's interests and feelings from the danger of being overlooked. Miles will be safe with him.

MILES IS TURNING ten and I let him decorate the cake I have baked for him. It's a round chocolate cake and he makes it a face with Smarties for eyes and licorice strips for nose and mustache, and then he carefully cuts a strip of fake red shoelace, the violent-colored sweet that dyes the children's mouths bright pink, to add a small, mean, down-turned mouth. When the time comes to cut it, *It's Mr. Palin!* he cries, who is the hated math teacher, and all the little boys join him whooping with delight as he plunges in the cake knife.

TODAY BIRTHDAY BANNERS have been strung across the room by the care staff, balloons are bobbing from the ceiling hoist and bright cards are out on display along the shelf above the suction machine. Later we will add our own and those from friends, the inscriptions tender, the truth unwritten. At midday we arrive to find Miles sitting in his wheelchair grim-faced amid the bunting, his jaw set and his mouth turned down, and with each breezy Happy Birthday Miles! from the nursing staff and passersby he looks more murderous. Their cheeriness, I suppose, is understandable, but each time it's said I want to block his ears. How can he want to be reminded that another year has passed?

He is looking painfully handsome in a deep green T-shirt the color of his eyes, a birthday present from the care home, and I can see that he's had his hair washed, as well as a good, close shave. Of course, it's a Monday, which is one of the three shower days of the week, and so this morning he would have been wheeled through on the gurney from his bedroom to the wet room, a sheet over his naked body for decency. The carers tell me he likes having his hair washed, it being so thick they can lather up the shampoo and give his scalp a really good long massage, and each time there is a slight lift to the left side of his mouth, an acknowledgment of pleasure if not quite a smile. I see from his file that the carers on duty today are Cheta and Joseph, two especially decorous, gentle Nigerians, and they are his favorites.

We have each brought presents wrapped as carefully as they would have been before, and we tear open the paper ourselves and tell him what we've bought. We read out each other's cards and the cards from his friends who aren't there. A new CD is put on to play, a T-shirt held up for inspection, a photo placed in a new frame; as each is put away there's a shifting sense of failure but it's difficult to know what presents to bring anymore. There have been some surprising successes: bought from a lurid junk mail catalog, a pair of soft corduroy boots lined with small sacs of lavender and wheat which can be warmed in the microwave, perfect for feet that by evening are marble cold from lack of circulation; or a small laser star projector, whose beams stream over the ceiling above his bed simulating an ever moving, softly lit night sky for company when he's not asleep.

Just when we can read that his mood has eased into calm endurance there's a knock on the door and we're invited with brio by the on-duty nurse to come and see the birthday cake they have waiting for him in the day room. We wheel him down the corridor and enter to a chorus of Happy Birthdays. He closes his eyes; I feel him retreating. The carers and nurses we know so well from the ward have been joined by some from the other wards, lured by the prospect of cake and festivities. And then there are Miles's fellow residents from this high-dependency ward, the men and women who live here together, unknown to each other or to Miles, each isolated in their own silent world.

The cake is standing proud in the center of the day room table. Every resident receives one on their birthday, along with a present, and though given with warmth and generosity the cakes are inevitably of the factory-made sort, garish and inedibly sweet. Today is no exception—huge, round, and squeamish-making with layers of shiny brown icing, it looks as unappealing as a rhino pat. It has been decorated with Smarties for eyes and sticky red syrup for a smiley mouth. I want to plunge the knife in deep and mourn Mr. Palin.

* * *

MARINA AND I are driving to Gael Lodge. We are on our way in the van to collect Miles and bring him home for the day, as we now do every Sunday. We hadn't realized how late it was and had to cut breakfast short—we like to collect him at 11:30 so that we can return just in time for his bedtime at 5:00 p.m. He can only spend six hours seated in his chair, his "seating tolerance," and we want to maximize that with us all at home.

Will, Claudia, and Marina have chosen to give over their Sundays to Miles. They could be having a lie-in followed by a late breakfast and a lazy read of the papers, or they could be seeing their friends and doing the things young people do on Sundays before the next week of commuting and work begins. Instead they travel across London, plagued by Sunday's continual engineering works, trains and underground invariably disrupted so that the journey becomes an obstacle course. One of them will either come home first or go straight to Gael Lodge to meet me there, and they take it in turns: one person does the collection journey, another the return, for someone needs to sit in the back of the van next to Miles. His head can slip forward out of the headrest or his arms or legs move into an awkward position, and he must always have his head supported as the van travels over the suburban speed bumps. Gemma told us that her worst thing when traveling is the way her head bobs about when the ambulance goes over a speed bump, so we can avoid that for Miles. If he is relaxed we play music and hope it's what he wants to hear, but I suspect what he likes best is the chance to hear us talking together without enduring the usual one-way conversation he must when we are alone with him.

Once home one of us wheels him down the van's ramp, hoping the man opposite is not out in the street or standing at his window. His Sunday treat is to stare at Miles, clearly his looked-forward-to weekly freak show. If he sees us in time he'll find a reason to walk by and say hello, hanging around to stare with open fascination at the sight of Miles in his chair. We try to thwart him, sending a lookout and not opening the van doors if he is around. If you see him you can tell him to fuck right off, growls Will as he fixes the hooks to Miles's chair and maneuvers the electronic controls guiding him down the ramp. It is with relief that we shut the front door.

Summer is best, of course, because we can take Miles out into the garden and leave his chair in a shady spot while we continue the day around him. Deck chairs are put out next to him and we read and chat, someone cooks lunch, maybe one of us disappears for a while to use the computer or take a nap. It's not easy for Ron to visit him during the week, so he loves to spend the time with him now, Sunday papers piled on the grass by his chair as he reads and Miles dozes next to him. In winter we might put the fire on in the sitting room and take him there, or we just stay in the open-plan kitchen and keep him warm with the soft small rug I've bought for him. At lunchtime we pull his chair up to the table. At the back of all our minds there is an ambivalence about this. Is it pleasurable for him to come home and be reminded afresh of what he is missing? How does he feel when he can smell the food we're eating and hear knives and forks on plates when he has not been able to eat a mouthful of anything in years? Does he enjoy hearing our animated chatter, as though everything is normal, when he is obviously there in his wheelchair beside us, mute, unseeing?

Are we doing this for him or for ourselves? The answer is, we can't be sure. We hope it is for him, because we all think that as wonderful as Gael Lodge is, it is soul-crushing on Sundays. Sunday is the hiatus in the week, the day of rest, no therapy or organized activities, only a half-hour church service held in the day room for those who wish, or whose relatives wish them, to attend. If he comes home he can have some peace—no background TV, no background sounds of choking or shouting from other residents, no well-meaning banter from their Sunday visitors—How we doing then, Milesy boy? Nice day for a little sit out in the sunshine, eh? Got to get a tan up for the girls, haven't we? Don't you worry, mate, you're doing well. At least if he comes home it might remind him how much he means to us, that we miss him every moment and have brought him home to be with us on the only day we can all be together.

We have been taught how to administer his medication through the PEG, flushing it through afterwards with sterile water, and how to use the suction machine to clear his throat of mucus when he coughs. There is a routine to the day and by four p.m. we need to think about taking him back. By now we are all weirdly flattened and this is the most difficult time, especially in winter when it's getting dark and Sunday's gloom has taken over what's left of the day. Then we must travel back in the fading afternoon and we start to snap at one another, the little things doing us in, like breaking a nail yet again on the van's chair hoist or spilling Miles's sterilized water as we gather up his belongings. At the journey's end we will have to wait while the carers put Miles to bed, hoping he will be comfortable and sleepy so that we can say good night and leave him to go home with an easy conscience. Because we are exhausted, and sad, and all we really want now is a stiff drink in front of the fire with an empty mind.

Some Sundays are easier than others. If the carers have done their job well in the morning he will be perfectly positioned in his chair and calmly waiting in the day room. That is always a good start and, if we're lucky, he will continue to be relaxed all day and therefore more likely to be awake and able to interact in his way. We will see him softening when Will's lovely girlfriend, Albi, is talking to him, and when friends drop in to see him and we all chat around his chair, he will lean back and look amused, the tiny movement of his mouth we love to see above all else. But then he has a bad day and we can't resolve the problem, despite checking that his Conveen hasn't leaked or his clothes aren't pinching or his headrest slipped. We can adjust his splints and give him the allowed extra acetaminophen but nothing helps.

Today has not turned out a good day. Miles has gradually become inconsolable. His spasticity has increased, his arms and legs pulled up tight, and he is coughing with the roar that I dread. Ashamed of myself, I close the door to the garden so that the neighbors won't hear. It is, truthfully, not a human sound, or rather, not the sound that a human being makes unless you imagine he is being tortured. Perhaps he has a migraine, or a terrible stomachache, or his stiffened limbs are especially painful, or maybe he is just confronting afresh the reality of his existence.

It is only 3 p.m. but we think we should take him back early. He needs to be repositioned, and maybe he would be more comfortable if he were put to bed. Claudia is next to him in the van and I can hear her soothing him. It won't be long now before you can go to bed. Lovely Moses is on duty, so he'll do it perfectly for you. We all love you, Miles. By the time we get there Miles is rigid in his chair, his roars of pain or fury or both deafening in the van's enclosed space.

Moses is as upset to see Miles as we are. He takes him straight into his room, calls another carer to help, and twenty minutes later when we go in Miles is still tense despite Moses's gentle, expert attention. Claudia puts on the Philip Glass CD that Miles loves and we stay with him, one either side of the bed, until eventually he falls asleep.

On the way home the traffic is dense and at the Lewisham roundabout a car cuts in front of us. I don't yield immediately and the driver, large, shaven, bull-headed, gesticulates through his window, mouthing the word clearly: *cunt*.

Bastard, I say, furiously following him. Fucking bastard, says Claudia. Fucking fat shaven-headed arsehole, I say.

Fucking fat cunt-faced arsehole, says Claudia. Ludicrous dickhead. We are beginning to laugh.

Clag-ridden arse flaps, I say. Gross fat wanking shitehawk.

Fucking prickface, says Claudia, fucking festering ululating farting arseholes.

I have to take off my glasses to wipe away the tears. Hold them for me, I say.

We feel much better.

CANCER DOESN'T SEEM real, the insidious way it hides silently inside Ron's body, still giving no outward sign even as it is spreading its poison. It is the antithesis of brain injury, which so soon makes such cruel and obvious wreckage of its victims. I'm worried that I don't give Ron as much time and attention as I give Miles. Ron is adamant in reassuring me. I don't want special attention, he says, I particularly don't want it. When people fuss over me and treat me differently, which some do, it makes me feel like a victim, part of a cancer club. I really don't want to be reminded of it. There is nothing you can do that I can't do for myself, unlike Miles. He puts his arms around me. Come on, my love, let's go out to dinner tonight and then we can give each other lots of attention.

But after four months of remission he has had to start another round of chemo. His cancer markers are back up again and the doctors are going to try a different treatment which they've warned him is stronger than the last. He is still working full-time and feels so well that the prospect seems bearable; hope on its gallant charger is still carrying us all high.

ON ARRIVAL AT Miles's ward this afternoon I am surprised to find the door shut and the day room in darkness. I open the door tentatively and as my eyes accustom to the darkness I can see the eight residents in their wheelchairs grouped in a semicircle in the center of the long room. It is an eerie Aladdin's Cave of music and moving lights, each person holding, or rather having had placed in their hand, a long coil of clear plastic tubing through which light is moving and pulsing in time to soft background music. The light coils emanate from a tall clear light stand, an updated version of those 1970s lava lamps in which bright viscous-looking blobs of fluorescent color move through each other, and these are now flowing out and over the laps of their silent audience. The organ of Pachelbel's *Canon* playing softly in the background adds to the ghostliness.

What different versions of this event are going through the damaged brains of the people in this room? Can they make any sense of this new Wednesday afternoon Sensual Experience Session that has been so carefully set up for them? However kind, I fear it is patronizing; these are grown men and women being subjected to a sensory experience at the most primitive level. You might wrap the light coils around a cot and play music softly to a baby in the same way, but a toddler would already be too sophisticated. A two-year-old would pull the coils, be bored after a few minutes of watching the light pillar, and be able to voice an opinion about it.

Miles has his eyes half open, directed somewhere above the light pillar; he is awake and I think he likes this quiet, passive thing that is happening. He is calm, his body relaxed; indeed all the residents are quiet and calm together, which is unusual. I take a chair and pull it up next to Miles and take his free hand and then squinting my eyes half shut I try to see it as he might. After a while the lights begin to merge and blur and I feel removed and more peaceful than I was; Samuel Barber's "Adagio for Strings" is playing now and I think they must have put on the *Relaxing Classics* CD, the one that we sometimes leave on for Miles when we leave him in the evening. I was wrong after all, this experience is not at all patronizing. I lean closer to Miles and rest my head on his shoulder, feeling his warmth and the slow rise and fall of his breath. I think of Marina's words not long ago at Putney: Here I am, hugging my brother, mourning my brother.

But now a sound is beginning to break into the peace. At first soft and intermittent, it begins to rise until there is no doubt: Petros is sobbing. Sweet Petros, the sixty-year-old Polish man who had built up his own business but had been waited for and set upon in the street after work by two young men, one of whom he had recently dismissed. He is a gentle-looking man, and after a year with no response of any kind so that he was deemed to be in a persistent vegetative state he suddenly began first to cry and then to laugh. It can be very upsetting when he cries because once it starts he wails from a depth of desolation that can't be stemmed, a primeval sound, like a banshee calling from the wild. It frightened his grandson so much that his daughter has had to stop bringing him. When he laughs it's hilarious, we all can't help joining in and hugging him with delight.

But now, terribly, he is sobbing. Pavarotti is singing "Nessun Dorma" and I wonder if that is what has reached him, Pavarotti's voice and that beautiful aria having become so inextricably part of a football fan's repertoire, and Petros, I know, was a keen Arsenal supporter. Denise, the gentle young Jamaican carer, is bending over him and soothing him but he is inconsolable, and she starts to wheel him out of the room and onto the wooden deck outside, to distract him but also to prevent the other residents from being distracted by him. Miles has remained impassive; more often he reacts violently to noise from the others, screwing up his face, clenching his legs into a rigid spasm of spasticity and sometimes roaring back at them. I am relieved he is peaceful, and I relax once more against his shoulder and close my eyes.

MILES AGED EIGHT. He has just returned from the birthday party of a little girl down the street. As he steps into the house he announces, When I grow up I'm going to be a homosexual. That's interesting, darling, I say. Why do you say that? Because, he growls, then I won't have to marry a *girl*.

Miles and Tamsin, his beautiful half-Italian girlfriend with the blackest hair and the palest green eyes, are going to Berlin for New Year. They agree to save Christmas presents until they are there. Miles has bought Tamsin a dress that he knows she wanted but couldn't afford, wraparound softest silk jersey the color of her eyes. He was with her when she tried it on and then went back later to buy it for her.

When they reach the hotel he manages to secrete the dress directly into the closet without her noticing. Later, when she starts unpacking she opens the closet. How weird, she says, the last person left a dress behind. Can you believe it, it's that Diane von Furstenberg dress I love! She lifts it out and holds it up. It's so gorgeous—how amazing that anyone could have forgotten it. It's my size too . . . And then she sees Miles's face and the weekend takes off from there.

* * *

TODAY WILL AND I are sorting through Miles's papers. The flat they share is being sold and Miles holds the original documents that are needed for the sale. As we search, Will comes across a poem Miles had written. He reads it and then hands it to me without saying anything; the look on his face tells me he has been caught unaware. And now as I read, Miles's voice is right here in the room with us, vivid, warm, wry, his humor and his deep seriousness.

The poem has a title: "The Basilica of St. Peter."

Another time, another girl. Siobhan was tougher than Tamsin, whose nervy, racehorse temperament was, in the end, not made for permanence. Miles visited Siobhan in Rome, where she was working at the time. His feelings for her were unrequited and he returned home subdued and rueful; he felt he'd made a fool of himself by making it clear she was the sole reason for his visit when he had obviously misread the situation.

He must have written the poem soon after his return from Rome, an ironic reflection on his miscalculated ardor. It feels an invasion of his privacy to be reading it, the tenderness of it, but I think it is beautiful, an example of his wonderful impetuosity; I wish someone had written a poem like that about me when I was young.

It is unfair, I know, the degree of dull anger I feel for Siobhan, that Miles should have suffered pain on her behalf. She is a lovely girl and kind, but the thought of his being unhappy or humiliated in love is quite intolerable now.

RAY HAS BEEN on the ward as long as Miles has and I have got to know his partner, Tracy. Volatile and voluble, her speech is richly embedded and spiked with expletives, a kind of default language that I think she has evolved as her safeguard through the chaos of her life. Armed with a voice many decibels above normal, she fires off the fucks, cunts, arseholes, shites like a spray of bullets; she sounds fierce but she is all at sea, confused and angry that she doesn't understand. I feel maternal towards her—I am old enough to be her mother—and she is always soft with me. Sometimes, after a grossly abusive rant delivered at top volume to the innocent carer or nurse who caught the edge of her misery, she apologizes to me in tears. Her immaculately made-up tough young face contorts with bewilderment at the pain and rage she can't articulate.

Sometimes, too, she talks about Ray. She tells me he is a traveler, a Romany, a "pikey" she calls him, one of eleven children whose extended family all still live in caravans in a travelers' community. When Ray moved in with her they broke off relations with him because she was not the same. She and Ray have a child also named Ray, who is now eight. Big Ray self-harmed and an unintentional drug overdose was the cause of his present state; drugs were a shared pastime. He has been severely deformed by the brain damage and subsequent lack of acute rehabilitation, his arms now permanently raised, the hands bent back in a claw so that his knuckles almost touch the forearm, his head and neck arched away from his chest so that his face is locked in a perpetual rictus. Like Miles he is in a minimally conscious state, but he can see and he will often blink in response to Tracy, while his expression visibly softens at the sight of little Ray. For four years Tracy has continued to be his loyal partner, as though he has not changed. She teases him, flirts with him, tells him off if he looks bad-tempered—I make this huge fucking effort to come and see you today and all you can do is look at me like a bloody old grump, I'm leaving, I'm not going to stay with you being fucking grumpy—and she attends to him physically with great tenderness, cutting the toenails of his rigid feet and wiping up the constant gobbets of thick phlegm; he is still her lover.

She plans to bring him home. There have been many discussions with Ray's primary care trust, which is funding his care, and these discussions appear to follow the same pattern of anger, confusion, and abuse. The social worker is an idiot, the PCT all wankers, the care home management up themselves. Tracy has finally found the house she wants, which has a garden so that little Ray can play in it, but it needs to be adapted. A lift will have to be put in to take Ray upstairs in his wheelchair and a bathroom converted into a wet room so that he can be gurney-showered. I ask if there will be live-in carers. No way, she says, I don't want nobody else living with us. I ask what she will do about the nights when Ray must be turned every four hours, requiring two people, and she looks surprised. I hadn't thought about that, she says. I'll find a way.

MARINA AND I are helpless with laughter. It is summer and we're on holiday in France for a week while the rest of the family hold the fort for Miles. Claudia has just been to see him and has sent me a text, and we're imagining her face as she typed the message. She is a kindhearted, generous girl, but she can be fierce, too. I love that about her, her warmth and vulnerability combined with her fierceness when unfairly crossed. She is tall, and her height and her dark, striking looks make the sudden flash of anger unequivocally intimidating: do not mess with me, it says. A frown as fearsome and quick as a crack of thunder crosses her face and then with a toss of her long hair it's gone.

Today she has had a run-in with one of the patients, Janet. Grossly obese, Janet has lost her legs to diabetes, both amputated above the knee, and she has suffered some brain damage as a result of a diabetic coma. Whether or not she has always been bad-tempered nobody knows, but her fury at the world and all the people she comes across is unremitting. Unlike many of the residents here, she is at least able to express herself, and her curmudgeonly behavior is tolerated with kindness by the care staff and management. I suppose she has become one of the characters of Gael Lodge—you know what Janet's like, we say.

Despite the doctors' pleas to the contrary, she continues to smoke. The care home is managed, unusually, for the comfort of the residents, it is properly their home, and smoking is Janet's greatest pleasure. She likes to drive herself in her electric wheelchair to the small covered entrance to the home where smoking is allowed and she will sit there for hours, glaring and muttering at the people in the street and at the cars going by. It is difficult to get past her in the narrow space, particularly when pushing a wheelchair, but we all say breezily, Hello, Janet, how are you doing today? Huh, she grunts tersely. She rarely speaks.

But today she did and Claudia is outraged. *Legless lump woman asked me if I was pregnant!* We know we shouldn't laugh but we can't help it. Claudia has been on a diet for weeks and this is not what she wanted to be asked. But it wasn't just that, she tells us afterwards. It was the build-up, struggling to get Miles in his wheelchair past her when she would not budge. Then, while I was talking to Miles, she interrupted me, Claudia says. It was difficult enough trying to understand what she was saying and not be irked that I'd been interrupted, but then I realized she was asking me if I was pregnant and of course I had to explain to her nicely and kindly that I wasn't. Her response to me then was, Huh, well, you look bigger. Never mind, I said. But just sometimes the extra effort is too much to bear.

Janet is an unwitting Cerberus to our hell; what lies beyond her is a place of emotional horror. The mental slide we have to make from one reality to another every time we enter is painful enough—the extra obstacle and the effort required to be bright with Janet as we try to maneuver around her only adds to the horror. She makes no effort to move even a little out of anyone's way; in fact she appears to enjoy the process, watching our maneuvers with interest. Perhaps it is the one small revenge she can take on the able-bodied world, and who should blame her?

Our laughter at Claudia's unexpectedly ruthless text is cruel, we know, but the sudden involuntary release of gallows humor is always wildly cathartic. Nevertheless the uncomfortable truth is that, however much we laugh, we could dismember anyone who laughed about Miles.

IN HIS SPARE time Miles had been writing a book, exploring the similarities between different schools of mysticism and religion and their link to modern discoveries in quantum physics. It is an affirmation of his idea of the interconnectedness of the universe and he was serious about the message he was conveying. Will has found the manuscript on his computer and sent it to me. It is still in rough draft, but I have it printed and bound at our local stationer. I will leave it in Miles's room, to read to him when the time seems right. I want to read his work to him during a good visit; I want to reassure him that what he has written has not been lost, that it will reach and touch people's lives. That is the only comfort I can think of that will have any real meaning for him—that his life has not been wasted. What does it matter if I play this imaginary card? It could be true.

Today when I arrive in the day room Miles is coolly awake, seated near the nurses' station and clearly listening to the banter of the two carers manning it. There is that slight lift to the right side of his mouth that could be the hint of a smile. Miles thinks

I'm being rude to Joseph, says Angela, who has been teasing Joseph about his uncool taste in music. She DJs with her Jamaican uncle at weekends and is into the latest hip-hop while Joseph likes Céline Dion and Robbie Williams. Can you imagine, says Angela, Robbie Williams! and she breaks into a ghastly crooning rendition of his latest song. When Joseph and Angela are on duty together Miles is invariably in a good mood, the result of the professional, respectful care they show all the residents here. I can see Miles is fully relaxed today, his legs and arms at ease in the chair, his awareness of what is going on around him palpable. His eyes are clear and alert, his whole body observing and listening.

Joseph helps me wheel Miles down to his room and pulls up a chair for me at his side. Claudia and Marina say Joseph would make the perfect husband, he is so gentle, so sensitive and understanding. I tell Miles this when Joseph has left the room and I think he shares the enjoyment of our affection for this kind man who is responsible for the sweet pleasure I am experiencing now, of seeing Miles relaxed, no sign of spasticity in any limb, his face clear. He has not retreated, as he does some days, when he is awake but unavailable, blocked off, deep inside himself. Today he is on the outside and it could be a fearful thing, the air so charged with his presence, the dimension he inhabits a force field too powerful for my everyday reality. I feel infinitely shallow by comparison, the banality of my existence exposed.

It seems the right time to read from his work. Will found your book, Miles, and passed it on to me, and I've had it printed and bound. I place his right hand on the manuscript and move his fingers over it, to feel the spiral-bound edges and the thickness of the pages together. It is incredibly exciting to have it, I tell him. I think it's brilliant and I'm going to make sure it gets out there. It is so right for the moment, too. I'll read you an extract now.

I start to read and as I do so he begins to move. He comes forward out of the chair in an alarming way I have never seen, did not think possible, his eyes fixed on me with a burning intensity.

Strip away the notion of a personal God, and the same message emerges from every world religion—be it Hinduism, Islam, Taoism, Christianity, Buddhism, Sikhism, or Judaism. This central spiritual message, common to all major faiths, can be summarized as follows:

> 1. *God is One, and encompasses all existence, including each and every human being.*
> 2. *This divine One is both infinite and eternal.*
> 3. *It is impossible to analyse this divine One, since any attempt to categorize or define it will diffract its ultimate simplicity.*
> 4. *In order to achieve enlightenment, therefore, we must free ourselves from all the trappings of such conscious, analytical thought.*
> 5. *Once the individual consciousness has been silenced in this way, the soul is free to become One with God.*

As I reach the end of the short extract I look up and see he has moved right out of the headrest, his upper body bent towards me in what can only be a superhuman effort of will. He is mouthing something, he is definitely mouthing something, his eyes wide, beseeching me to understand. The look on his face is one of utmost pain, unbearable to see.

What have I done? Has his experience given him new knowledge and this is no longer what he believes? Was that what he was trying to tell me? Does he still believe in what he wrote? Or—this is the dreaded fear I try not to think of—does he now believe that his rejection of conventional religion is the cause of his being damned in this hell? He loved and celebrated every blade of grass, every cloud, every star, every quiver of life he *celebrated*. What can he think is the reason for the unspeakable horror he now inhabits?

Or is he asking me to set his soul free to become One with God?

JANCIS, A YOUNG neuropsychotherapist, has come to work at Gael Lodge while completing her PhD. She engages with Miles in a particular way, as though he were a friend and fellow student. She discusses her research with him and asks him questions about it, watching him intently for his response. She asks me about his life before the accident, what his interests were, what he was like as a small boy and as an adult, what were his defining characteristics. Miles has affected me deeply, she says to me one day. He is remarkable. It seems to me vividly apparent that he is present when I'm with him, there is a power emanating from him. He has taught me a lot; getting to know him has entirely changed my ideas about consciousness and communication. I hope that what I go on to do will make a difference to the lives of other people in his situation.

LOLA HAD A stroke when she was thirty-two. She was a fitness instructor at a gym in West London, with a lean muscled body like Madonna's and a charmingly mobile face. I have seen the pictures pinned up in her room, flamboyant in a purple leotard among the machines, energy and humor booming from her—a magnificent *jolie-laide*. Fitness classes with her would undoubtedly have been fun.

She is forty-five now, her once toned body slack and soft in the wheelchair. But the humor is still there, though it has taken a particular turn. The brain damage she sustained appears not to have affected her IQ but it has disinhibited her, exacerbated by an obsession with sex. Do you know when I had my stroke? she asks people. I had it in the middle of a *huge* orgasm. When she asks me I see her looking at me slyly, judging my reaction; it's the only fun she has, harmlessly goading people to be embarrassed, seeing what she can get away with. After the Sunday service in the day room the priest speaks to each of the patients passing him on their way out. Lola gestures for him to come closer and as he does so she reaches out in a flash and grabs him in the crotch, laughing with delight as he pulls himself away in horror. Hey, she calls out to Tom, a young friend who is visiting Miles, hey you, what's your name? Tom, he says, how are you? Have you got hairy balls, Tom? she asks.

Lola has a daughter and a granddaughter, but they don't come to see her much. It is difficult for the daughter, especially with her little girl, when her mother is lewdly interrogating everyone she sees. We have all got used to her by now, are in fact fond of her brazenness. Come on, Lola, we say, when she asks yet again if we prefer the taste of sex to chocolate. You've asked us that before, it's boring! You're beautiful, she says, disarmingly. Then she adds, mischievously, But us black women have the advantage, you know, Lu. Black don't crack. She means the wrinkles on my face, her head tilted sweetly to one side as she looks at me. You're too damn right, Lola, I say, it's not fair, you don't look nearly old enough to have a granddaughter, and she doesn't, her skin still perfectly unlined.

She is Ghanaian from a well-to-do family, sophisticated, she speaks French with an excellent accent. Her mother is as good-looking as Lola is plain, but both are glamorous, Lola still choosing her clothes with care—she tells the carers what to put together each morning. Her mother comes to visit and is as imperious with the staff as she is with her daughter; Lola looks a little crushed each time, has been admonished for her loose language and for eating too much, for she has been gaining weight. Please can I have a chocolate biscuit? she asks the visitors if she sees them with a mug of tea, for she knows there is a tin of biscuits in the kitchenette and that the visitors are a soft touch.

The kitchenette is more like a large cupboard, situated just off the day room on the ground floor. It is for visitors' use only and it has come to represent a retreat, the only place where for a moment I can imagine I am somewhere else. The small fridge in which we can leave snacks to chill, a little history of the relatives as I see a cream bun alongside a pot of zero percent fat yogurt, a bowl of spiced yams, a small quiche. There is a large tin with a Brueghel-like snow scene on the lid that seems never to run out of biscuits, the overly sweet smell as I open it a comfort while deciding what sort to have today. But as I'm deliberating I can hear Lola's voice. Her wheel-chair is blocking the entrance and she is asking me for a biscuit. Go on, Lu, she says, just one, please. I've really been good lately. Please, go *on*, be nice to me! I find one without a cream center and hand it to her. Just one more, she says. Please, a creamy one—you know, sugar and spice and all things nice, like s-e-x, and she grins delight-edly. Do you like my earrings?

I finish making my tea and Lola moves to let me leave. Thanks, Lu, you're sweet, she says. Which do you prefer . . . I must go back to Miles, I tell her firmly. Lola is kind, without malice, adrift in her strange world, and yet I am exhausted as I return to Miles's room with my tea and biscuit. I feel adrift in a strange world too.

THE END OF a long afternoon and I am sitting in Miles's room, watching him. It has not been a good visit; nothing I've done has helped and I feel sullen and useless. He is seated in his wheelchair, his mouth open, jaw juddering rhythmically. Every now and then he coughs, his face turning a deep red as he fights for breath.

Always the same cough: first a sudden shout—it takes him by surprise—then a long drawn-out *aaaargh* before it comes, a roiling, choking sound, a gasping for breath, his whole body tensed, legs raised, arms clenched, and then, as the cough subsides, a final, bellowing roar of rage.

After a few minutes the juddering spasm in his jaw begins to subside and his limbs slowly relax down. Eyes half closed, he stares into something far beyond the distance. I move my hand gently across his field of vision and he doesn't register it; at least he is calm.

The room is quiet now, the silence respite for us both. Through the bay window that gives onto the street outside I watch a mother unloading the boot of her car with the familiar blue-and-white Tesco bags while her small daughter tries to help her, carrying one bag to every four or five that her mother manages to lift at once. She must have more children, this is a mountainous shopping she's just done, surely for a large family. I remember the weekly visits to the supermarket when the four children were all at home, how starving the boys were when they came back from school and how they ate at least double the amount the girls did.

I turn to look at Miles and can suddenly picture clearly the exuberant small boy tucking into his giant pile of toast at teatime: gray shorts, wrinkled-down gray socks, scuffed black shoes too big for his skinny boy's legs, the gray shirt hanging out from under his too-small navy blazer, and his eyes alight as he tells me the day's news. The time he came back in a furious grump, marching into the house with a gruff hello, flinging his rugby bag down on the hall floor. He scowled through teatime, ignoring Will and the girls' chatter, until finally he blurted it out: Matron is a sex *maniac*. Goodness, darling, I say, why do you think that? He answers darkly, She made us each take our pants down and she squeezed my *balls*. Oh dear, I reassure him, that's part of Matron's job, it's an important health check to see you're all growing up properly. But he's not convinced. I don't care, I won't let her do it again, he growls.

He is asleep now, breathing deeply, calmly. This room is his home; he has been here for a long time and there is no reason to imagine that he might ever live anywhere else. The neurologist told me, when I asked him, that yes, Miles could outlive me. He is a healthy young man and short of a sudden, drastic infection, unlikely because the nursing in this home is so good, he could survive for decades in his condition. An old man stooped in this chair, his body atrophied through disuse, his face strangely unlived in, without frown or laughter lines; their absence the testimony to decades of life as existence only.

We have tried to personalize the room, but it's difficult. Looking around it now I feel a dull anger. I hate the room, I hate its implacable possession of Miles. Let me confront it, then; I'll take it on and reveal it for what it is. It's almost pleasurable—I want to feel the hurt, punish myself with it, dare to observe precisely the details of this room that I habitually blur into a cowardly soft focus.

I begin with the bed, set into a small recess on the right of the bay window. It is undoubtedly a hospital bed, high, metal, white-painted, on wheels. The special pressure mattress to avoid bedsores, plastic-covered to repel soiling, the adjustable metal side bars that are pulled up to prevent him falling out. But Miles can't turn himself.

To the left of the bed the children have tacked some pinups of girls, in line with his pillow. The girls are models, of the long-legged and sexily elegant sort, not the pneumatic Page 3 variety; his preference used to be for natural beauty. I say used to—I don't know now, but I hope he can still dream about them, feel desire.

On the wall behind the bed, a large white plastic board, fixed there so that when his feed—his *feed*—inadvertently sprays while being opened it can easily be washed off. There is a spray of it at home, on the kitchen ceiling, from a Sunday visit. The feed is beige, the color of school gravy, the consistency thick and viscous. Once dried and stuck to the wall it is impossible to wipe off, has to be chiseled or scraped with a knife. I imagine it in the stomach, heavy, like fresh cement. But it contains all recommended vitamins and minerals and, importantly, it eliminates wind and emanates as odorless waste. Miles has no bodily smells now; even that, the primitive, personal essence we each own, even that has been annulled. He has one liter of feed per night, which starts at six p.m. on slow release into his PEG, the feeding tube inserted directly into his stomach, the bag of beige liquid hanging from a metal stand at the side of his bed. Hydration is delivered during the day, a liter of sterile water injected at intervals into his PEG. A friend of mine who could not eat or drink for eight weeks after surgery described the yearning for a sip of water as purest torture.

A shelf by the bed supports his CD player, the suction machine, a tray with jug and utensils for drug dispensing, and an electric fan. Shasha, the Chinese acupuncturist, has told us never to allow the fan to blow directly on him because it will damage his chi, already struggling for survival. But the suction machine—what does that do to his chi? It takes his breath away. It is a portable one, so that we can bring it with us when he comes home on Sundays, and it's rather like a Magimix, with its solid electronic base and removable plastic container, though the receptacle is for saliva and phlegm that has been suctioned out through the attached long clear tube, to help him when he's choking. Traumatic brain injury invariably compromises the swallow, which, if you think about it, is one of the most complex neuromuscular interactions in the body. Your saliva glands manufacture between two and four pints of saliva daily, which you swallow without thinking about it. Without a swallow, all this saliva pools in your mouth until you choke and gag.

A small metal medicine cabinet hangs on the wall opposite the bed. Only the nurse on duty has the keys to this; neurological pain-relieving drugs are much sought after on the experimental drug scene. Above the cabinet, fixed to the ceiling, runs a mechanical hoist with T-bar and remote control, a lift system that allows Miles, his body held in a sling, to be hoisted from bed to chair and back again. The humiliation, swinging helplessly in the air like a failed circus act.

On the wall facing the bed, a large, framed montage of photographs. I hope that something is released from this carefully assembled collage of his life, though there is a nagging worry that perhaps the photographs only taunt him, as the pinups may also do. During his sentient moments, does he want to be reminded of what he was? A tear fell down his cheek when Will told him he was buying a flat; they had lived together and it must have signified the permanence of his situation. But the photographs are there for another reason: our defense against his annihilation. They tell people he was *this*, this powerful, humorous, handsome young man, not *this* that you see now.

On top of the chest, a vase of garish orange tulips; I try to buy the brightest-colored flowers available, not always the most pleasing.

And finally, in the corner of the room, by the sink and antibacterial hand wash and paper towel dispensers, is the mirror.

As always, I dread catching his reflection in the mirror. My equilibrium is hard won; always a tenuous contract with reality, the dishonesty of it is laid bare in that uncompromising silver surface. Each time it happens I experience the same shock of unwanted recognition: there, that not-in-this-world young man, his green eyes fixed in a long, faraway stare, that is in reality my son. The Miles I hug and kiss hello brightly and wheel to his room because I want privacy, where I will make a cup of tea for myself and draw up a chair to tell him the day's news and try to think of what else might still interest him—he is a myth of my making, necessarily.

I need the soft focus. We are living with horror, he and I.

But it is Miles alone who is living it. He has no escape. I have had the luxury—it depends how you look at it—to build layer upon layer of self-protection, have spun a cocoon of opacity between the Miles I interact with and the unconfrontable truth.

SINCE RON'S CANCER was diagnosed a year ago I have tried not to let my involvement with Miles's care overshadow my time with Ron. I visit Miles during the day when Ron is at work and on Sundays when we bring Miles back we are all at home together, with friends or Belinda and Amelia dropping by. On Saturdays David visits Miles. Let's make Saturday our day for treats, Ron says, and so we do, having lunch out on our own and going to exhibitions and films that we have spent the week planning to see. The day takes on a celebratory, festive air, a beacon of color in an otherwise subdued stretch of grays and darker days, the time together charged with an intensity we don't refer to. It is extraordinary that Ron simply never complains about his illness, despite the sometimes grueling side effects now of his treatment, the nausea, cramp, dry skin that splits and cracks, the hair loss and the fatigue, the battery of medication he must remember to take every day and the long fortnightly sessions at the clinic being given his intravenous chemo.

But now the tumors have returned. Ron's doctor has not lost hope and is recommending a further, different course of chemo. Something, though I don't confront it, warns me it's possible this may be the last.

Ron has decided to semi-retire, which means he will be at home for two days a week. I must make more time for him, I don't want to lose a moment of this time. Miles, at least, is healthy.

I speak to Rachel, the care home manager, who understands the situation. There is a young trainee occupational therapist at Gael Lodge who has struck up a rapport with Miles, interacting with him in a natural way that Miles seems comfortable with. Glenn has been working with him on a new form of therapy we have discovered, a "touch-free" device that uses sensor technology to translate body movement into music. Miles used to make music with a bank of sophisticated electronics; now voluntary or involuntary movements of his arms past a sensor will trigger programmed sounds. I ask Rachel if it would be possible for Glenn to be assigned to Miles as a personal therapist two days a week for the foreseeable future. I don't know how long it will be, but the truth is that I suspect we have less than a year left. Rachel agrees.

It is a new luxury, being at home together during the week. We talk and we read, Ron does some work at his desk, and we go for long walks in Greenwich Park. Soon, though, I begin to notice him tiring easily, something he has never done. He watches the news or sport on TV and when I take him a cup of tea I find him asleep in his chair, the television still on. His walk is changing, no longer a vigorous stride but muted now, so that I have to slow my step to keep pace with him. These changes I must adapt to; Ron's vigor and energy were so much a part of his character and I fear the loss of them, fear his knowing he is losing them. I don't want him to fall asleep. I find it difficult to walk slowly. I hate what this disease is doing to him.

We go together to see the oncologist at the end of this course of chemo. It has not been successful and Ron is exhausted. He will take a break from treatment over the next few weeks before meeting again to decide what happens next.

* * *

WALKING ACROSS THE heath this morning on my way to play tennis I find myself shouting at the gods: Come and get me, you bastards! Shaking my fist at the sky like a madwoman. Come on, you fuckers, come on, just try! I'll show you.

Ron is dying. It is only palliative care from now on; he has said he does not want further treatment. Sixteen months since his diagnosis and we have talked and talked, we have sheared our souls, there is nothing left unsaid. We have had ten years together and if I had not met him ten years ago I could have lived without knowing. We had hoped to stay out our love, to fade together into old age, but he is becoming frail now before his time. I must support him when he is standing in the shower lest he falls, I must help him out of the bath, I must stand below him on an escalator and brace myself for his weight. Yesterday he fell in the street getting out of a taxi, the driver already alarmed by the gauntness of him, his bones gleaming under pearl-taut skin.

He wakes one morning with the whites of his eyes the color of tea, his face a bilious yellow. He is jaundiced and he knows what that means as for the first time he cries out loud, Oh no, no, no, I don't want to go, I don't want to leave you! I call the doctor for steroids and lie on the bed alongside him, his body as fragile as fine glass.

At night the children and I take it in turns to be on duty. Thank god for Will, Claudia, and Marina.

I HAVE BEEN driving for an hour and I'm lost. It's early evening and darkness has fallen during the journey that I have done so often now I know every twist and turn of it. Miles has been put to bed and I'm on the way back home from Gael Lodge. It takes around twenty minutes and I know the route by heart, I need not think where to turn left or right, but somewhere tonight I went wrong. I don't know where I am. Hunched over the steering wheel, gripping it so hard my neck and jaw ache, something has snapped and I'm shouting, screaming into the dark: *Where the hell am I? Where am I, where am I, where AM I?* Pulling on the wheel, bouncing backwards and forwards on my seat like a broken jack-in-a-box.

It's early summer and unseasonably cold. Inside the car it's too warm, I can't get the temperature right and the heated air is burning my feet and drying my eyes. Outside the streets are empty, glistening with a light sheen of rain and the windshield wipers scrape like razor blades. The darkness looms menacingly, I don't recognize anything and I don't think I can ever find my way out. Another junction ahead and again I have to choose left or right; I don't decide until it's almost too late, turning left with a squeal of tires.

Having made the decision I put my foot down and race down the empty street. I'm lost but at least there is the sound of the engine gaining speed, the hiss of wheels on wet tarmac, the wall at the end of the street coming nearer. I could solve the problem, put my foot down further, keep going until the wall obliterates everything and I will no longer be lost. Just as I begin to accelerate I recognize the block of flats on my right and the street suddenly falls into place: this is the route I take every day on my way to Gael Lodge. I'm going in the wrong direction, but I know where I am.

Slowing down, I turn into the driveway of the flats so that I can reverse out and drive back in the other direction, back home. The flats look desolate, bare bulbs dimly lighting the long balcony corridors that give onto the street. As I pull off the road and stop the car to change gear into reverse, something knocks on my window, a dark shape. There is no streetlight here and I recoil, desperately fumbling the gears to get away, but a person has pushed their face right up against the glass. It's a woman, her hair bedraggled with the rain, her hands cupped together in front of her face, mouthing, please, please help me, I need money, I've got no money. Her eyes are wild, there is too much white showing. I roll down the window an inch and hear myself screaming hysterically at her: Go away! Get out of my way! You frightened me! You can't do this, you can't frighten people like this. Why should I help you? My son is in a coma, my husband is dying of cancer, how can I help you, for fuck's sake? Get out of my way! She stands still, shocked, as I back the car out of the driveway. I can't see properly through my tears but I know the way home now.

Some months later, driving down the same road one afternoon with Marina on our way to see Miles, the woman suddenly appears at the side of the car. She is in the middle of the road and her eyes lock with mine. I speed past her. She had appeared out of nowhere; neither Marina nor I can understand how she got there. She's terrifying, Mum, says Marina, she's a really terrifying crackhead. She feels like the Grim Reaper to me.

TODAY A HOSPITAL bed is being delivered for Ron. I want him to stay at home, I cannot contemplate his dying in a hospital or a hospice. I think of Miles lying awake on his own at night, the horror of imagining his loneliness. At least Ron will not have to suffer that.

His absence from the double bed seems cruelly symbolic. It makes a rupture in our domestic lives that so vividly signifies the finality of the situation; his departure has begun. Neither of us wants it, but after discussion with the palliative care nurse we know it is the right thing. Bedbound now, too weak to stand, Ron needs a special pressure mattress and one that is soilproof, while a mechanism at the pillow end that allows him to remain propped up will make him more comfortable and, I hope, help him sleep.

Thanking the two burly porters from the Greenwich Palliative Care Team who have carried the bed upstairs and set it in place in our bedroom I am in tears, and when Ron thanks them too I am undone. The gratitude I feel for this amazing team of people is overwhelming, the two nurses who have been taking it in turns to visit, the carers who come morning and evening to manage Ron's ablutions, the doctor who is so understanding about prescribing his pain relief. As a result of their care Ron and I and all the children have the luxury of his remaining at home. Time together, the last remaining luxury.

IT HAS BEEN a long night and dawn is here at last. Soft tendrils of light are just beginning to curl around the edges of the curtains and outside the bedroom window the family of starlings who've nested in the wisteria have begun their chittering. I wonder if Ron can hear them; he loves to be woken by the sound, though I always find it too early for comfort.

Lifting my head from the pillow I can see the still dark mound of Ron's body in his new high bed across the room. I think he must be asleep at last, so I don't suppose he can hear the birds. Marina has just fallen asleep too, next to me in the double bed. She and Claudia are taking it in turns to stay down here with me, for Ron's restlessness at night is demanding. Around dawn, Will will appear and take over and then we can sleep.

With relief I hear the bedroom door opening and Will comes in carrying a cup of coffee he must have just made himself, the rich smell of it a comforting reminder of something familiar, normal. Hi, darling, I'm awake, I whisper. How has he been? he asks, and I tell him I think Ron's asleep for the moment after what was a long, uncomfortable night. His restlessness is getting worse and I think I will have to see if a Marie Curie nurse can come at nights from now on. This is not sustainable.

Will goes over to sit on the chair next to Ron's bed and I settle down and try to sleep. Just as I'm beginning to let go I can hear Ron waking. He's saying he needs to sit up and as I look across from my bed I can see Ron's frailty apparent even in the half-light, Will lifting him up into a sitting position, sliding his legs gently over onto the side of the bed and then supporting him. For a few minutes Ron remains sitting quietly and then he says, I want to stand, and I watch Will now bending forward to put his arms around Ron and lift him to a standing position, holding him securely upright. I know this is a difficult balancing act because Ron's body without the ability to maintain his posture has become a deadweight. They remain like this for a minute or so, merged together in one dark shape outlined against the pale curtains behind them. Down again, Ron says suddenly, and Will lowers him. I wonder what is going through Ron's mind as he sits on the edge of the bed as though poised for flight, despite Will having to support him. The room is silent, the birds outside have stopped their chatter, and the only sound for the moment is the soft in and out of Marina's breath next to me. I want to get up, Ron says. It is a new thing, this agitation of his, a private thing we can't be part of. Will lifts him again and holds him up and they remain standing in silence for some time before eventually Will lowers him back to a sitting position. It is like watching a kind of strange and tender dance ritual, of shadows and silhouettes and movements performed with intense concentration, everything narrowed down into this one urgent, unknowable need of Ron's. Thanks, Will, good man, Ron says. Sorry. It's okay. I love you, Ron, Will says, surprisingly and simply. He has never said this before. Very gravely, Ron looks up at him. I love you, too, Will, he says.

RON IS BECOMING delirious. The only comfort we can take is that he is here at home, everything around him familiar for his rare moments of lucidity. The Marie Curie nurses come at night. Early in the morning the young one, Wendy, wakes me. I don't think you have long, she says. I sit up. How long? Perhaps some hours. The beginning of a perfect summer's day, mid-July, light sifting in through the east window of the bedroom and Ron so beautiful in repose, eyes closed, his breathing as delicate as being brushed by a butterfly's wing. I call Belinda and Amelia, who arrive within minutes, and wake Will, Claudia, and Marina. We are all there.

It is the first time I have seen someone die. A strange privilege. Calmly, peacefully, Ron leaves, his eyes opening one last time, unfathomably blue, before they slowly close.

RON'S FUNERAL TODAY, a Monday, two weeks since he died. How protected from death has my life been that I've only ever attended two funerals and have never had to organize one. There has been so much to do these past two weeks, the distraction almost a comfort. Waking too early this morning I feel a new sense of peace in the knowledge that Ron will finally be free to go.

Downstairs in the kitchen making tea, the kettle crackles and sighs in the morning silence. It is a beautiful day for Ron's departure. His idea of heaven, the air already warming up as I open the doors out onto the garden, and everywhere a tumble of scents and colors. This garden has become a barometer of my state of mind. It died with neglect the first summer after Miles's accident, but I remade it for Ron, planted wildly last autumn thinking if I brought it back to life it might keep him alive too. I failed, but it will do him proud today. How it will fare after this I don't know. But for now the borders are brimming with wild geraniums, feathery-headed Annabel hydrangeas, pale roses.

Taking my mug of tea with me I wander through the downstairs rooms. People will be in the garden today, but I want to make sure the house is ready too. With Ron upstairs in our bedroom in the weeks before he died, the children and I lived only between there and the kitchen. I haven't set foot in the drawing room for months. A cool green north-facing room, it's our place both for special occasions, champagne and Christmas, the log fire rustling, birthdays and friends, or in between a place in which to retreat, to read and listen to music. Going into it now I wonder when Ron was last here. He seems very close. It is deathly quiet, too early for cars or people outside. I feel porous in the quiet. Books are piled, spilled over the floor by the bookshelves, so I put down my mug and tidy them up as best I can. There is never enough shelf space. A book catches my eye, *Love Letters*, which Ron gave me, a collection of the letters between Leonard Woolf and Trekkie Ritchie filling in the little-known relationship they had after Virginia died. As I open it a piece of folded white paper floats to the ground. It's Ron's inky embroidered writing.

> *L*
> *Love totally and completely*
> *for ever and ever*
> *As ever and for ever*
> *R xxx*

I've never seen it before. I don't know when he put it there—he didn't give it to me with the book, which at the time I read to the end.

* * *

MILES IS NOT coming to the funeral. It's been a painful decision, but the children and I don't want him to be on show, which he would be with so many people coming who have not seen him since his accident or who don't know him and might be curious to see a young man whom they think of as in a coma. We remember the time we took him out in Queen Square, how he hated it, or the dreadful staring he experienced on hospital visits. It's too painful to contemplate. He will come to the cremation afterwards and I have asked for Joseph to accompany him from Gael Lodge. Only close friends and family will be joining us there. Joseph and he are waiting at the entrance to the crematorium when we arrive. The shock of seeing him, so handsome, so as he always looked. Joseph has dressed him in black trousers and the black short-sleeved Hugo Boss shirt with a thin orange stripe down the side that he loved. It is much easier for the carers to dress him in T-shirts; so typical of Joseph to have gone to this extra trouble today. Miles appears fiercely awake, his stern composure intimidating. Does he know where he is? He must understand the gravity of the situation. The children gather around him as I go to greet the friends who've arrived and we talk about the funeral, about Ron, how he would have loved the music. When the priest invites us to go in I am relieved to attend to Miles, to wheel him down the aisle to the front and take my seat at the end of the pew next to him. Leaning over I whisper in his ear, Ron would be so proud of you today, Miley. I am so incredibly proud of you. He sits erect, unmoving, formidable. How strong a support he would have been for me. The overture for *Parsifal* begins to play and now I'm dissolving, Ron is here in front of me, unreachable behind the bland wooden surface of the coffin I chose so carefully as though it mattered, the cream and lime roses draped and scenting for an instant this ugly space. He is here and not here. Miles is here but not here.

"GRIEF IS NOT an achievement," I read, in a trenchant review of a memoir in a literary magazine. No, indeed; it is as random as death, which is not an achievement either. It just happens, to anybody, anywhere, anytime, just one part of what we otherwise call life. This writer admits he has not yet had to suffer grief, but he is concerned that for some it is abused, exploited, a badge of honor. Am I exploiting my grief, writing about it? And then I read the poet Mark Doty, immersed in the deep, darkest moment, writing to wrest some sense from himself at the death of his lover: "Being in grief, it seems, is not unlike being in love." How those words ring like a bell through the echoing cloisters of this cold new world without Ron. Of course. In love, or in grief for love lost; one segues into the other, a continuum of love.

WE SCATTER RON's ashes, the children and I, at the house in France that he loved so much, our first house together. A white butterfly follows us as we move through the garden in the early cool of dawn. A dance of the ashes. Pearl-like, mother-of-pearl, the wind blows the ashes on our hands, clothes, hair, in our mouths.

I'VE GONE TO Paris again, to stay in the quiet of our friends' apartment and try to understand what has happened. Sitting in the sunshine on the window ledge with my cup of coffee, the church bells opposite begin to ring in a strange way. It's mid-morning, they don't normally ring at this time. Each toll of the bell is stark, it stops dead instead of lingering and melding into the next, and the tone is different, harsh, alarming. Something is wrong. As I open the window to look out, the old familiar melodious bell begins to toll over the first, becoming louder and louder until it is an unapologetic riot of sound. I wonder if it is a wedding and the bell ringer is new and got it wrong to start with. There is no one about, only a dark car with its tailgate open parked at the entrance to the church, and then I watch as four men in black suits appear, slowly descending the steps carrying a pale wooden coffin. Not a wedding but a funeral; the bells are inviting us to celebrate this life that has just ended. A priest in rich purple and gold follows the men down the steps and stands to one side as they lower and slide the coffin into the open car. People in dark dress are coming out of the church now, embracing one another, stepping aside as the four men reappear down the steps carrying out great stiff wreaths of flowers which they place on top of the coffin, leaning in carefully one after the other. The back door of the hearse is closed and as it is driven away the mourners begin to disperse. The priest in his splendid robes waits on the steps until there is no one left and then he is gone too.

THE JOURNEY BY car to Gael Lodge is an easy one, driving through the alternatingly elegant and bleak residential streets of South London. I listen to the radio, music or people talking a necessary distraction. Today Bruckner's Seventh Symphony is playing, one of Ron's favorites, and I am thinking of him as I turn up the last long hill, past the delicatessen where I sometimes stop to get an instant supper on the way home and then the Baptist church whose Sunday crowd are so colorfully dressed it could be a carnival. Reaching Gael Lodge there is nothing to signify it being an institution, comprising as it does three conjoined houses in a street of similar Edwardian detached and semidetached homes. It is a quiet street and the residents appear unconcerned about their proximity to a home for seriously brain-damaged people.

What must have once been large front gardens of the three houses are now paved to allow for a small number of staff and relatives' cars to park. Miles's room is on the ground floor, his bay window facing the street, and today there is a free space right in front of it. His blinds are open so he must be in the day room; when he is in the room the blinds are kept at an angle to allow for privacy. I pull in and park, but the Bruckner is still playing and for a while I remain in the closed car and luxuriate in the music, my eyes closed. It ends and I turn off the engine, get my bags together, and open the car door.

What I hear then is the deep, bellowing sound of a creature in distress, a sound so loud and so terrifying I'm gripped by a kind of primeval fear. I've never heard anything like it. It does not sound human; such distress, such pain, could not be borne. It's coming out of Gael Lodge; how can the residents of this street live with such a sound? Another drawn-out, anguished, roaring cry of pain— it is coming from Miles's room. The blinds have just been angled down. This is my son I am listening to.

When I reach his room I find Miles raised up in midair in the hoist, being moved from his chair to be put to bed. His face is puce, his jaw rigid, his eyes dark with a rage that says everything there is to say. The two carers are distraught and they are frightened by him. He suddenly started doing this in the day room, they tell me, so we thought it might be best to put him to bed. We can't understand what's wrong.

Oh my god, Miles, I understand. Your frustration—that is too weak a word—your total powerlessness to control any single aspect of your life, every moment of every day. How can you bear it? How can I help you? He leans forward in the hoist, he is staring at me, beseeching, demanding my help, but I am powerless too. I cannot help him.

* * *

SUDDENLY, IN THE midst of the bleakness there is what feels like a glorious blast of joyful news. Will is getting married to Albi, and the girls and I could not imagine anyone lovelier or more loved to be joining the family. To compound the happiness, Albi is pregnant.

It is going to be a private civil wedding, because more than anything Will wants Miles to attend. There will be just the two families present and Belinda and Amelia, followed by a festive lunch at home; a larger party for friends will be held in the months to come. Will searches for a venue for the ceremony that can accommodate Miles; there must be either ground-floor access or an elevator that can take him in his wheelchair. His left leg is now rigid, the knee locked in extension, which requires a minimum of two meters in all. After numerous unsuccessful visits he finds the perfect place, ten minutes from home. Rangers House is an English Heritage Georgian house set into the wall of Greenwich Park and the wedding will take place in the beautiful second-floor gallery, the elevator unusually large enough to take Miles.

Claudia has offered to drive to Gael Lodge to collect him and take him to the ceremony, and Moses will accompany him. It was extraordinary, she tells us later. Miles was waiting in the day room with Moses when I arrived, and I have never seen him so alert and so intensely calm at the same time. He knew where he was going. Once he was in the van I told him I thought he should try to rest on the journey, or even sleep if he could, because it was so important he should be awake for the ceremony. He closed his eyes—he understood.

Claudia and Miles are early and waiting in the gallery when I arrive with Will and Marina. I almost cry out on seeing him; he looks so intimidatingly alert, strong, normal, that for a ridiculous flashing moment I think he's back just as he was. His chair is facing the door and he is clearly calmly waiting for things to begin.

I had feared this moment, as much as I am thrilled the wedding is taking place. I had feared he would be having a bad day, might be contorted with spasticity, or coughing, or doing his signature roar of frustration. Albi's large family has never met him before and I know how difficult people can find it, being exposed to his situation. I want to protect him from their embarrassment and, in truth, protect us, the family, too. I have spoken to Moses, have asked that, should Miles make a noise, could he please take him quietly from the room. It would be so very painful for Will to have the ceremony ruined in that way.

But now I am standing next to Miles, introducing him one by one to Albi's parents and her three siblings, and I am brimming with pride. Miles is formidable, his interest in them a tangible thing, his authority palpable. When we move on to the ceremony he remains vividly alert, his body quite still, looking intently in the direction of the registrar as she performs the ritual of joining Will and Albi in marriage.

Back at home we stand around the fire in the drawing room and toast the newlyweds and Miles is still actively with us. There is a point when I look across the room and see Albi standing by him. She has taken his hand and is holding it on her pregnant stomach and they are sharing an intense communication. He is looking up at her with an expression of great tenderness and pride mixed with fierce protectiveness; I can imagine him looking down at her with the same expression if he had been standing here today, undamaged. It is unbearably poignant, not just his love for this beautiful girl, but also as though he is more attuned, now, to an existence beyond the present everyday, that he knows he is feeling a new life under his hand, in the way a blind person's sense of touch and hearing are made keener through their loss. Look at Albi and Miles, I say to Claudia, who is standing next to me. I know, Mum, she says, a few moments ago I went to join them and I had to leave, I felt as though I was interrupting a very private conversation.

Finally the time comes for us to have lunch. An ambulance has been booked to take Miles and Moses back to Gael Lodge; he has been in his chair for five hours already and to stay on for the meal would take him too far beyond his seating tolerance. His absence leaves a space that can't be filled, but he has clearly and generously given Will and Albi the most precious thing he could have given them.

RACHEL, THE FORMIDABLE manager of Gael Lodge, has her office situated immediately after the entrance to the building. The glass wall and open door exemplify her management style: open and direct, she misses nothing. This morning she calls me in as I walk past, as she does every now and then. We chat about Miles for a while and then she says, I must ask you something, Lu, which I'm afraid I have to ask all relatives connected with the high-dependency wards. Have you ever thought about Miles being considered NFR—Not for Resuscitation? This is a shock. No, never, I reply. Not at all. Must I be on the alert again? Only here at Gael Lodge have I never felt the need to be in armed combat on Miles's behalf, as I was before he moved here and as I still must be whenever he visits another hospital or even enters an ambulance. But I know Rachel understands Miles and she understands the family; I know, too, that her first concern in every instance is for her patient.

If he suffers a cardiac arrest, she asks, do you want us to apply CPR?

Cardiac pulmonary resuscitation. I think of Ellen on the ward, whose heart five years ago stopped seven times and seven times the paramedics started it again. Pictures of her before her heart attack show a slight, sweet-faced girl with two small children, her tall, shy husband, the sense of a quiet, self-contained family. Her husband no longer brings the children to visit because they suffer nightmares afterwards, remain withdrawn for days. Ellen must wear a gum guard to stop her grinding her teeth, for her mouth works continuously, gaping open, lips bared, her expressionless face frozen in a scream without sound, blank eyes roaming unaligned before suddenly she clamps her jaws down together with shocking force. *Clamp*, open, freeze, *clamp*, open, freeze, all day long. Nothing else. I have to think how much better for her, her husband, her children, if the dedicated paramedics had not restarted her heart the seventh time. I would agree to NFR for Miles.

So I tell Rachel I will speak to the family and get back to her. Four years ago I would have wanted to destroy anyone who dared to suggest NFR. I think of Dr. Mosley back at UCH; part of his cruelty lay in saying what he said to Will when he did. I understand how difficult it must be for doctors who see the MRI of a patient's brain and foresee the consequences of their injury, but must face the relatives who have no knowledge, no comprehension at all of TBI. How could they, unless they have had firsthand experience? Believing, hoping their loved one will recover is a necessary part of the means to cope, a crucial survival mechanism in those early stages of fear and confusion. It is the doctor's responsibility to respect this.

I leave Rachel's office and go to find Miles. It's late October, winter is near, the sky a wash of pale blue and a feeling in the air of snow having fallen somewhere far away. Despite the sunshine the garden is empty and I want to take Miles out into it. I need to be on my own with him, away from people. A carer helps me wrap him up, two rugs, the striped multicolored scarf he always wore snowboarding, gloves, and a beanie; if it weren't for the rugs he could be relaxing in a ski resort. He's vividly alert, one of those days when his nearness to the surface is electric, a force field around him. Hey, handsome! Denise calls out from behind the nurses' desk as I wheel him through the day room, and I think, she's right, he looks magnificent today.

There's a bench under the pergola at the end of the garden that has the sun all day and is sheltered from the wind. I wheel Miles there and for a while we sit in silence in the enclosed warmth and stillness. I love you so very much, Miles. You know that, don't you? I take his hand and he looks at me, clear-eyed and calm, but it's a look of such intensity I could believe he knows what's in my mind. Rachel spoke to me today. He continues to look at me and I feel the familiar crumple of pain somewhere deep inside me. I'm doing everything in my power to help you get out of this, my darling. But if there is a risk of further damage, a setback—I don't want you to take it. I don't think you would want that. Would you? He closes his eyes slowly and then he opens them again, and his expression has changed, softened, it speaks to me in the clearest way of love and *pity*. How can I burden him with pity as well? Miles, you know I sometimes think now that you don't want to continue. Am I right in thinking that? Still looking at me his right thumb begins to tremor and then slowly, unbelievably, quiveringly he presses down on my hand. It is the movement he used to be able to make to signify affirmation, before his spasticity became so severe. I thought he could no longer do it. It is the lightest pressure, but there is no doubt it happens.

The children come home for supper and we discuss Rachel's question. Our individual journeys to this point have been gradual and though shared there are things that have not been said, perhaps because they have been too difficult to confront. We now all accept that Miles will not recover in any meaningful way; we all consider his life to be an unbearable existence for him. We see it as one long stretch of unremitting misery, the agony of absolute loneliness, punctuated by extreme pain, discomfort, anger, irritation, humiliation, boredom, and only perhaps the very occasional, slightest relief, like being turned by gentle carers rather than careless ones when he has been too long in one position. What can be pleasurable, apart from the oblivion of sleep? Our armor throughout these past few years, the protective shield of hope, has gradually worn thin, but we have not fully confronted that yet; its admission would be too final an acknowledgment of loss. I will continue to push for any treatment that can ameliorate his condition, but really I know it will only alleviate the discomfort. We all know that nothing can bring him back across the void that separates his life now from his life as it should have been lived.

I tell the children about my conversation with Miles this afternoon and my thoughts about Ellen. As painful as it is, I think NFR should apply to Miles's future treatment. If I were in Miles's position, Will says, if I was told that some amazing treatment might be available in ten, five, even, actually, a year's time, I would still not want to continue my existence. We're all silent. He has a knack, Will, of articulating succinctly something which one has not yet thought through. If it were me, he continues, I would definitely not want to be resuscitated after cardiac arrest, especially if the chances are that I'd be even more damaged than before. Claudia agrees with him. It's unthinkable to have to be talking about Miles in this way, she says. But I try to imagine him in the circumstances. I imagine if he was here now, having to make this decision about one of us. He would never tolerate the prospect of dragging on such a life.

Marina has been quiet throughout the conversation, and now she is quietly adamant. I think NFR is a decision only Miles can make. I don't think we have the right to make it on his behalf, much as we all agree that his life is not worth living anymore. We all understand what that means. It is a decision we respect, and so the next day I tell Rachel that until Marina changes her mind, NFR does not apply to Miles.

ONE EVENING SOME weeks later Marina returns home from visiting Miles and tells me she has changed her mind. She accepts Miles should be considered NFR. If he were given the chance to die it would be a cruelty to condemn him to a longer existence, she says. He was so bitterly unhappy today. It was the darkest, bleakest misery. He can't bear it. It's the least we can do. I ask her what happened. I can't describe it, she says. It's too painful. But he made it clear. I am quite certain he does not want to continue in this way.

I think now of Marina's words all those years ago in Innsbruck, that our hope for Miles was like a love affair; now they seem even more apt. A failing love affair, only ever some small epiphany, some small climax, but never resolution, never full emotional satisfaction. The hope we sustained at the beginning slowly destroyed in the end by ennui, by the burden of reality.

BEFORE I RETURN to Rachel with our decision I speak with Miles's GP, Matthew. He confirms what we already know, that resuscitation in Miles's current condition would be likely to leave him in a significantly worse state. Remember, though, he reassures me, that you can always change your mind if you have any doubts about what Miles would wish, or if at any time he gives an indication about what he wants. His opinion and his well-being will continue to remain our first priority.

CLAUDIA HAS JUST returned from Gael Lodge and we have poured ourselves a glass of wine and settled on the sofa in the sitting room to watch the Channel 4 news. Miles wants to die, she says. I turn off the television. What do you mean? I ask her. What made you say that? He told me today, she replies. It was extraordinary. He had already been put to bed when I got there and he was coughing really badly. The carer on duty said they had given him a nebulizer but it made no difference. I raised the pillow end of the bed to try to help and I suctioned him, but nothing worked. You know what it's like when he coughs and coughs and cannot clear it. And then he did one huge, terrible cough that made him retch violently and after that he just roared like I've never heard him before. It was the most wretched sound I've ever heard. I'm so sorry, Miley, I wish I could help you, I said to him, and with that he just lifted himself right out from the pillow, staring at me with such intensity, such anger, that I knew exactly what he was saying. He was saying, You know you can help me. Do it. Please do it.

There is nothing I can say. I understand what she is describing, have seen and felt that anger directed at me and have dreaded its meaning. Claudia takes a long sip of wine, puts down her glass, and then looks at me carefully. I told Miles I would, she says. I told him I would help him die. I said I couldn't do it for a while but I would find a way. I promised him. You cannot imagine the look of relief on his face as he sank back onto the bed.

I know Claudia is serious. She means to do this. Perhaps it is strange, but I am not surprised. You cannot possibly do that, darling, I tell her. Apart from the fact that you don't know what the appropriate drugs are or where to find them, you would go to prison. I don't mind, Mum, she says. You'll all come and visit me and I'll study there, do something. I know I've got an unrealistic view of it, but the most important thing for me is that Miles will be free from suffering. He would do this for me. I know it won't be easy—it will be horrifying, terrifying. But it wouldn't be a fraction of the hell he is suffering.

It's out of the question, Will says when I tell him. We can't let her. I won't let her. It would destroy Claudia, Marina says, she hasn't thought it through. She would not be able to live with the knowledge of what she had done, even if it had released Miles. I realize how far we have traveled that there is no shock for any of us in hearing Claudia state her intention. The truth is, we all believe it is exactly what Miles does want. For the moment only she has the recklessness to say it, and mean it.

I MISS RON. *Miss*, such a slight, quiet word, but it says everything. He is missing and his absence permeates every moment of my life like an elusive scent that reminds me of something familiar but never present. I carry it with me day and night. Private and invisible, it sustains me. How I need him here now.

THE SPASTICITY IN Miles's left arm has got so bad that there is no option left but surgery. The muscles of the arm and the hand have now contracted so that the arm is permanently bent at the elbow, his hand clenched into a fist pulled up to his shoulder, the fingers so tightly clamped it is almost impossible to pry them open. This attempt at prying open has to be done daily, because the skin inside his hand has broken down into weeping open sores. He is in permanent pain but the added pain of having his fingers bent back to clean the hand is quite clearly excruciating.

As I start to warn him that we need to open his hand to clean it he hunches back into himself, presses the fist further into his shoulder, both legs lift from the chair, and his face contorts in anticipation. To wash his hand is to perpetrate violence. No compensation that the cruelty is imperative, that however painful, infection of the skin will increase his spasticity even further. I begin by touching his hand and holding it for a moment. I'm so sorry, Miles, I wish this didn't hurt you, but I have to do it. Your hand is getting infected and it needs to be kept clean and dry. I love you so very much, my darling, I hate to inflict this pain on you. Please let me try to open your fingers, I'm going to do it as gently as I can. But as I try to open the hand I am entering into combat with Miles and he is so furiously strong my frustration eventually turns to irritation—*open* your hand, for god's sake. I am fighting him with all my strength now, I am his enemy, the enemy of this heinous thing that has destroyed him, reduced him to a dumb, suffering parody of the powerful young man he was. Teeth clenched with the effort, I feel the tremors of a violence that would destroy us both.

An appointment is made for Miles to see an orthopedic consultant, a hand specialist. There is nothing for it, the surgeon explains to me, after examining Miles. The only way to relieve him of this problem is to sever the ligaments of his hand and arm. I'm afraid he won't be able to use the arm or hand again. The surgeon looks at me and it is unspoken, that that won't be a meaningful loss for Miles. But, he says, with sudden fierceness, I can relieve him of this pain. He looks at Miles and I see what he sees, a healthy young man utterly dependent on somebody, anybody, anybody at all, to help him. He looks back at me and I can read the pain refracted in his eyes; he understands. I will put Miles's procedure at the top of my list, he says. He should not have to endure this one day longer.

Sunday evening and Marina and I have arrived at the hospital early to be in time for Miles. We stand at the entrance, watching as yet another ambulance parks in the reserved space and the driver and his assistant hop down from their seats to walk around and open up the back. The doors are opened, the mechanical ramp activated, and the two men wheel down a stretcher with prac-ticed ease. What I see is a handsome, dark-haired young man lying frozen on his back, one arm disturbingly bent back on itself and one leg strangely raised, pointing into the air, as straight and stiff as a gymnast's. He has got stuck in the middle of a complicated move-ment and so too has his face, frozen in a long-drawn-out moment of raw misery. Jesus Christ, that's Miles. Marina and I turn to one another; our clarity is shared.

There are times like this when reality suddenly intrudes through the fragile lens of normalization that makes participa-tion in Miles's world bearable. In the way that the safety glasses a welder must wear will save his eyes from the sparks of burning metal, we have acquired a protective filter that allows us to deflect the small, constant shocks. But sometimes, like now, the lens fails and I'm caught off guard. It can happen when I see Miles reflected in a mirror, or when I suddenly see him in the distance, perhaps a carer or a friend in the garden talking to him or pushing his wheel-chair, or like now, looking down from the top of the hospital steps. I have remained outside the scene, looking in. And how can Miles bear this? There is no protective lens for him; he is living it from the inside every moment.

We walk quickly down to the ambulance. Hello, Miles dar-ling, I say, kissing him hello, Marina and I are here. Marina leans down to kiss him too and as she does so his face softens and he closes his eyes as though savoring the moment. We're at the hos-pital, Miles—that surgeon who was so helpful when we saw him together last week will operate on your arm tomorrow. He is certain he can release you from the pain you're enduring. We're going up to the ward now, Marina and I are coming with you. Yelena, the carer from Gael Lodge who is accompanying Miles, appears from the other side of the ambulance carrying various bags, the paraphernalia of Miles's existence—his medication, splints, sanitary pads, Conveens, his toothbrush and razor, some clothes. Marina and I take them from her as the three of us follow the men pushing the gurney through the hospital foyer and up to the ward.

It's a men-only surgical ward, a cavernous room that looks as though nothing has changed since the First World War. Metal beds in rows down each side, wooden locker on one side and chair on the other, dreary blue curtains on overhead rails an attempt at privacy. It is clearly not an acute ward, since none of the men in here looks particularly unhealthy, though each is either waiting for surgery or recovering from it. Some of the men have visitors but everyone falls silent as Miles is wheeled down the center aisle to his bed at the end of the ward. Perhaps he is too unnerving a reminder of what can happen. Perhaps he makes them feel more vulnerable at a time when they need reassurance.

The operation is scheduled for 8:00 the next morning. I get to the hospital early, and buying a takeaway coffee at the café in the huge domed atrium, I feel the charge of the place. At this hour everyone has a clear purpose, greetings ring out, brisk footsteps echoing as doctors, nurses, therapists, technicians, cleaners, all the cogs of this vast machine of expertise and dedication arrive for the day or leave after the night's work. On accompanying Miles down to the operating theater I find the place is already abuzz, the surgeon transformed from elegant-suited doctor to virile man of action. I could fall in love with this man for what he is doing for Miles. He greets us both, greets Miles so respectfully, before introducing his anesthetist, a small wiry South African who puts me at my ease. You can stay with your son while I give him the anesthetic, he says. That's not normally allowed but this is kind of different. Miles is wheeled into the pre-op room and the anesthetist chats to me as he makes the preparations. I watch Miles's eyes close as he drops straight into unconsciousness and I don't have time to ask how much anesthetic is required in the circumstances, to go from minimally conscious rather than from fully conscious. I hope it is the same; the experience of pain is certainly the same.

Three and a half hours later I am called to see him in the recovery room. My trepidation as I enter is replaced by the sweet thrill of relief and gratitude—the surgeon has worked a miracle. Miles is transformed, his face calm, his body relaxed, and—the miracle—his left arm, though heavily bandaged, is resting for the first time in years in a natural position in front of him, supported now by a pillow on his lap. I feel the familiar stirrings of hope begin to rise; I am hoping with all my heart that this operation has removed the pain and maybe, *maybe*, if he is no longer distracted by pain and no longer muffled by heavy pain relief, he might start to communicate. Just maybe. But then I hear myself being admonished by despair. Don't be a fool, it tells me, you know how long it's been. You know there is no hope for the sort of life Miles wants to live. We'll see, says hope. I'm walking the tightrope again.

Miles remains comfortable throughout the day, cushioned by the slowly waning aftereffects of his anesthetic. When Will, Claudia, and Marina arrive to see him in the evening I leave them, reassured that the operation has been a success. Yelena is back for her night shift and the nurse on duty seems competent; Miles appears set for a calm night. I plan to come in early again tomorrow, to meet with the surgeon on his rounds before surgery.

It's still dark when I leave home the next morning. Ordering my coffee in the hospital café I feel a strange, subdued but growing sense of excitement—I am about to see Miles and he may be pain-free. That will be a new and wonderful thing, a black knot of horror excised. When I arrive on the ward the curtain has been pulled around Miles's bed and I imagine he is having his early ablutions before the surgeon arrives. But when I pass through the curtain what I see is a young man who could have spent the long night in a bombed-out crater in no-man's-land, wounded, alone, in agony. His back is arched away from the bed, his face mottled purple, his eyes wild and staring, his teeth bared. He is pouring with sweat, his T-shirt dripping wet. I can see even the sheets are soaked through. I have never, not even in a horror film, ever seen any person or animal in this state; I could not possibly have imagined it. WHAT is happening? I shout and then I see Yelena, terrified, on the other side of the bed. For god's sake, Yelena, what's going on? I try to touch Miles but he arches still further away from me, eyes now staring into my eyes, my son, my beloved son, staring at me like a wounded wild animal in a trap. Where is the nurse? I go out into the open ward and find the nurse. Come here, I say to her, please come here immediately. She looks annoyed by my peremptoriness but follows me. Look at him! Just look at him! I'm ice cold with anger. What has been going on? What pain relief has Miles been given? I'll have to check, she says coolly, but I know we gave him a thousand milligrams of acetaminophen an hour ago. You must be joking, I say, you gave him acetaminophen? Acetaminophen! What does that do for pain like this? Is that what you would give yourself in the circumstances? Miles can't tell you but couldn't you *see* it, for Christ's sake? *Can* you see it? You're a nurse, you're meant to care for people. Bring me the drug chart, I want to see what he was given last night. She goes out and returns with the chart.

The only pain relief Miles has received all night is acetamin-ophen. The anesthetist omitted to prescribe any pain relief for Miles. And, I see with even colder fury, the junior doctor on duty on the first night omitted to enter the prescribed neurological pain relief he receives every night, 400 mg gabapentin to top up the

600 mg he has already been given during the day. With no pain relief at all after the operation he has not even had his regular nightly dose. The doctor hadn't bothered to turn the last page of his medication notes from Gael Lodge. The ligaments of Miles's upper and lower arm and his hand have been severed during a three-hour operation, with the attendant deep wounds carefully stitched and bandaged. The violent pain he experienced during the night triggered severe spasticity spasms, as a result of which powerful involuntary movements of his arms occurred which Miles could not control. When Yelena asked the nurse on duty for help turning him, she complained that it was not her job, that the care home should have sent two carers to look after him. By early morning the stitches had split open and the bandages were soaked with blood. A junior doctor was the only doctor available and was busy, so took some time before attending to Miles. He did not prescribe further pain relief and all he did was rebandage Miles's arm.

For the past ten hours at least Miles has experienced no pain relief of any kind. What was going through his mind? Where did he think he was?

I am ready to destroy the entire medical staff of this hospital in a hail of bullets. But when the surgeon arrives he is on my side, is as appalled as I am, immediately instructs the nurse to get some intravenous morphine. He examines Miles's arm. I don't understand, he says. She returns and he injects Miles, watching over him as his body slowly subsides onto the bed. I don't understand, the surgeon says again, Jack is a very good anesthetist. Well, I understand, I tell him. It is simple—because Miles is unable to speak for himself he was treated with contempt. We've seen it before. If you are helpless, if you are damaged and can't communicate, there are people who will treat you in a way they would not dream of treating an animal. I could destroy them all. I understand, the surgeon says.

MILES SHOULD REMAIN in the hospital for a further five days, but I want him out of that ward as soon as possible. After telling Rachel about his experience she immediately agrees to have him back at Gael Lodge. We are perfectly capable of giving him postoperative care here, she says, and what's more he won't risk picking up any of those awful hospital infections. She always bangs the drum for Gael Lodge and she's right; in fact he will receive the sort of post-operative care that NHS hospital managers can only dream of, professional, scrupulous, and attuned to Miles's individual needs.

Rachel asks if I will make a formal complaint to the hospital. I don't have the extra reserves of energy, I tell her. I am so hugely grateful to the surgeon for his compassionate treatment of Miles and I'm certain he won't let that happen again under his care. He told me he has dealt with the anesthetist; the experience with Miles has been a salutary one, in particular as the hospital has just been designated one of the four major stroke and trauma centers in London.

But I think somehow the experience has been salutary in a personal sense for him too. On his final round before discharging Miles I take the opportunity to thank him for the manner in which he has treated Miles. I want to remain unemotional, but as I speak the vivid memory rises unbidden, Miles, wild-eyed, arched up in his bed, and the matey little anesthetist beforehand, chatting casually to me as he administered the drugs. If only you had known Miles before his accident, I say to the surgeon. He was so much the greater man—he would have seen off that little anesthetist. I've lost it now, the tears are coming fast, but looking up I could swear there is a tear in the surgeon's eyes too.

MARCH IS THE cruelest month, unraveling memory as it brings with it Miles's birthday and the anniversary of his accident, one week apart. I thought at first that March 19 could be no worse than any other day, but it always is. However hard I try not to think about it, each moment of the day takes on a painful significance, a slow countdown of retrieved memory as vividly recalled as if I were living it again.

Today is the fourth anniversary and the children are all at home for supper. Four years ago Miles was in the operating theater and we were on the start of our journey, flying out to Munich. Four years have passed for Miles and nothing has changed. We talk about that and somehow, tonight, it becomes clear that because nothing has changed, everything has changed. We are reaching the end of our long journey of hope. Like a tree planted to block out an unwanted view, hope has slowly, unnoticed, been withering at the root. Now it has fallen away and all of a sudden the view is visible again. It's no use continuing to pretend it isn't there; we all now acknowledge the bitter truth, that there can no longer be any hope of recovery for Miles.

What has brought us to this point is that Miles knows nothing has changed. He *knows*. He has been making it clear. For some time we have noticed the shift in his mood, a darkness of expression, a marked stiffening of his jaw, a dismissive shutting of his eyes whenever we make our usual upbeat statements. You're looking wonderful today, Miles. I've just seen Shasha and she says the acupuncture session yesterday went really well. She thinks you're getting more movement in your right arm. It's great to hear you managed the tilt table twice this week, the physiotherapist says he'll try to fit you in for two sessions next week as well. You're going to make it, Miles, you're going to come back and do all the things you planned to do. Only ever upbeat, over and over, the words worn thin with overuse. He never could tolerate dissembling.

Over supper the children and I discuss tactics, as we so often have over the past four years. We have to change our approach with Miles. We all feel certain he is asking us to stop the false rallying, the pretending to be hopeful; we have all seen him shut down as we begin to be upbeat. How can we be honest with him? It would seem cruel beyond imagining. Or would it? Jean-Dominique Bauby, Tony Judt, Tony Nicklinson come to mind, all of whom found relief in stating the truth about their existence. Knowing Miles is to know he would take the same approach. If only he could communicate, he could direct us. I can't help thinking—perhaps he is directing us?

Together we make the decision that we will no longer refer to Miles's future when we're with him. It begins to feel as though we have been unthinkingly callous, putting impossible pressure on him to try to meet our apparent expectations. All we can now do is continue to be there for him, try to interest and distract him, let him know how central he is and will always be to this family that loves him so intensely. How proud we are of him, how much he has achieved, how loved he is.

What else is there, in the end, but love?

Some days after we take this decision Rachel calls me again from her office as I walk past on my way to see Miles. I wonder if you think I'm right, Lu, she says, but I have noticed a difference in Miles. In what way? I ask her. I can't put my finger on it, he just looks more relaxed. His spasticity has decreased and he hasn't seemed as angry or frustrated as he so often has been lately. It's very strange, she says, really a marked difference, as if he is in a sort of Zen place, waiting calmly for something. I could hug this remarkable woman; her dedication and sensitivity to each one of her fifty-five patients is borne out over and over again. I tell her about the family's discussion and that the children and I have also seen the change in Miles in these last few days. Since putting our decision into practice it is as though a huge and terrible burden had been lifted from him. He no longer has to perform. I wish we had understood what demands we were making on him, I say to her. We were always urging him on, thinking we were helping him in keeping his spirits up when instead we were simply asking the impossible of him. But you had to do that, Rachel says, it was entirely necessary, both for him and for you all. You had to give him every chance. The most important thing is that you and he have reached this point together.

THE FOLLOWING SATURDAY I have friends over for lunch. Will is due to join us but he's late. I know he was going to Gael Lodge first before coming and I wonder what has happened to hold him up. He arrives halfway through the meal and, although I suspect our guests haven't noticed, I can see he is preoccupied. As soon as they leave I ask him how the visit went.

Something extraordinary happened, Mum, he says. The consultant rehab guy was there, Dr. Davies, doing his Saturday rounds and he asked to speak to me privately. Then he asked me if we had ever considered the possibility of applying to the Court of Protection to end Miles's life. Will gives me a quick concerned glance, checking to see how I react. He continues. Dr. Davies said he believed Miles was on the outer edge of MCS, that he would continue in this condition indefinitely and that, having come to know Miles, he did not believe he wished to continue living. He said he had been wanting to speak to you for some time but had not been able to bring himself to do so.

I know Dr. Davies, a consultant who treats all his patients at Gael Lodge with a scrupulous old-fashioned politeness, though he is proactive in his treatment. I am shocked and—what?—strangely elated by his statement to Will. It is as though I can see a light flickering in the blackness that descended after our discussion the other night and I realize, with absolute clarity, that to release Miles would be the greatest gift we could give him. Will and I look at each other for a moment in silence. It's what Miles wants, isn't it, Will? I say. Yes, Will answers. He puts his arms around me and we stand for some time in silence. What a roller coaster you've been on, I say to him. First Dr. Mosley all those years ago and now Dr. Davies. I know, Will says. I thought about Mosley when Davies was speaking to me. The weird sensation, having more or less the same conversation, but delivered so differently, under such changed circumstances. And this time feeling that I was being given good news for Miles.

I put off contacting Dr. Davies; I'm not ready to have this conversation. I have spent so long keeping reality at bay, have become an expert at it. Four weeks later I arrange to see him on the ward. Miles is asleep in his chair so we leave him in the day room and go out to the wooden deck that leads onto the garden. There is no one else around. I am about to have a conversation to discuss the death of my son. What does that make me? There is no dilemma. I am still certain the greatest gift I could give him now would be to release him. Will told me you wanted to speak to me, I say to Dr. Davies. He told me your thoughts about Miles. Dr. Davies looks apprehensive. I have watched you with Miles, he says, and your dedication, your family's dedication . . . He hesitates before continuing. Dr. Davies, I say, wanting to reassure him, Dr. Davies, we could not be more grateful for your intervention. It shows us your extraordinary, real concern for Miles, because you have understood him, understood that he doesn't want to go on. We know that. He has made it clear to us. I look at Dr. Davies and his eyes meet mine with a look of such compassion I wonder how he can bear to do the work he does, every one of his patients so impaired, their lives so impossibly reduced.

I am grateful to him but I don't think he's right. As it currently exists, the law allows for the Court of Protection to make end-of-life decisions only for people who are clearly diagnosed as in a permanent vegetative state. Miles has been diagnosed MCS, minimally conscious state. The formal definitions could not be more precise: patients in PVS are in a state lacking all consciousness. MCS patients show minimal but definite evidence of consciousness. To apply to the court on Miles's behalf would be to ask for the law to change.

Dr. Davies thinks it is worth looking into, that it is possible the court might consider his case. Miles has not improved and in his view he has no hope of recovery. Both the medical staff treating him and his close relatives believe he does not wish to continue living. The law is an ass, I say to him. Either PVS, lacking all consciousness, or MCS, minimal but definite consciousness and able to suffer. Which life is worse *for the patient*? If only Miles were PVS and knew nothing, felt nothing. We would not be having this conversation.

I thank Dr. Davies again for his concern and tell him I will seek advice on the matter. He leaves and I return to Miles. He is still asleep in his usual position in the day room, tucked away behind the pillar and facing out into the garden. I pull up a chair next to him and take out my book to read. I can't read. He looks so peaceful asleep, his face in repose void of any pain. In the background the television is blaring out, MTV and gyrating girl dancers providing the backdrop for a strutting, bejeweled rapper. The music thumps through the room. From where I'm sitting I can see two of the patients whose chairs are facing the screen, Ray and Alex. Like Miles, both men are MCS, but unlike Miles their vision is intact. They are watching the dancers with interest and, it is obvious, with pleasure, Alex with his sly, quiet smile and Ray waving his arms about and grinning wildly.

I watch them with a sickening envy. If you were to ask them, I do not think either of these two men would wish to end their lives, despite the catastrophe that has decimated them. Ray's moods are complex and much of the time his unhappiness is painfully obvious, but the joy he expresses when seeing his son overrides everything—in those moments he clearly loves, would celebrate, being alive. Alex I have never seen look even mildly unhappy or uncomfortable. He appears content with his life as it is, sitting in his wheelchair with his arms folded, observing the world around him with his quick, dark eyes or humoring the carers when they tease him fondly. You like the pretty girls, don't you, Alex, they say and he giggles delightedly. They're right; Marina and Claudia find his observation of them unsettling, for somehow he conveys a lewd interest. And why not? If it gives him pleasure, it does no harm.

Turning back to Miles I take his hand in mine, gently so as not to wake him, and as I feel his living warmth something deep inside me tears in half. I have failed him. I have not been able to help him. His predicament has been too profound for me. With a new dead-ened anger I think: What Miles has to suffer is greater than most of the abhorrent things humanity has inflicted on itself throughout the ages. Being stoned to death, burned at the stake, drawn and quartered, crucified, is to endure a horror that is, mercifully, finite. Six hours on the cross seems infinitely more bearable. The impo-tence of my anger, the thing that cannot be squared, is the knowl-edge that it was the laudable, civilized, humane response to Miles's accident that has put him in this position. Modern medicine and technology saved him from dying but could not give him back a life worth living. I think of the words I read in a legal journal on the sub-ject of the Mental Capacity Act: profound cognitive impairment as a result of traumatic brain injury leads to "a twilight zone of suspended animation where death commences while life, in some form, continues." In some form. When we talk of the sanctity of life we think of *life*, not existence in some form. For someone like Miles, to lack autonomy and the capacity for self-determination renders life meaningless.

And if, by any wild chance, the Court of Protection allows Miles to end this existence, the death it authorizes will be barbaric. The doctors will be given permission to stop hydration and nutrition, setting in motion a process that can take anything from ten days to three weeks or more before his body, starved and dehydrated, finally gives up. The doctors may treat his distress, but despite having permission to end his life they may not hasten his death in the way a dog would be relieved of its suffering. It seems pure cowardice on the part of the legal system. One precise dose of barbiturates, given by a doctor who understood and cared for Miles and with all the family present, would give him, at least, an easeful death.

I wish Miles had died the beautiful, violent death he faced that ice-clear morning. Then it would have been as it should, a quick, brilliantly lit thing, a leap for joy into the glittering sunshine and the high blue air. No suffering, no pain, just an end, clean and quick, like his clean, quick, brilliant mind.

The music continues its inane background thump. Miles's hand is wet with my tears. He is still asleep. Taking a tissue from my bag I dry his hands and kiss him on the cheek. I should go home and reassemble myself.

THE PERSON I need to speak to is Matthew, Dr. Jensen. I want to know his views on Dr. Davies's comments. He is the doctor most familiar with Miles; he talks to him, and talks about him to us, just as if he is still the person he used to be, and I see Miles responding to Matthew's quietly authoritative voice with a particular attention, his body stilled, intent on listening.

On my way into Gael Lodge the next afternoon I see him in the distance and we arrange to meet at the end of his rounds; he says he will come and find me in Miles's room when he's finished. Miles is awake in the day room as I arrive, sitting in his chair with the bleak, resigned, fed-up expression he mostly has nowadays, and as I hear myself greeting him brightly as usual the inanity of what I'm saying reverberates through me. Anything other than acknowledging the hopelessness of his mood and his situation feels like a betrayal, a betrayal of the honest and direct relationship we have always had. By not acknowledging the truth I am also infantilizing him, and yet to speak the truth is simply not possible.

Miles is asleep when Matthew finally comes to find me. Even so, I don't want to have the discussion in Miles's presence and so Matthew finds us an empty office. As I start to tell him what Dr. Davies has said, the reality of what I'm saying confronts me afresh: I want Miles, my precious oldest child, my extraordinary, beloved Miles who has so enriched my life, I want him to be allowed to die. No: face the truth. I want someone to be allowed to end his life. I am unhinged; I am no longer normal. What mother can let herself think like this? In the silence that follows Matthew looks at me in the way I have so often seen him, listening, observing, but not judging. Dr. Davies has spoken to me, too, he says. I share his belief that Miles's frustration at his situation has made his life intolerable for him now. He understands, and I believe he does not want to continue. However, he is not PVS and even though we all may think it is clearly in his best interests, I do not think a court would allow withdrawal of nutrition and hydration. Unfortunately I don't believe they would see the futility of Miles's present situation in the same way. I have watched you fighting for Miles's life, and I understand why you would now be prepared to fight the case for his death. But you have all been through so much already, and this application would be a protracted process, long and difficult and, I believe, ultimately unsuccessful.

Whatever Matthew's views of the court, I am not unhinged, I am not abnormal. He cares for Miles, and he understands.

SOME YEARS AGO, after Miles and I had both read *The Diving Bell and the Butterfly*, we discussed the tragic events of the story and our admiration for Jean-Dominique Bauby's extraordinary lack of self-pity. I remember we were sitting on the veranda of our house in France. It was early evening, the light was softening over the hills and sea below us, bats swooping under the eaves. We were having our first glass of St. Raphaël, an aromatic local aperitif which none of the others likes but we loved, served on cubes of ice with a quarter of a lemon squeezed in first to counteract the heavy sweetness. Ever since he was a small boy we had loved our talks together, the sense of intuitive intimacy in whatever we discussed. We talked now about the horror of being sentient but unable to communicate. He thought there could be nothing worse and in those circumstances he would not want to be kept alive; he was emphatic about that. I agreed. Now I know there is something worse: to be partially sentient, and unable to communicate.

Miles's partially sentient self—is it the same self as before? If it is a different self, is he still the same person? The children and I drew up a list together once with a friend of Miles's. It was a list of what had defined Miles, and what defines him now.

Before	After
A protector	Defenseless
Determined	Helpless
Powerful	Vulnerable
Intellectual	Brain-damaged
Decisive	Unable to make decisions
Strategic thinker	Unable to think ahead
Articulate	Mute
Witty	Mute
Funny	Sad
Proactive	Unable to initiate
Irascible	Long-suffering
Impatient	Long-suffering
Artistic	Impaired vision
Enjoyer of good food	Unable to swallow

We could have continued; the point was that in every conceivable way we could think of Miles had been rendered the opposite by his accident.

Now something else comes to mind, to complete the list:

To be	Not to be

WHEN MILES WAS thirteen he was chosen to play Hamlet in the annual school play. The actors' parents helped backstage if they had the time and I was put in charge of doing the makeup. It was huge fun for me—small boys between nine and thirteen are a joyful species—but the English master was serious in his aim of showing what his boys could rise to; he told me he had always wanted to produce *Hamlet* and knew when he first taught Miles aged ten that he had found his man, as he put it. The school gym was adjacent to the main hall where the production took place and a number of thick mattresses were laid out on the floor for the boys to sit on while they waited to go on stage. I would wait there to touch up their makeup if necessary, and I have fond memories—I think of Ophelia, a slight eleven-year-old as pretty as a girl in his pale makeup and long white dress, coming off stage and in repressed exuberance taking a flying leap onto a mattress with a resounding tearing of lace.

But at thirteen Miles was beginning to leave that exuberance behind. The painful clouds of adolescence were lowering on the horizon and with them came sudden unexpected squalls of introspection and self-doubt. The newness of them informed his delivery and Shakespeare's words were expressed with a moving rawness quite different from that of a more mature actor. Now when I read those words they have quite another resonance for me: To be, or not to be, that is the question . . . To die—to sleep, No more: and by a sleep to say we end the heartache . . .

I HAVE MADE an appointment to see an eminent barrister, a Queen's Counsel who specializes in Court of Protection and medical decisions. The children and I meet with my solicitor Brian and his assistant at the barrister's chambers and make small talk as we wait. Brian has advised me kindly throughout the raft of administrative measures I have had to deal with in my position as Miles's legal guardian and I know he is concerned about this new situation. He is involved with both his local church and local hospice and I am sure it runs against his belief. What he would not understand is the bitter irony in me feeling that I am about to appear before a judge of the highest court to plead *for* Miles's life, not its ending, as though everything that has happened over the past four years now hinges on me to resolve.

I have done my homework for this meeting as requested, have sent the QC in advance a summary of Miles's life and his character before the accident and a chronological assessment of his life and treatment since the accident. The barrister arrives and ushers us into the meeting room. He looks every part the classical lawyer, silver-haired, distinguished, but his manner is immediately informal and he puts us at our ease as we hesitantly seat ourselves around the intimidatingly large and gleaming boardroom table. He is empathetic about Miles's predicament. He asks us all our views and listens respectfully. He has clearly read everything we sent him and he has got the measure of Miles's character.

By the end of the meeting he has reached the opinion that he is prepared to take on Miles's case. Having listened to what we have all had to say and having read the two doctors' reports, both Dr. Davies and Dr. Jensen, as well as the reports from Miles's time at Putney and Addenbrooke's in Cambridge, he is of the opinion that the court might consider Miles's case sympathetically. From these reports he understands that Miles is not aware all of the time but is definitely aware some of the time. He tells us that, as a barrister, he has seen many families who interpret signs from loved ones optimistically, but it seems to him that we are not such a family. He understands the irony of our situation, that we had spent our time since Miles's accident arguing that he should be receiving better treatment but that now we are fighting for Miles's life and his suffering to be ended, which is a total shift from our initial feelings. He understands that it is no longer in Miles's best interests to continue; were he in the family's situation, he would feel the same. If we are prepared to face the very difficult and long process of an application to the court, he is willing to help us. We should discuss among ourselves what we have learned of the process and whether we still wish to go ahead and instruct him.

As we leave the chambers and walk together down the Embankment to Charing Cross, the Thames flowing calmly alongside us, I think about that sunlit walk four years ago along the river in Innsbruck. So much has happened, and so little.

THE GRAVITY OF our situation is onerous. Our lives, the children's and mine, are weighted with the knowledge of what we may be embarking on, though there is no dilemma as to its rightness. It is a mission of mercy. I speak about it with a few very close and trusted friends, Jennifer, Matthew, Andrew, a lawyer, and his wife, Madeleine; their support and advice is invaluable. I'm given the name of a rehabilitation expert, Dr. Lazard, who has acted in end-of-life cases as the patient's so-called litigation friend for the Court of Protection's official solicitor and I contact his secretary. She tells me a good time to call him and when I do we speak on the phone for over an hour; though he doesn't know Miles or me, his experience allows him to understand the situation precisely and he is unexpectedly supportive and sympathetic. But his advice is clear: the law allows end-of-life requests to apply only to patients who are PVS. He does not believe a Court of Protection judge would grant the request. In his view it would be a long, painful, expensive process for nothing. And then he confides in me that he knows there is a groundbreaking case going through the court at the moment for a person who is MCS; he can't tell me more than that but we should wait to hear the result before we embark on any proceedings. Call me in six months' time, he says, and I will be able to tell you more.

This news is both reassuring and frustrating. I wish I could know the story behind the other application, could contact the family to share our experience and give them our support. If they are successful it will pave the way for our application, just as the initial PVS case of Tony Bland, a victim of the Hillsborough stadium disaster, changed the law in 1993. If they are not successful, Miles's situation will be even more difficult. We must wait and Miles must continue to endure his existence.

RAY HAS BEEN in and out of hospital for the past month, and one day Tracy asks me what the word *palliative* means. I've been told a palliative care doctor is coming from a hospice to see Ray, she says. He doesn't need a new bloody doctor. What's he coming for? She has no idea what it means but she knows what a hospice is and she is alarmed and angry.

I don't think it's for me to tell her that the doctors believe Ray's life is nearing its end. All I can do is suggest that she telephones the hospice, explain who she is, and ask to speak to the palliative care doctor who is going to see him. I hope the doctor will be understanding and undeterred by her anger. I wish I could protect her from the horror that must surely engulf her when Ray dies, for I fear her love for him is the one stable thing in her life. It has been an illuminating experience, a privilege, to witness the courage of this young woman whose life has been so narrowed down in every way, and her refusal to accept that the tragedy of Ray's situation should have made him any different.

Four days later Ray died. I was away for a long weekend and Joseph told me what happened. Ray had been readmitted to the hospital and then was sent back to Gael Lodge. There was nothing more that could be done for him and he was put on a syringe driver of morphine with no further treatment prescribed. When it became clear he was dying Tracy spent the night in his room, and in the morning she went to Rachel to explain that she would now have to call his family because in the Romany tradition all his relatives must come to see him before he dies.

The first one arrived at 10:30 in the morning and by the end of the day more than two hundred people had come to see Ray.

All of them were travelers, large men and women who crammed themselves into his small upstairs room while their children ran about through the day rooms and in the garden, shouting happily at each other and throwing snowballs at the windows. The adults brought in alcohol and smoked in the ward. One man fell over in Ray's room and cut his head so badly the nurse on duty had to attend to him; another fell off the chair in Rachel's office while asking her to phone Croydon police station because he was on bail and due to report there in an hour—could she explain to them that his brother was dying so he wouldn't be able to make it? Despite the care staff putting up a large makeshift notice warning that the elevator could take no more than six people, in the early evening it finally broke down completely between the two floors with ten people in it. One of the men tried to force open the metal doors, cut his hand, and bled all over the elevator.

Throughout the day Tracy remained at Ray's side. Her behavior was impeccably restrained during this final time; she understood what was happening. Little Ray was not with her; he played with the other children. Around seven that evening Ray died and the last travelers took their leave.

The ward is small and there is only one elevator. Repairing it is an expensive and complicated procedure. Luckily Miles's room is on the ground floor, but for the next few days the patients upstairs are unable to be brought down for treatment.

Ray's death affects us all deeply. The ward feels a much colder place without him, without Tracy and little Ray, their exuberance and their innocence.

SIX MONTHS HAVE passed and I call Dr. Lazard. He says that the MCS case he had told me about is still under review and he does not think it will be resolved for some considerable time, probably not until next year. He reiterates his view that there is absolutely no point in our applying to the court until we know the result.

Miles's mood is increasingly bleak and nothing we do appears to distract or engage him. Claudia returns from a visit one day in tears. He seemed so depressed, so utterly desolate, Mum, that I just couldn't help slipping into the old thing of telling him how well he was doing and how he would recover. And then the same thing happened as before—as I said the words he did that awful tensing up he does, his legs lifting rigid and his head pushed forward out of the headrest and he glared at me with such undisguised fury it was obvious what he was saying, he was telling me to stop the lie. It was frightening. I felt I had to apologize and I said, I'm so sorry, Miles, it's not true. You understand your situation. I know what you want, and I'm going to look into ways of doing it for you. I will help you get out of this. As I said that he relaxed back into the chair and closed his eyes in the way he does when we've understood him and the effort is over. His anger was shocking, Mum. He still feels so passionately. I can't bear him suffering like this.

None of us can. I see how it is affecting Will and Marina too, the solemn tenderness with which they engage with him and their extreme sadness after each visit, the sense of defeat. We try to make a point of having Miles's friends around on Sundays, so that his visit home is lightened with outside banter to lift the atmosphere. But while the children and I continue to wait for the results of the Court of Protection case, our mood is darkening. How can I describe the fact that we now sit around the kitchen table and discuss how to end Miles's life ourselves? We have heard that it is quite possible to buy the necessary fatal drug over the Internet, but the dread-filled, restraining fear is that we don't know the precise, correct dose. I have a number of friends who are doctors. Could I ask them? Do we really have the courage to follow this through? Our desire to help Miles is now accompanied by a growing anger at the realization that one man or one woman, a judge, a person who does not know Miles and most likely has no personal experience of traumatic brain damage, will be the ultimate arbiter of his life. How can his or her personal beliefs not influence the outcome? It is a deeply sensitive, personal, *moral* issue; it should not be a legal one.

I think of the moment when Miles pressed his thumb down on my hand under the pergola, his look of deep, yearning pity. I can't help but believe that at the beginning, in Innsbruck, he stayed for our sake, the ultimate protector. He has suffered enough for that decision. It is our duty now to let him go.

In cold desperation one morning I contact Dignitas. As I dial the number I sense that the line I am crossing with this call is irrevocable. I explain the situation to the person who answers the phone, though all the time I am aware that Miles will certainly not be eligible because he is not able to express his intention to end his life or to undertake the last act himself, either to swallow or to administer the drug via his gastric tube. The woman I am speaking to confirms my fears, but she is so understanding and sympathetic that I find myself crying on the phone with this stranger. I feel so helpless, I tell her. My son falls outside every avenue of hope—he is not PVS so he doesn't fit the British legal qualification, he is not eligible for Dignitas, and he can't do it himself. Yet he is aware enough to suffer, and to convey his suffering to us and to the doctors treating him. I wish I could help you, she says. Maybe in the future you will be able to help me personally, I tell her. I strongly support the view that, when facing the end of life, if it is what a person wishes, he or she should be allowed to choose the time and the manner in which they die. I do not think it should be for the state to decide.

Putting down the phone I think: I have cut the very last thread of hope. We are in a different place now. And then I think: maybe all four of us should hold the fatal syringe together. We will gift Miles this last thing as one, loving him as one. Let the judges do with that what they will. Put the four of us in jail. How the tabloids would love it. Perhaps it would finally make somebody understand the wretchedness and indignity of the lives so many people are currently condemned to live.

TALKING TO JENNIFER I tell her of the call to Dignitas. She is one of my closest friends and I am losing her to the breast cancer that has now metastasized, though for the moment she is in remission. She is a doctor, a consultant psychiatrist. She has known Miles since he was a boy, has three children of her own, and the prospect of losing her warmth, vitality, humor, wisdom, I cannot absorb. I will do it for Miles, she says. While I lay in the hospital bed after my last treatment I could only think of Miles. I understood, for a while, what he is going through. I had to ask the nurse to stop the hands on the clock above the door—I could not endure the seconds passing by. Time was a terrible thing, unbearable. I would gladly release him from that and you know I no longer have to be concerned with jeopardizing my career. But I cannot let her; her remaining life is fragile and I don't want her to take on such a responsibility. It is entirely ours to resolve; and yet we cannot bring ourselves to act.

In a way Jennifer's offer clarifies my dilemma, our dilemma. The desire to help Miles is clear and fervent, but it is a matter of principle, a thing of the mind. The physical act, however we use words, language, to describe our desire for it, is different. It is not our place. We need instruction; we are not doctors, we do not know how. We fear getting it wrong. Compassion is not enough; skill is required too. I have followed the story in the press of a mother who tried to end the life of her son who suffered a traumatic brain injury when, following a pub fight, he was taken to the hospital by ambulance but managed to open the back doors and fell out while it was still moving. Two months after his injury she injected him with street heroin in an attempt to end his life, but instead he suffered a heart attack. He was resuscitated, following which his disabilities were even more profound and he was now deemed to be in a vegetative state. She was banned from seeing him, but some months later she gained entry to his rehabilitation unit under an assumed name and this time the dose of heroin succeeded. At her trial the doctors said that her son was showing signs of possible recovery before her first attempt disabled him further. She was jailed, after appeal, for five years. I do not identify with this woman, though I feel immense pity for her. I find it incomprehensible that she did not give her son a chance to recover, that her first injection of heroin took place only two months after his injury. But then I do not know her story.

If the law were changed, if consent were required and properly given both by the doctors treating Miles and by us, his family, then Miles could be released without dilemma, helped by his doctor as he should be and allowed to go gracefully and painlessly. It is what he wants, but it cannot happen. Perhaps in fifty, a hundred years' time we will have learned to accept death when it is necessary, instead of keeping it in abeyance at all costs.

VI

It is the Easter weekend and spring has come early. How blithely the year comes around without Ron, the new buds and growth disconcerting in their tenderness. We bring Miles home on Good Friday and, wheeling him out into the garden, we set his chair in the shade and draw up the deck chairs alongside him in the sun for ourselves. How glad I am the children are all here, books and newspapers piled next to us on the grass and the peace of this garden behind its high walls, all luxuries to be savored. But Miles is uncomfortable and tetchy, coughing more than usual and finding it difficult to clear his throat. I fetch the hated suction machine, draw out the phlegm from his mouth and the back of his throat, and watch it fill the machine's container. As I stand over him my mind wanders back and I think about how at the beginning Miles would obstruct us, biting the hard end of the tube and not letting go, and then suddenly, today, as he looks up at me with the helpless passivity with which he now allows us to do this thing, it is too much to bear. Stopping the machine I put away the tube and bend down and put my arms around him to bury my face in the curve of his neck as the familiar wave of pain engulfs me. When it begins to ebb away I realize Claudia has left what she was doing and is here too, her arms around us both in a silent embrace. Miles is starting to cough again, so we move and I resume the suctioning. You're a darling, I say to Claudia. My back aches slightly; hugging Miles when he is in his wheelchair is never comfortable, you have to bend forward in such a way that the small of the back takes all your weight and I've never found how to solve the problem.

ON SUNDAY MORNING Marina and I drive to Gael Lodge and we talk about that first Easter in Innsbruck, the earliest memories, fragile now with retrospective knowledge of our naïveté. The colorful stalls on the cobbled plazas of the Old Town selling painted eggs, elaborate breads, marzipan cakes, stout men and women dressed in their surreal Easter rabbit costumes regaling the children, the shock of confronting the festivities as we walked through the April sunshine to visit Miles lying unreachable on his hospital bed. The fantasy, it turned out, that none of us could suppress, that he would wake and rise up from his bed and talk to us, tell us where he had been, what he had experienced. We were sure that could happen. How strange it is now to imagine ourselves then; we are no longer the same people.

ARRIVING AT GAEL Lodge we find the in-house service in full swing in the main day room, wheelchairs drawn up and carers in attendance. Some of the residents are able to sing and the priest is helping them along in his splendid baritone. There are bowls of small chocolate eggs dotted around and a lunchtime barbecue in the garden is planned; today is going to be fun for the residents who can join in.

When we get home the day starts peacefully. Miles is awake and we all chat to each other, reading bits out from the Sunday papers and trying to find things that might amuse or interest him. But then the day deteriorates, his cough constant and the effort to clear his throat becoming more and more difficult. By early afternoon he is exhausted, but his coughing has not been followed by the usual roar of anger and frustration; instead he coughs, chokes, arms and legs stiffening with spasticity and his face growing purple before he manages the final gasp of air, then silence, broken only by heavy breathing as his limbs slowly retract.

The silence is such a marked change that I am alarmed, his passivity, his slumped calm like the deadened, glassy inertia of someone at the deepest reaches of their depression. I take his hand and find myself pleading with him. Miles, darling, please don't go away like this now. We are doing everything we can to help you, though I know how unendurably slow it seems. I cannot bear to lose him like this before he has gone.

Will and I drive him back and I tell Jana of my concern. She will call the doctor on duty. I know there is the ever-present danger of chest infections turning to pneumonia for people who are bedbound. We exist in a strange paradox. While we dread the ordeal he endures day after day and long for his release, the reality of his becoming ill and suffering further is terrifying, to be prevented at all costs.

ON EASTER MONDAY the infection escalates. Claudia and I arrive in the morning hoping to bring him home, but it's clearly not possible. He's still in bed, flushed and sweating. When he coughs he struggles to get his breath, but he does not look fearful; it is I who am afraid. There is something about him that makes me feel his acceptance of this is willed, for I am aware of that fierce determination that used to be his defining characteristic, a sense that at last he is back in control. Eventually he falls asleep and we stay on in his room, watching him, checking his oxygen levels, reluctant to leave. Matthew is coming and the nursing here is skilled; there is no more we can do but we don't want to go. He sleeps for the rest of the day and in the evening we leave.

Before going to bed I call the ward and speak to the nurse on duty, who tells me Miles is sleeping well, despite his raised temperature. We will keep an eye on him through the night, she reassures me.

TUESDAY MORNING, THE Easter weekend over and the children back at work. Fran, an old friend of mine who lives in Hong Kong, is in London and has asked to see Miles. Our two families would often join together for Christmas in the Alps. Her son, Paddy, became a great friend of Miles and Will, little boys creating snow forts only to destroy them in furious battles and then, as teenagers, snowboarding, finding ever more perilous jumps. When Paddy fell into a crevasse off-piste Miles grabbed hold of him, clinging on while Will left to find help. The story still haunts Fran, though she laughs as she remembers that instead of falsely reassuring Paddy when he asked, terrified, Am I going to die? Miles responded frankly, I don't know.

This will be the first time Fran has seen Miles since his accident. I call her and tell her that he is unwell, but I can hear how upset she is at the thought of not seeing him. I won't stay long, she says, I would like just to see him again. I've thought about him so much over the years. He was exceptional. She continues and I'm in tears when I put down the phone. I'm reminded afresh of the waste, the senseless waste.

Jana is in Miles's room when I arrive. He seems more settled, she says, though I'm a bit concerned we haven't been able to lower his temperature. Again the unspoken fear is pneumonia, the sudden escalating of his chest infection. Miles looks more drowsy than usual, neither asleep nor awake, and his breathing appears more shallow, but an infection always does that, especially in his compromised condition. Matthew has seen him and for the moment there is nothing more that can be done. At least, as drowsy as he is, he does not look as though he's in any discomfort. Fran's impending visit may not be as difficult as I thought.

I should not have worried about her. She is immediately at ease with Miles, goes straight to his side and quietly and warmly engages with him. He appears to rouse a little at the sound of her distinctive voice, but it's short-lived. His face resumes the bleak, resigned expression he has nowadays and he closes his eyes. She is undeterred, pulls a chair up to the bed and, holding his hand, begins to reminisce about his escapades with Paddy when they were small boys. Maybe Miles will enjoy that. As I always do when friends come to see him, I'll leave them on their own. I'm going to make some tea, I tell her. Call me when you feel you've had enough time. I'll be in the day room.

The making of tea here is a ritual, a necessary punctuation of the time. I don't want it particularly, nor the stodgily sweet biscuit I take from the guest biscuit tin, but the process is soothing. I will be alone in the small cubbyhole of a kitchen off the ground-floor ward and as I wait for the kettle to come to the boil I can stand with my back to the world outside and just for those few minutes let my mind go blank. Then the swirling of the tea bag in the boiled water, concentrating on ensuring I get the right color and strength before removing it and adding the milk. Putting the milk away in the small fridge, finally selecting a biscuit, the ritual is over and I set off, no different, I suppose, from tea or coffee breaks in offices everywhere.

Walking back into the day room there is the usual social banter of being here, greeting a nurse or carer or relative, engaging with the residents from other wards who sometimes wander in. Really I lead a double life; this is my other social world now, a gentle world, a place of curious harmony. There are tiffs and crises, but everyone is safe here and people are kind. All the while the residents who belong in this high-dependency ward are ranged around the edges of the day room, facing each other in their wheelchairs, their world a different one, mute, excluded even from this.

Eventually I pull up a chair and take out my iPod and something to read from my bag. Unwinding the knotted earphones I put them in, scroll through the titles to find something, and stop at Adele, recently added to the list for me by Marina. "Set Fire to the Rain" is playing, Adele's pure, rich voice taking me with her, when I realize Fran is standing at the entrance to the day room, calling me urgently, Lu, Lu, come now, come right now. She looks strange, something about her eyes conveying more than the words, her face ice pale, and then she is calling for a nurse, a doctor, Help, please, she calls, as I run past her to Miles's room.

Please somebody come, he needs help, Fran cries, I think he's choking, somebody, please, Miles is not breathing properly. I run to the bed and lean in to lift him, hold him up, Miles, Miles, are you all right? What's happening? What's wrong, my darling? His face is darkened, his breathing rapid and shallow, but his expression is calm, clear, as though he is seeing through me, past me, far beyond this place and the moment to something infinitely understandable at last. I love you, Miles. A long shuddering breath, his eyes wide open so deep green, so deeply peaceful I freeze. I remember Ron, his last breath, his eyes. I don't understand. It is too sudden. Is Miles dying? Is this what's happening? I know he wants to go but I don't want him to go now, I want him to stay, I cannot endure the loss. I have not confronted the loss. My mind cuts loose and from somewhere far above me I look down and observe a woman holding a young man in her arms, see his strong face, his clear jawline, the thick dark hair and long lashes, so dark now resting on his paling cheek. The woman, me, I am gazing down at them both.

The silence is absolute.

There is no next breath.

Miles's breath erased, breath ephemeral as consciousness.

THE DOOR OPENS and the silence is broken in a blur of activity as Matthew and Jana enter the room. Matthew strides towards the bed and I step aside as he bends over Miles, speaking urgently to Jana, who has joined him on the other side. I am suspended, useless, I don't know what's happening and I can't help. Eventually Matthew stands up and looks at me and then I know. Now I want to hold Miles and I climb straight up onto the high bed, the first time I have ever done that. Aware how preposterous and undignified I must look but not caring. Why haven't I done this before? All those times I could have hugged him properly like I am now, my arms around his strong back, my face in the sweet hollow of his neck; it seems unbearably sad that I have never done this before. I'm so sorry, my darling. I'm crying, a strange new sound. I love you, Miles. I love you, my darling, darling Miles. Lying there, even now his face cooling to stone, his chest, his heart beneath my heart holding its warmth. He wanted to go; I must not hold him back. You can go now, my darling, you can leave us, you need stay no longer. You have stayed long enough and we will survive now. You've taught us how to survive. I tighten my arms around him and we have melded, together we are crossing the divide and he is leading me, taking me with him, our bodies on the bed in the small room that is too full of people all disappearing far, far beneath us. Now there is only emptiness and absolute peace. I am void of all feeling; it is the pure peace of nothingness.

Miles, my son, has died.

Some time later—I have no sense of how long I have been there, with him and not with him—I climb down off the bed. The room seems strangely light, the silence immense. Huge Jana hugs me. Fran is sitting down on the only chair in the room, her head in her hands. She looks up and she is crying, Oh Lu, I didn't understand, I didn't know what was happening. I knew he had a chest infection, I thought it was just that, I'm so sorry. Her words float in the silence. I put my arms around her, detached, aware only of this sense of intense calm and emptiness. Please, Fran. He wanted to go. I must call the children and David. I call them, their shock, they will all come immediately.

I can't access what I feel. I remember the Sunday five years ago, watching myself sleep-walking, the same out-of-bodyness. There are things to do. Later I will talk to Rachel, ask about undertakers, know what happens next. But for now we will stay until they come to take Miles's body away. I don't remember any more.

I HAVE MADE an appointment with the undertakers to see Miles in the mortuary. At the end at Gael Lodge he was surrounded by people and by all the paraphernalia of his damaged existence. I want to see him again, unencumbered, on his own. I did not need to see Ron again; his death at home was private and complete. I had told the undertakers to come and collect Ron's body in the evening and we had time to be alone with him, at peace in the quiet room and his death so gentle.

Marina wants to come with me. It is a comfort, for there is something, we are not sure what, that feels shared in our relationship with Miles. Perhaps, we say, as we drive to see him, perhaps it is his particular protectiveness of us. A kind of paternal protectiveness, Marina says, even of you. Arriving at the undertakers we are both guarded, this thing so private, Miles so much *ours* that it feels wrong to have to ask to see him. Who does his body belong to now?

A middle-aged woman is at the reception and she is expecting us. Her manner is restrained without being falsely respectful and I am grateful to her. She leads us down the stairs to the viewing room. You may stay as long as you like, she says, and disappears.

We stand still for a moment, bracing ourselves, taking it in. The lighting is subdued, the atmosphere hushed, reverent, ecclesiastical. Two great vases of white lilies are set on gilded wooden pedestals, their scent filling the room, obscuring faint echoes of something more clinical. Above them hangs a painting of a sun setting over a darkened ocean in a rapturous splash of greens and gold and pinks, the well-intentioned metaphor ghastly in its sentimentality. Heavy purple curtains are suspended from rails that cross the ceiling, which I see can be pulled for further privacy. In the center of the space stands a table, the top and sides draped in the same purple velvet as the curtains. A wooden coffin lies on the table, pale grained ash with brass handles; I recognize it as the one I chose from the brochure for Miles.

The absolute shock of seeing him. I had thought I was braced for this, but I am not. He lies on his back in the coffin, dressed in the dark green shirt and sweater I had given the undertaker. He looks so *present*, so strong, his face perfectly composed. Realigned in death to what it had been, there is no single indication or sign of the past five years, all the damage, the tension gone. Erased in death, no trace of it remains. Such strange beauty, a body without breath. His face freshly shaved. So cold when I kiss it, freezer cold.

I think, here he is on display again, as he was in Innsbruck that first day all those years ago, a magnificent specimen of young manhood. His presence is palpable, a field of energy that emanates from his stilled body. There is a sense of something distinct and contained, as it had been in the hospital room, though this time there is no conflict. In the first instance death was defeated but now it is his choice; he desired this end. What word is there to describe Miles as he is in death? *Awe*, above all.

Awe for him, for the grace that resides in his tangible, residual power; awe for death, its omnipotence. Its unequivocal magnificence. And with this comes a sudden and unexpected sense of deep calm and comfort: we are alive and then we die and all of it is magnificent and *right*. Grief will resume, but for now, standing here in this alien underground room, I am suffused with reverence for the life that Miles was given to live and lived so intensely.

Marina takes my hand as we leave. He loved us, too, she says. That is ours to keep.

A WEEK LATER and Miles's funeral, the day as beautiful as Ron's, a sky the texture of watercolor blue. The crematorium chapel is local to Gael Lodge but none of us has noticed it before, hidden away from the high street behind what appears to be a lush private park but is in fact a tree-lined cemetery. It rained last night and as we drive up the long driveway towards the chapel everything looks newly washed, the clean gray of the old chapel at the end and the surrounding headstones set against a verdant green of massed sycamores and flowering chestnuts. How can it be, that Miles is dead and yet the world renews itself, quivers with fresh life.

Madeleine, a friend and interfaith minister who has known Miles since he was a small boy, takes the service. We are a small group, the children, David and his two brothers, Amelia and Belinda, my nephew Sean and a few close friends of Miles's; we want this funeral to be private. Later we'll hold a big memorial at home and celebrate Miles with all his friends and the carers and medical staff who know him so well.

The coffin stands alone in front of us, draped in the same cream and lime roses I chose for Ron, their velvety lusciousness comforting. It is a strange thing, knowing how Miles looks now, lying there under the plain ash and roses; I know what he is wearing, the precise unearthly coldness of him. I can see that expression on his face, imagine him listening intently the way he does as he hears Will and Marina read from his book and registers the ringing, defiant ending Claudia gives to E. E. Cummings's "Buffalo Bill":

Jesus
he was a handsome man
and what i want to know is
how do you like your blue-eyed boy
Mister Death

MADELEINE TALKS ABOUT Miles with tenderness and a deep understanding of his and our predicament throughout the past five years. Intimate, personal, and loving, this is a profound validation of Miles. He really *was* exceptional, extraordinary, she says. Miles was so richly gifted in every sense, his crystal-sharp mind, his joy-filled physicality. She describes his moments of deep connection with what he called the "nameless One," how he transformed them into poetry, music, right into the way he lived; she talks of his joyful seriousness and his clear, honest, searching inquiry, always stripping away nonsense, claptrap, mumbo jumbo. And then, she says, there's Miles the hilarious spontaneous rapper: who else would rhyme *Chaucer* with *flying saucer*? She has been listening to his electronic music, not the sort of music she normally listens to, but she is absorbed by it, sees the connection with his writing that marries mysticism with quantum physics and language. "A Quantum Leap" she names the composition we are about to hear and then a recording of the music begins to play. Hesitant and tender at first, the hauntingly eerie electronic sounds start to merge and rise and unfurl themselves until Miles's wit and wild exuberance are filling this old gray chapel, his energy ricocheting against the walls in bursts of color that defy the final silence he endured for so long.

SOUTHWARK CORONER'S COURT, weeks later. Though Miles's death was the result of his initial brain injury compromising his health, it was nevertheless sudden and unexpected, a situation that requires a coroner's inquest. His assistant explains to me over the phone that it is a formality and that I don't have to attend; the coroner dealt with the matter at the time and released Miles's body for the funeral. Perhaps she is concerned to protect me, but of course I must go, I tell her. I can't endure the idea of Miles's end being discussed by strangers in an anonymous court without anyone present for him.

Walking from London Bridge Station to the court I think she may have been right. The pain I have been carrying with me since Miles died is melting, rising, forcing itself to the surface and I can't quell it, my face contorted and running with tears as I scrabble in my handbag for tissues and sunglasses and then must stand still to take a deep breath and hold on to myself. An elderly woman passing by looks at me with concern and then distaste; I suppose I appear mad or drunk or both, a woman hunched crying in the middle of the pavement. You're right, I think, I must pull myself together, I cannot let Miles down and I am due at the court in five minutes. What you don't realize, you old bat, is that everything is coming to a head; the horror of the past five years and now this, this final thing, yet another claim on Miles's life. For five years his life has been other people's business. I just want him to be left in peace at last. Anger helps, as it always does; the tears stop coming and I arrive at the court more or less intact.

My anger is entirely misjudged. From the moment I arrive at the court everybody I deal with is unfailingly kind and considerate. When the coroner's assistant comes out of her office to greet me her kindness disarms me completely and now the tears really come; I can barely breathe. I'm so sorry, I keep saying hopelessly, I'm so sorry, I don't know why this should happen now, I seem to have managed so far. I completely understand, she says, as she hands me a box of tissues from her desk, this is very normal. You have lost your son. Her kindness is matched by the young man whose job it is to show me to the courtroom and the counselor I am surprised to discover has been assigned to accompany me. The coroner himself is exceptional; both a lawyer and a doctor, he reads out Miles's history, deals with the formalities of the inquest, asks me to go into the witness box to answer questions, and does it all with great authority but with such sensitivity and respect for Miles that, far from an intrusion, the process feels like the proper and dignified end to Miles's years of suffering. He talks of Miles's youth, of his career so far and the loss of his potential, and he imagines the distress his plight must have caused the family. His recognition of Miles and of us all is an unexpected validation I will cherish.

THE FORMALITIES OF death have been dealt with, the legal paperwork, the letters, certificates, notifications, and coroner's report, all the paraphernalia of closing down a life. The distractions of organizing the funeral and then, six weeks later, the memorial party are also over, the latter held at home with more than a hundred of Miles's friends arriving and much food and wine and music. All these things, in retrospect, have carried us through the first turbulent, raw months of grief.

There is nothing left to do, and now with his death there comes a silence that is the depth of oceans. Even surrounded by loving family and friends, I feel alone, submerged in my grief. The full impact of Ron's death was muffled by Miles's continuing situation; now as I mourn Miles I am freshly, vividly aware of the loss of Ron. How time passes, how I manage the mundane daily acts of living, I have no idea. Trying to retrieve those memories now there is nothing, only a void.

It is summer and I go out to the house in France and for the first time in over five years I stay longer than a week. I am a double amputee, carrying the constant pain of phantom limbs, convalescing in the sunshine. The children come out to join me and together we reconvene, slowly consolidate our depleted group and we reminisce. For what we do have are our memories of Miles and Ron. We share them, watch Miles running across the grass to leap off the dangerously high garden wall into the pool, or we see him arriving back from the morning bread run, glowing with sweat from having run up the steep hill that leads to the house, his rucksack full of baguettes and flattened croissants. We remember Ron lying in the sun with his Discman, in his element, eyes closed and unconsciously and adorably conducting the music as he listens. We see them both coming back from the supermarket with a box of fresh squid to barbecue, neither having ever cooked them before. Or Miles, in the boiling heat of a summer's night, pulling his mattress into the windowless laundry room and sleeping there so as to shut out the noise of a neighbor's party.

In death Miles returned to his former self, five years receding into bleached-out images of a dreamlike otherworld. Our foremost memories now become those of the vital, powerful Miles, embracing his future, regaling us, enlivening our lives. More vivid than ever, we have those memories back and we indulge ourselves, luxuriate in them. But our mourning is a doubled thing, for the double loss of Miles both as he was and as he became. We have lost the powerful Miles; we have also lost the vulnerable, hurt, sweet Miles that we loved in a different way but quite as much.

The memories do not overlap; they remain separate, distinct. Remembering Miles as he was is accompanied by the fierce agony of knowing how young and *alive* he was at the moment he was cut down, the terrible waste of his vibrant potential; remembering him as he became is to relive the poignancy of his helpless, unalleviated suffering. In the months before Miles died Claudia had described her fear that she was losing the memories of Miles as he had been before the accident. It's distressing, she said, I'm finding them difficult to retrieve. They're being submerged by the Miles we see now. I can't bear the thought of not remembering him active and vital, the old Miles. I don't know what to do to stop it. What she did do was to order ten large photograph albums to be delivered to the house and then spent the following weekends sitting at the kitchen table sorting out thirty years of pictures in chronological order and pasting them into the albums. Only weeks before Miles died my hopeless mess of photos in the old copper trunk was transformed into a coherent memory bank, just in time.

Looking through the later books I'm aware there are no photos of Miles taken after his accident. None of us could bring ourselves to photograph him, just another small way of saving ourselves from confronting his reality. Nothing concrete remains of that time. And suddenly that seems to me a gross and cowardly misrepresentation of Miles's life. We should, we need to honor his years of suffering and not allow them to be forgotten or pushed into the background.

TODAY I READ in the paper that the Court of Protection has refused an application by the family of "M," a severely brain-damaged woman in a minimally conscious state, to withdraw her feeding tube and allow her to die.

This must be the case that Dr. Lazard had told me about. I discover that eight years ago the woman referred to as "M" suffered viral encephalitis, which put her in a coma. Her mother, sister, and partner made the application; they were unanimous in their view that she wished to die. Before her illness she had expressed the view that she would not want to remain alive in such a situation, but they had no proof. She had not taken out an advance directive.

When refusing the application the judge said: "'M' does experience pain and discomfort, and her disability severely restricts what she can do. However, I find she does have some positive experiences." Apparently he had formed this opinion as a result of the care home assistant's claim that "M" cried when she heard Elvis Presley and appeared upset when she heard a Lionel Ritchie love song.

WILL AND I are sorting through Miles's belongings. For three years, since the flat he and Will shared was sold, they have lain untouched in his old room here at home, the door closed; sorting through them remained on my To Do list, the job undone. The pile of books, CDs, personal files, notebooks, music-making paraphernalia, boxing gloves, snowboard and snowboarding gear, motorbike helmet and biking gear, his laptop, speakers, ornaments, wallet, rucksacks, suitcases, briefcase, all an inventory of his former life, and even though I knew he would never use any of these things again, clearing them out remained impossibly final, an admission of the end of hope.

Will and I start off by dividing everything into two piles, to keep and not to keep. The latter pile requires decisions—throw away, give to charity, or sell? We intend to be businesslike about this but very soon we are floored. Every item is a graphic personal remnant of what he was, each thing has a history, evokes a particular memory that spools out into a fresh story. I stand holding the hammered brass bowl I gave him one birthday, when he surprised me by asking for something decorative and surprised me even more by how delighted he was with it. I want to smarten up the flat, he had said. I don't know where to get those kind of home things. Why don't you be my interior decorator? But once he knew where to look his natural flair took over, just as he had personalized his rooms at university. I had not expected him to be domesticated; how he would have loved a home of his own.

We can give his clothes to the hospice shop, I say to Will. That seems simple, but it isn't, each piece as I fold it away releasing a fresh image of how he looked wearing it, how casually he wore his clothes, how little he cared for them. I'd know he'd come home even if I hadn't heard him come in because of the trail of dropped coat, jacket, keys on the floor in the hall, even the jacket of the Paul Smith suit he bought when he began his last job. I remember the ridiculous fun we had choosing it despite his hatred of shopping for clothes, the lunch we treated ourselves to, his exuberance talking about his new job and his future and his protectiveness of a waiter who irritated me by getting the order wrong. Be kind to him, Mum, he's trying hard, he's probably new here. How handsome he looked, finally wearing a smart suit. His dislike of shopping was a family joke, the grumpiness that accompanied it, his decisiveness—that's fine, I'll have that, let's go now—and his incredulity that the girls and I could happily spend half an hour deciding on whether or not we should buy something.

While I sort the clothes, Will goes through the electronic equipment, putting the music-making kit, the keyboard, synthesizer, and other complex-looking instruments aside for safekeeping. It was a shared hobby and they could spend hours riffing together. I imagine them now, the way they sparked off each other's humor, their adorable energetic boyishness I would think, listening to them, no different from their shared excitement dressed up and playing Starsky and Hutch aged five and six. And though I never understood the instruments I loved the haunting futuristic sounds of the digital music they made. Will hasn't done anything with them since the accident and looking at them now I think that their silence—silence altogether—is the purest reflection of our loss. All the particular resonating sounds of Miles silenced, the only noise he could make for the past five years that roar of frustration and misery that we dreaded.

We are almost finished. Around us lie the remains of Miles's life, sorted and labeled in black plastic bags and boxes. Will and I are still intact but we are wrung out and facing us now is the final pile stashed in the corner of the room, the thing we have both been avoiding. Miles's snowboard leans against the wall, its sleek shape and colorful design of snowboarding graffiti still in perfect condition, not a scratch on it. Like a riderless horse after a fall, it stands quietly innocent of the disaster it carried. I don't want it in my house. Would you sell it, Will? I ask. No, he says, I couldn't let someone else use it. I understand; innocent or not, it has bad feng shui now. Next to the board is the battered leather and canvas holdall, still with its easyJet label for LGW, Gatwick, that Ben and Charlie brought back with them from Munich, the bag that Miles packed that Sunday morning. Beside it is a pile of snowboarding clothes, boots, gloves, hat, scarf, the wide waterproof trousers and zipped jacket and, Oh Jesus, Will, I say, that's the helmet. This is what Miles was wearing when he fell. Will puts his arm around me as I pick up the helmet. How slight a thing it looks. How lethal. I turn it over, run my hand around the padded interior, weigh its lightness in my hand. His brain rotated. Not even a scratch or dent on it. Get rid of it now, get rid of these things, throw them all away, immediately. Bending down to scoop them up I see underneath them all his vest, one of the cream-colored thermal ones I bought so long ago for the boys when they were teenagers and we still had the chalet in the Alps, and as I stand up it falls apart in my hands. It has been ripped up the front, slashed from waist to neck in one long jagged cut. Of course, the paramedics. Dropping the rest of his clothes I close my eyes and bury my face in this torn old remnant and suddenly I'm drenched in the smell of him, the distinctive acrid smell of his perspiration, vivid man smell, still alive. The essence of him, still here, that final moment of pure exhilaration perfectly preserved. He is about to leap into the boundless blue air. And now I am standing next to him and I say, Go for it, Miles. Go for it.

Acknowledgments

My heartfelt thanks:

To Clare Alexander, Margaret Stead, and all at Atlantic Books, Blake Morrison, Francis Spufford, Tamsin Shelton, Erica Platter, Eileen Horne, Genevieve Fox, and Tricia Gilpin, for their encouragement, and for their invaluable help in the completion of this book; similarly to Pat Strachan, Nell Casey, John McGhee, and all at Catapult; to all my friends, for their kindness and support, and to Teresa and Jonathan Sumption, Benjie and Sarah Lister, Liv Lowrie, Jane Custance Baker, Pete Gingold, Nicky Thomas, and David Mitchell, for their sustaining practical help as well; to all Miles's friends who continued to visit and support him; special thanks to Tom Lister, Zach Leonard, Caroline Kamana, Jason Blain, Freddie Sumption, and Simon Rucker; to Richard Greenwood, Christine Quisel, Daniel Atkinson, Suzanne Davey, Khanye Lembethe, and David Echendu, my deep gratitude for the outstanding care they gave Miles at all times; to the many medical staff and carers who looked after Miles with gentleness, respect, and understanding; to Belinda and Amelia Spinney, for their generous encouragement and support; and finally to Will, Claudia, and Marina, to whom I owe everything.

In grateful and loving memory of Jennifer Mitchell, Angharad McAlpine, Josef Barbach, Martin Coleman, and Shasha Li.

About the Author

Lu Spinney was born in Cape Town and spent her childhood on a farm in the Midlands of KwaZulu-Natal, later moving with her family to the Indian Ocean coast north of Durban. After university, she left South Africa to live in Nice and Paris, before settling in London. *Beyond the High Blue Air* is her first book.